Collective Enforcement of Consumer Law

Europa Law Publishing, Groningen 2007

Collective Enforcement of Consumer Law

Securing Compliance in Europe through Private Group Action and Public Authority Intervention

Edited by Willem van Boom & Marco Loos

European Studies in Private Law (1)

FACULTEIT DER RECHTSGELEERDHEID
Amsterdams Instituut voor Privaatrecht

Rotterdam Institute of Private Law

Europa Law Publishing is a publishing company specializing in European Union law, international trade law, public international law, environmental law and comparative national law.
For further information please contact Europa Law Publishing via email: info@europalawpublishing.com or visit our website at: www.europalawpublishing.com.

Typeset in Scala and Scala Sans, Graphic design by G2K Designers, Groningen/Amsterdam

NUR 822; ISBN 978-90-76871-80-6

British Library Cataloguing-in-Publication Data
A catalogue record for this book is available from the British Library

CHAPTER I

Introduction

Willem van Boom and Marco Loos[1]

On Friday 15 September 2006, the Symposium 'Collective Consumer Interests And How They Are Served Best in Europe' was held in the building of the *Koninklijke Nederlandse Akademie van Wetenschappen* in Amsterdam, co-hosted by the editors of this book. This symposium coincided with the onset of the institution of a Dutch Consumer Authority, which was scheduled to officially come into practice on 1 January 2007. In the Netherlands, such a 'consumer watch dog' is new. However, in several European countries consumer authorities or other regulatory bodies have long since been established. The symposium was meant, first of all, to hear about and learn from the experience of these foreign consumer authorities and regulatory bodies. However, and moreover, the symposium also served a more profound goal.

Since the 1975 Consumer Policy Programme, consumer law in the member states of the European Union has developed especially within the framework of the European Union. The vast majority of substantive consumer law in the member states of the European Union nowadays is of European origin, varying from legislation on consumer health and safety, including the regulation of foodstuffs, toys etc., doorstep selling, package travel and timeshare, insurance law, product liability, unfair contract terms, unfair commercial practices, distance selling of goods and services, distance marketing of financial services and consumer sales and consumer guarantees. As the key areas of substantive consumer protection have now to some extent been harmonised, the interest of both the consumer rights movement as well as the European Commission seems to be slowly shifting. In the 1970s and 1980s, the consumer rights movement in the European countries primarily focussed on the acquisition of consumer rights, i.e. on improvement of the position of the consumer by way of changes in the substantive law.

In the eyes of the European Commission, consumer law was and is instrumental to the establishment and completion of the internal market. As a result of the instrumentalist view on consumer law, the emphasis in European consumer law lies more and more at correcting information asymmetries by imposing duties to inform on sellers and service providers, often combined with the introduction of cooling off-periods and rights of withdrawal.

Since the beginning of the 21st century, a new trend seems to be emerging. Next to legislation supporting the development of new markets and marketing techniques (e.g. e-commerce), the attention has somewhat shifted from improving the position of the consumer in *substantive* law, towards improving the possibility of the consumer to actually realise his right.[2] This trend has two different aspects: on the one hand, the European legislator (as the national legislators) focuses on alternative dispute resolution schemes (ADR), such as mediation. On

---

1 Willem van Boom is professor of private law at the Rotterdam Institute of Private Law, Erasmus University Rotterdam (the Netherlands). Marco Loos is professor of private law at the Amsterdam Institute of Private Law, University of Amsterdam (the Netherlands).

2 Cf. OECD, *Consumer dispute resolution and redress in the global marketplace*, OECD (2006).

the other hand, following the experience in especially the UK and the Scandinavian countries, the individual enforcement of consumer rights was supplemented by collective action schemes, either entitling private consumer organisations to act on behalf of the collective of consumers, or establishing regulatory agencies in public law to do so.

On 27 October 2004, the European Council and the European Parliament adopted Regulation (EC) 2006/2004. The regulation lays down the conditions under which the competent authorities in the Member States will have to cooperate with each other as well as with the Commission in order to ensure compliance with and enforcement of consumer protection laws (art. 1). The Regulation has led the Dutch government to establish a Consumer Authority. The Consumer Authority is to provide its services to the consumer authorities in other European member states in the enforcement of European legislation in crossborder situations. The government decided, however, to broaden the scope of the Consumer Authority's competence also to national situations, implying that the Consumer Authority will be authorised to enforce European legislation in domestic situations as well.

The proposal of a bill to introduce such a Consumer Authority gives rise to the question whether consumer rights are indeed best enforced by public law regulators or agencies. At the conference, this matter was looked at from various angles. One of these is whether it is private organisations such as consumer associations and foundations that should take care of the collective enforcement. Professor Dr. Hans-W. Micklitz (Bamberg University) set out the strengths and weaknesses of such collective private enforcement of consumer law. He distinguished between the different collective enforcement instruments, which include actions for injunction, test cases, skimming-off procedures, and collective damage procedures on the basis of either opt-in or opt-out. He contrasted these schemes with enforcement of private individual rights through consumers, consumer organisations, trade organisations and/or consumer agencies. In the opinion of Micklitz, collective private enforcement provides adequate answers to current societal changes.

Professor Dr. Gerrit Betlem (University of Southampton, UK) addressed the European directives and regulations pertaining to the public law enforcement of consumer interests by regulatory agencies. In his presentation, Betlem focused on the two main EC law instruments containing specific provisions on powers to enforce consumer law: the 1998 Directive and the 2004 Regulation. The focus of both instruments is on intra-Community infringements, the envisaged enforcers and their powers, and extraterritorial consumer protection. Betlem argued that the combined effect on a number of conceivable transnational enforcement scenarios is considerable. Conclusions were drawn in the light of the 2003 OECD Guidelines on transnational enforcement of consumer law, in order to answer this central question: What progress has been made with the 2004 Regulation and how does it fare when judged by the standards set by the OECD? Despite some shortcomings in the private law sphere – the public law aspects are largely satisfactory –, the legislative framework improves on the ECJ's case law by requiring equal protection of consumers based in the home State and abroad.

Although the EU law framework does not impose any obligations on watchdogs to assist individual consumers who litigate against foreign traders, and there is insufficient detail on legal action by watchdogs against traders based in other countries, including the freezing of assets, Betlem did find that the EU framework makes a useful contribution by stipulating that watchdogs must protect foreign as well as indigenous consumers. This ends forms of discriminatory enforcement which have occurred in the past. It is also an improvement in the case law of the ECJ.

In the discussion that followed the presentation, interesting insights in the cross-border enforcement issues were dealt with. The overall conclusion was that mainly public authorities will benefit from the new transnational enforcement system and that private consumer organizations seem reluctant to tackle cross-border issues.

In order to gain from the experience with regulatory agencies abroad, two speakers were invited to illustrate the effectiveness of such bodies. In his contribution, professor Dr. Geraint Howells (Lancaster University, UK) made a presentation of the OFT (Office of Fair Trading) and its enforcement strategy in consumer affairs. From a policy point of view, this presentation facilitated comparison with the recent Dutch approach. In short, the OFT has returned from the heavy enforcement strategy and is now inclined towards stimulating communication and self-regulation. Criminal prosecution as a means of enforcement is on its way out, so it seems. As regards the OFT its willingness to bring legal action has been seen to vary depending on the inclinations of the organisation's leadership. The present hierarchy certainly stresses the desire to educate and achieve market-based solutions by working with businesses. It is thought important that enforcement remains a last resort, but one that is available to the regulators. In this respect moves towards higher and more easily imposed administrative fines are to be welcomed, so Howells argues. Furthermore, he argued that it must be possible for regulators to take matters to court. In recent times there seem to have been an increased readiness to take matters to court where traders do not accept the OFT's line. The OFT's enforcement work has involved cross border practices. Undertakings of two Dutch companies in relation to bogus prize draw mailings were investigated. Moreover the OFT pursued the Belgian company D Duchesne SA to the Brussels Court of Appeal and may have to go even higher in the Belgian courts. This point sparked discussion with Betlem and the other participants.

The Scandinavian experience was demonstrated by Dr. Klaus Viitanen (Helsinki University, Finland). In his presentation, Viitanen gave an in-depth report of the typical features for the Nordic system of consumer protection, whereby regulation of marketing and unfair contract terms by general clauses go hand in hand with special state authorities, Consumer Ombudsmen. For the supervision of marketing and unfair contract terms, special courts – often called the Market Court or Council – are competent for cases pertaining to the collective interests of consumers. Furthermore, the residual role of consumer organisations in the supervision was highlighted. The most noticeable part of the presentation was the twin avenue approach of enforcement of consumer collective interests by regulatory agencies in the four Nordic countries (Ombudsmen) on the one hand and the Market Courts on the other hand. An important element in the success of this twin avenue approach is that the Ombudsmen has acquired authority and can 'speak softly and carry a big stick' whereas the Market Courts are specialized courts consisting of professional judges, expert members and representatives of interest groups. The role of private enforcement through consumer organisations and business organisations is residual, possibly because consumer organisations were in practice non-existant when the Nordic system was established in 1970's. Later, the need to come into action was obviously not as big in other European countries because the system seemed to work rather well.

Mr. Sjoerd Ammerlaan (Dutch Consumer Authority, Ministry of Economic Affairs) presented the Dutch bill. In his presentation, Ammerlaan gave an in-depth insight into the legal framework of the Consumer Authority in the Netherlands, how it operates within the European enforcement network, and how it wants to develop its strategy for the coming year. In the discussion that followed, specific points of comparison were raised. The presentations by Betlem and Howells proved a valuable background for analyzing the Dutch approach from a European and the UK perspective.

Dr. Katalin Cseres (University of Amsterdam) discussed the competition law implications of finding effective means for the enforcement of collective consumer interests. She dealt with three main issues. First, she indicated the legal possibilities consumers have in order to enforce their rights by making use of competition rules. Second, she set out the competition law perspectives of enforcing consumer interests by applying consumer protection rules. Third, the institutional side of this discussion was studied. On the one hand, she addressed the question whether it is the public agencies or the private organizations that are better placed to enforce the law. On the other, she addressed the question how competition authorities, consumer organizations and courts can or should cooperate in order to make enforcement of collective consumer interests a success. Cseres argued that in European consumer law the shift from substantive rights to procedural rights has been gaining more weight. Previously Directives in the area of consumer protection have left enforcement of the law entirely to the Member States. It is obvious, however, she argued, that effective legal redress for consumers constitutes a corollary of the substantial rights conferred by any legal order. If consumers are granted substantive rights without providing mechanisms to ensure their effective exercise, these rights have no practical value. The development of European law that has evolved along the lines of the Injunctions Directive as well as the Enforcement Cooperation Regulation has led the discussion on the one hand, to finding effective means of collective consumer redress providing an efficient supplement to individual redress schemes such as small claims procedures and ADR. On the other, the deterrent effect of currently available remedies and sanctions are being reviewed. The question is whether the present arsenal of remedies and sanctions (mainly consisting of injunctive relief and fines) should be extended to the recovery of damages. With regard to providing consumers with meaningful compensation for damages suffered as a consequence of 'anti-consumer' practices the discussion taking place in competition law can provide useful insights. Cseres indicated that the application and effectiveness of procedural rules directly depend on consumer and business behaviour. As regards consumer behaviour, she remarked that consumer complaints are influenced by the general attitude of consumers towards seeking redress and situational variables. In this respect, questions such as to what consumers want when they seek redress and how they seek it, are important. As regards business behaviour, the impact of the enforcement of consumer interests on businesses and the influence of (the threat of) legislation is of primary importance. An effective institutional framework is equally important to achieve an efficient redressal system. Whether it is public authorities or private organizations who take consumers by their hands can make a difference not only for consumers but for businesses, too. The role of competition authorities is perhaps more obvious in cases where consumers enforce their rights on the basis of competition law. Whether they could assist consumers in other ways by, for example, enforcing fair trading rules requires a more careful consideration.

Dr. Chris Hodges (Oxford University, UK) evaluated the effectiveness of public and private models for regulating consumer protection. In his presentation, Hodges made a critical analysis of the policy considerations underlying European consumer law enforcement. In particular, he focussed on the role and involvement of consumer organisations in enforcing regulation, and in regulation by private litigation. According to Hodges, the evidence is that consumer involvement in regulatory enforcement is ineffective and inefficient. The data may be limited, and further empirical research is called for. But if this conclusion is correct, it has profound implications for Community policy on regulation and enforcement, as well as tort law. The 'responsive regulation' structure deserves to be far more widely understood – applied in practice. Theoretical considerations indicate that we should be suspicious both of regulation of business by consumer interests, and equally of consumers by business interests. If consistency, quality of output, and accountability are important, balanced regulation through public institutions seems the optimal solution, although self-regulation under a 'responsive regulation' structure. If costs are a barrier to current public policy in strengthening public regulatory bodies, then it needs to be understood that these are necessary costs but also that solutions can and should be made to make regulatory systems more efficient. Further EU harmonisation, the involvement of approved consumer bodies in surveillance (but not in enforcement), and extension of co-regulation within defined parameters, all appear to offer potentially useful ways forward. A further point of criticism raised by Hodges concerned the area of resolving multiple private damages claims. Experience clearly raises concerns about enforcement of regulation through civil litigation. The development of excessive and disproportionate transactional costs, self-interested lawyer-led litigation and excessive claims culture, would appear to harm the economy rather than encourage competition, decrease prices, and increase employment or innovation. There are many similarities between the functions and powers of the British OFT, German, Austrian and now Dutch Consumer Authorities, and the Nordic Ombudsmen. Although some may differ in the extent to which they are formally part of government, they essentially operate as public authorities, rather than consumer organisations. If this observation is correct, there is considerable scope for proceeding by way of ensuring that such bodies operate as public authorities in the 'responsive regulation' mode. Further, an important part of their functions could be to facilitate low cost, extra-court mediation systems, rather than expensive and aggressive enforcement actions. The central proposition put forward by Hodges was that policy should be more evidence-based. The discussion that followed did in fact support this idea.

This book contains the presentations of the symposium as they were subsequently developed by the authors. It also concludes a presentation which was developed for the symposium, but could not be delivered there. Prof. dr. Roger Van den Bergh (Erasmus University Rotterdam) had hoped to give a presentation on collective enforcement of consumer law from the perspective of law and economics. Van den Bergh doubts that a lenient enforcement of consumer protection laws in a Member State alone will effect the relocation of traders looking to profit from that lenient system. He feels that other factors (taxes, wages, infrastructure) are likely to have a much greater impact on location decisions as these costs are a far greater component of the costs of doing business. He equally doubts that consumers will more often engage in cross-border transactions when consumer protection laws were better enforced as, again, other factors seem more relevant, e.g. language, culture, distance and travelling costs. Nevertheless, he argues, there is a case to be made for better enforcement of consumer law. Like Cseres, he relates the enforcement of consumer law to the enforcement of competition law and argues that the former may learn from the experiences of the latter. Van den Bergh warns his audience that overenforcement of consumer legislation would be counterproductive as it may stifle innovation, whereas underenforcement of consumer law could lead to (or increase) market failure. In his view, both instruments – consumer and competition policy and law – may contribute to the development of healthy markets and redressing existing market failures. A proper mix of private and public collective enforcement will yield the best results, Van den Bergh argues. In this respect, he criticises the otherwise positively evaluated Regulation 2006/2004, as it seems to favour public enforcement even in areas of consumer law where private parties possess better information than public authorities and there is no serious risk of under-deterrence. Unfortunately, Van den Bergh could not deliver his speech due to other pressing obligations. He nevertheless kindly agreed to submit a contribution to this book.

In the final chapter of this book, we will draw together the main issues discussed and arguments presented by the other authors and make some suggestions for finding the right balance between private and public enforcement efforts.

We hope this book may provide the tools for the Dutch Consumer Authority to achieve the goals it has set for itself, and moreover fuel to the debate on the proper enforcement of both domestic and European consumer law.

Rotterdam/Amsterdam, April 2007

CHAPTER 2

Collective private enforcement of consumer law: the key questions

Hans-W. Micklitz[1]

1 Expansion of collective redress in Germany

1.1 Action for injunction, *Sammelklage*, skimming off procedure, model lawsuit under the investors' protection laws

The action for injunction in favour of consumer organisations was established in 1964. In the year 1976 it was used by the Unfair Contract Terms Act as an adequate legal instrument for the abstract review of general business terms. The European Commission took over the German approach and expanded its concept to a minimum protection scheme by adopting a variety of directives governing unfair commercial practices – including Directive 84/450/EEC misleading advertising; Directive 97/7/EC distance contracts; Directive 97/55/EC comparative advertising; Directive 2005/29/EC unfair commercial practices and Directive 93/13/EEC unfair contract terms. The Injunctions Directive 98/27/EC intends primarily, but not exclusively to improve cross-border enforcement.

Since January 1, 2002 the legislator eased the strict restrictions on legal advise that many regarded as out-of-time to enable class action and model lawsuits. Since then, according to Article 1 § 3 no. 8 of the Legal Advice Act (*Rechtsberatungsgesetz*, 'RBerG')[2] it does not fall under the legal advice prohibition, if a consumer organisation that is supported by public funding enforces by legal action a claim of a consumer or such a claim that was transferred to it by the consumer for collecting purposes, as long as such action is necessary for consumer protection. Thereby, the consumer organisation is given the opportunity to pick one or a limited number out of a variety of involved parties and conduct in their names (model) processes. However, it is also possible to file class action type lawsuits. If the overall number of injured parties is high enough and the parties are relatively easy to identify, the consumer organisation

---

1 The article summarises the results of two studies on association rights for suing in Europe that my colleague Ms. Stadler and I conducted during the years 2004-2005. One of the studies was requested by the Austrian Ministry for Social Security, Generations and Consumer Protection and published under the title 'Gruppenklage in den Mitgliedstaaten der Europäischen Gemeinschaften & den Vereinigten Staaten von Amerika', in: Gabriel/Pirker-Hörmann (ed.), *Massenverfahren – Reformbedarf für die ZPO?* Verbraucherrecht, Verbraucherpolitik Band 33, 2005, pp. 111-310, the other one by the (former) German Federal Ministry for Consumer Protection, Nutrition and Agriculture under the title *Verbandsklagerecht in der Informationsgesellschaft* 2005. Those publications also contain various references to the legal systems of the member states and the U.S.

2 See A. Stadler, *Musterverbandsklagen nach künftigem deutschen Recht, Festschr. Schumann 2001*, 465 et seq.; H. Heidemann-Peuser, 'Neues Klagerecht der Verbraucherverbände nach dem Rechtsberatungsgesetz', (2002) *VuR*, 455; more reserved B. Heß, Sammeklagen im Kapitalmarktrecht, AG 2003, 113; H.W. Micklitz / H. Beuchler, 'Musterklageverfahren – Einziehung einer Forderung im Interesse des Verbraucherschutzes', (2004) *NJW*, 1502.

can have itself been authorised by the parties for collecting or have the claims been assigned to it and thereby prevent a flood of individual lawsuits with a great number of parties involved. Thus, Article 1 § 3 No. 8 RBerG entails the opportunity of actions for damages initiated by consumer organisations and also for other actions for performance, e.g. for recession or contestation. Notwithstanding the narrow wording ('collect' [*"einziehen"*]) and the connection with an assignable claim, consumer organisations should according to the *ratio legis* and due to reverse interpretation also entitle for affirmative, non-performance actions, e.g. regarding the nullity of contract clauses.[3]

By amending the Unfair Commercial Practices Act in 2004, the German legislature introduced skimming off lawsuits. Consumer that suffered a minor loss as a result of unlawful contract terms, defective products, or misleading advertising often waive the assertion of their claims, because the expenses are disproportionate to the revenues. Until then, businesses that widely benefited from such waivers at large, had to fear at the worst a consumer organisation's action for injunction bearing no retroactive effect. § 10 of the new Unfair Commercial Practices Act (UWG), by which the legislature for the first time provided a so-called skimming off claim (*'Gewinnabschöpfungsanspruch'*), now aims to counter such strategies within the range of unfair market behaviour. Whoever purposefully violates commercial practices law can from now on be called upon by certain consumer and trader organisations for recovery of ill-gotten gains.

The provision tries to compensate the legal enforcement deficit by introducing on an organisational level – so to speak in the public interest – an additional right to sue, which constitutes a claim *sui generis* located between tort and unjustified enrichment law. Pursuant to legislator's intention such claim does not aim at compensating the capital loss suffered by each individual and therefore does not fit within the category of the traditional liability law. Rather, the point is to deprive – for general and singular preventive reasons – the wrongdoer from the economic advantages he received as a result of his illegal behaviour. The claim's preventive function is justified by the fact that liability law does not get to grips with individual claims for such minor damages.

On November 1, 2005 a special model lawsuit procedure as part of the German investor protection scheme came into effect. The regulation is a legislature's reaction towards the large quantity of lawsuits in the Telekom-case in Frankfurt and undergoes – with a restriction to the investor law – a 5-year test

[3] The planned fundamental reform of the Legal Advice Act and its conversion into a Legal Service Act would have brought a clarification. Under an amendment of § 79 Abs. 2 no. 3 of the Civil Procedure Act consumer organisations would generally have been entitled to represent persons in court, if this was necessary for the consumer protection interest. However, the reform has only produced a draft (available at the homepage of the German Federal Ministry of Justice under http://www.bmj.bund.de/enid/41550 9b54407a389639b6430b1edb5c5,0/Rechtspflege/Rechtsdienstleistung_00.html (last visited August 14, 2005)) and is not going to be further pursued during this legislative period.

phase, followed by a possible extension of its scope of application. The basic idea of the new law, which is contained in a separate Act, is to select in the event of parallel lawsuits a model lawsuit and then have common factual and legal questions decided only once with binding effect for all claimants concerned. Because of the scope and importance of the decision made in the model case it is settled before the Appeal Court (*'Oberlandesgericht'*) and shall facilitate the judges' specialisation. The regulation is triggered by damages that occur to capital investors on a serial basis – independent of the amount.

If several claimants sue for damages because of false, misleading, or omitted capital market statements or fulfillment of a contract resulting from an offer that falls under the Securities Acquisition and Takeover Act, the claimants of the defendant can henceforth in every pending case file a motion for a model case decision. Along with the Capital Investors' Model Proceeding Act ('KapMuG') a new § 32b was introduced in the German Civil Procedure Act ('ZPO') which establishes an exclusive place of jurisdiction for all lawsuits that fall under the KapMuG's scope of application. However, as far as the European Regulation on Jurisdiction and Enforcement of Judgments in Civil and Commercial Matters applies, it can not be ruled out that lawsuits are also filed at the consumer's place of venue (Article 15-17 EuGVO) or where the tortious act took place (Article 5 no. 3 EuGVO) at home or abroad. The binding effect of the model case decision shall also influence to an extent all cases that were pending in court at the moment the model case is decided.

To achieve better cross-court information the KapMuG establishes an electronic claim register to be used for publishing and exchanging announcements and information that are relevant for the proceeding. If ten applications for a model lawsuit are filed, the court where the first application was filed will submit the case to the competent Court of Appeal where the model lawsuit proceeding will then take place. The latter chooses out of the group of plaintiffs who have already filed a lawsuit one claimant as a representative plaintiff and decides those issues by affirmative judgment that are common subject to all proceedings. KapMuG § 8 para. 2 no. 1 establishes – in line with the selection of the 'lead plaintiff' under the US-American *Private Securities Litigation Reform Act* 1995 – the assumption that the plaintiff with the highest single claim has the most interest in the model proceeding and therefore provides the best possible guarantee for a diligent conduct of the proceeding.

The individual lawsuits that are pending with the court are suspended for the duration of the affirmative model lawsuit proceedings. After an affirmative decision, which can be appealed to the Federal Court of Justice, has been reached the proceedings of the individual lawsuits are resumed, whereby all parties are in essence bound to the affirmative model decision. The defendant and the chosen plaintiff are the only parties of the model lawsuit proceedings. All other plaintiffs with their lawsuits being temporarily suspended are given the status of an admitted third party, which under the conventional terminology of the German Civil Procedure Code corresponds with the position of an intervener.

1.2 Deficiencies of the KapMuG

The KapMuG is limited to 5 years. Subsequent to the test period, the legislator will have to decide on a renewal and possible extension of its scope of application. However, a discussion on the possible disadvantages and advantages of the KapMuG should already start now, if a well-balanced solution is to be reached.

If the statute is measured against its target to combine effective legal protection with the relief of the judiciary, the concept that appears simple at first sight loses its persuasiveness. The intended relief effect will hardly occur. The model decision of the Court of Appeal must bind those plaintiffs that cannot participate as party in this intermediate procedure. Otherwise the whole procedure does not make sense. However, their right to be heard must be respected. The KapMuG solves this problem – allegedly elegant – through third-party-admittance. With the decision to suspend all other cases the individual plaintiffs automatically obtain the position of admitted third parties within the affirmative model procedure. This gives them basically the right to bring both aggressive and defensive legal action as well as, of course, the right to be present during trial and taking evidence. The informational obligations towards the third-parties might widely be met through the electronic claim register which should be in line with the constitutional requirements.

Obviously, the concept is driven by the hope that the admitted third parties will largely remain passive during the affirmative model lawsuit proceedings, so that de facto there would only be the model plaintiff and defendant acting before Court of Appeal. This might be so in an ideal case. However, as soon as the admitted third parties get the impression that the model plaintiff does not lead the case in the direction, they want to see it, they are more or less forced to make use of their participation rights. After the conclusion of the affirmative model lawsuit they only have a small range of possibilities to proceed against already decided factual and legal issues. In order to avoid liability claims, the respective lawyers must assert their legal position during the affirmative model lawsuit proceedings. Legally speaking it hardly makes a difference whether the person involved is a 'party' or an 'admitted third party'. Therefore the KapMuG is not able to provide for a substantial procedural simplification. The only effect might be that complex law suits have to be settled before the Court of Appeal.

1.3 Thoughts on the future form of group actions

The presentation is limited to group action claims for damages and sets other forms of collective legal enforcement aside, such as the action for injunction as a minimum standard in the EC, the skimming off procedure, the *Sammelklage* and the model law suit in investor protection law. It deliberately avoids the use of the term class action as this alludes straight away to the American class action which is mainly used in Europe as a deterrent against further legislative activities to strengthening collective actions. The centre of group actions pertains to the phenomena of mass damages that affect a certain amount of people differently, but that is characterised by more or less similar factual and legal issues. My remarks draw an ideal picture of a European group action that integrates the experiences gained under American class action lawsuits and already existing types of group actions within the Member States of the European Community.

2 Justification of group actions

2.1 Procedural economy

There is one major reason for the implementation of group action lawsuits: the procedural economy. Ample evidence can be derived from Member States where the individualisation of legal disputes not only burdens the judiciary, but also deteriorates individual defence and recovery of the affected persons. One of the central mass incidents in Germany was the struggle of consumer against overpriced credits.[4] Do-it-yourself builders who had 'beautified' their houses with wood preservatives had to realise that the wooden parts turned out to be contaminated by pentachlorphenol and lindane.[5] 'Heininger' – which became a keyword for junk real estate – has not been overcome,[6] yet, the attention is already drawn to mass damages that private investors might have suffered due to incorrect or incomplete capital market information. The case against the Deutsche Telekom pending in Frankfurt/Main involves 16,000 plaintiffs.

2.2 Justice

Bundling consumer claims might create 'more' justice than individualising litigation. While individual lawsuits are said to increase justice pertaining to each particular case, they necessarily neglect collective justice which can be represented only by all consumers concerned. Therefore group action lawsuits may contribute to improve justice – here not being understood as an optimisation of individual interests but as a collective justice that gives individuals at least the option to achieve indemnification, also in cases where they cannot prevail on an individual level. The experience with the wood preservatives cases shows the problematic consequences resulting from the

4 Cf. Reifner, *Kreditrecht (Credit Law) – Handbuch zum Konsum- und Hypothekenkreditrecht*, 1991 (2nd ed. 1999) Kreditrecht.

5 Hänsel/Micklitz, Holzschutzmittelprozesse, (1994) *VuR*, Sonderband.

6 Judgment, October 25, 2005, Case C-229/04 – *Crailshaimer Volksbank*, ECR 2005, I-9273; Judgment, October 25, 2005, Case C-350/03 – *Schulte*, ECR 2005, I-9214.

individualisation of parallel legal disputes that privileges the active plaintiffs to the detriment of the more passive ones.

2.3 Regulatory functions of group actions

Eventually group actions may have a market regulatory function. Such target is often neglected in political discussions despite its accentuation by supporters of the economic analysis of the law. Ideally, group actions create an additional incentive for companies to bring informational, supervising and controlling obligations, that the state imposes upon them, into practice in favour of the potential beneficiaries, i.e. in fact of consumers (but not only them). Group actions may thereby fill gaps resulting from incomplete or insufficient market control of public authorities agencies.[7]

3 Position and function of the group action within the collective legal protection

3.1 Group action and skimming-off lawsuits

In theory it is possible to expand skimming off proceedings in such way as to be also suited for collective mass events. However, two arguments can be raised against it. On one hand, it is a legal construction that still has to prove its worth in practice, especially because the law as it stands in its present form is nothing more than a 'nice colourful paper tiger'. On the other hand the skimming off procedures are only suited for minor and scattered damages that lie below the value that encourages a consumer to enforce his legal rights. Typical cases of skimming off claims are the direct discrimination of the consumer (groceries with incorrect filling quantity), misleading advertising and unfair direct selling strategies. The overall damage can be extensive, the individual loss, however, is minimal. Group actions should not be dealing with such minor and scattered damages.

3.2 The long shadow of the American class-action

In Europe the term class action has not gained any clear contours, yet. As regards content it comes close to the American *class action*. After all the American *class action* has lost most of its scare since more and more Member States of the European Community tend to bundle damage claims. Sweden, Spain and Norway adopted respective laws, France is currently launch-

7 Criticising such argumentation, F.J. Säcker, *Die Einordnung der Verbandsklage in das System des Privatrechts* (München 2006).

ing an attempt to establish corresponding collective redress schemes,[8] in the Netherlands a respective Act passed both legislative chambers in 2005, Ireland, too, is contemplating to take such steps. In Greece, a group action is at least subject matter of discussions. The Civil Procedure Rules of England and Wales contain special regulations for the bundling of multiple individual lawsuits that conceptually depart farthest from the *group action* picture influenced by the American *class action*, but sure enough cannot completely deny their source of inspiration. Even though it is not a group action in its actual sense, the reference to the American *class action* as well as the identical initial situation and objective target nevertheless justify the inclusion of the English model in the discussion.

3.3 Group action and model lawsuits

According to its definition a group action lawsuit constitutes a bundling of individual claims for reason of procedural economy. This leads to distinction problems, in particular with regard to model lawsuits. While within the context of a model lawsuit the adequate case must be detected that exemplarily – so to speak – condenses the legal issues of multiple claimants, the problem with group action lawsuits is the other way around. Mass events and mass damages connect the injured parties to a relatively homogeneous group of plaintiffs. Such group of plaintiffs aims to receive compensation for suffered losses. As a group they feel more powerful standing vis-à-vis the major wrongdoer. The bundling of interests serves for an optimisation in the administration of the interests. As conspicuous as these differences may be – on one side the solving of a fundamental problem, on the other side the bundling of interests for purpose of an improved individual improvement – the borderlines blur when also the group action deals with non-similar case constellations where a compensation for suffered losses cannot be reached by way of a single lawsuit.

3.4 Coping with mass damages

Besides the classical damage constellations, being part of product liability and capital market law, there are also mass events that in the narrow legal sense do not aim at compensation payments for suffered financial loss and/or personal injury, but from a legal point of view concentrate e.g. on the rescission of contracts or the assertion of a right of withdrawal. The group action lawsuit must insofar be adjusted in such way that it can react to damaging events in the broadest sense. 'Damages' means financial loss, property damages, however, also bundled performance interests. Thus, a flexible definition of damages is necessary.

---

8 On June 6, 2005, as a response to the initiative announced by President Chirac, a hearing was conducted at the Cour de Cassation with the intention to prepare the formulation of a statutory regulation. The report of the working group (December 12, 2005), which was lead by *Guillaume Cerutti* and *Marc Guillaume*, is available on the internet.

4 Questions of principle pertaining to group actions

4.1 Opt-in or opt-out?

The 'American class action' has been on scholarly focus for the last 20 years. The latest development shows that the American legislation saw the necessity to confine certain excrescences of 'American class actions'. Simultaneously, forms of collective legal enforcement boom in Europe. There are not only the usual suspects among the supporters of collective forms of legal enforcement, i.e. representatives of associations with bound interests and their apologists.

It can however not be ignored that the United Kingdom, Sweden and also Germany with its KapMuG did not choose an opt-out solution. Within the European context the development in Sweden deserves particular attention. For the Swedish legislator contrary to Professor *Lindblom's* scholarly groundwork argued – probably not least due to political considerations – for an opt-in solution. By moving from opt-out to opt-in Sweden seems to have found a concept that holds the balance between the extension of collective legal enforcement mechanisms and the conservation of conventional European legal traditions.

The development in England was similar to that in Sweden. In his report, by which he performed the groundwork for the later draft act, Lord *Woolf* discussed both systems – opt-in and opt-out – with their respective advantages and disadvantages. Eventually his recommendations were more leaning towards the opt-in system. Nevertheless he suggested leaving it to the judges' discretion to apply in individual cases the opt-out approach. He thought it was possible to combine both systems, for example by way of commencing the procedure on an opt-out basis and having the group of plaintiffs later sieved through an opt-in mesh.

Pragmatic considerations speak in favour of a group action introduction on the basis of an opt-solution. Its limits are known. Only those affected persons can profit from group action proceedings who agree to participate in the procedure. Such an opt-in solution requires the accessibility of the potentially affected persons as well as education and information to create the necessary basis for a mass procedure. It reduces the potential for a possible clash between the right to be heard under the human rights convention. However, an opt-out solution guarantees to a completely different degree as could ever be reached by an opt-in solution that negative market effects are being corrected. It must nevertheless clearly be emphasised that – apart from constitutional and human rights implications – it is mainly a political decision, which way the state chooses.

Regarding the recovery of ill-gotten gains resulting from violations of the unfair commercial practices and the anti trust law, there are – as far as minor damages are concerned – indications for a consensus on the necessity of an opt-out solution.

4.2 The appropriate group representative

A group action lawsuit can only be performed effectively if out of the mass of individuals affected and potential participants a single group representative steps forward acting on behalf of the group and leading the whole case. Several constellations must be distinguished, the leading question, however, stays the same, how to find the *appropriate* plaintiff. Whether it is an individual plaintiff or an association is in principle irrelevant.

4.2.1 The chosen group representative

In theory it is possible that the group of claimants organises itself and thereby creates the basis for the appointment of an internal leader who could then take the position of a group representative within the legal proceedings. Such self-structuring processes can in particular be found with mass damages where the cause of the damage can exactly be located. In most cases the legal form of an association is chosen. The advantage lies in the high legitimacy of a democratically chosen group representative. If the potentially injured parties organise themselves, independent of the particular legal form chosen, the legislator should refrain from influencing the process of self-organisation.

This does however not mean that the judge has to accept the election of the group representative at any rate. Sweden grants to the judge at least a veto right to assure that the group representative has the appropriate qualifications. Under the 'American class action', as it stands today, it is the exclusive responsibility of the judge to determinate the group' lawyer. The same applies in England. Thereby it must be determined whether and to what extent the judge can be bound to statutory guidelines if he intends to make use of his veto right. An examination of the relevant legal systems demonstrates that the judge's decision is inherently discretional.

4.2.2 'First come, first serve'

In reality it will often be a team appearing, one or more group action plaintiffs accompanied by one or more lawyers. As far as statutory rules exists, they concern the question whether it is possible to filter the appropriate plaintiff out of a number of possible representatives and which role the plaintiff's lawyer can be given within the group action lawsuit. The question, however, becomes obsolete if one assumes that as it is in Sweden the plaintiff who files the group action automatically becomes its group representative.

In the U.S. originally the principle of 'first come, first serve' applied. Here the party who was the first to file a claim with the court became class leader and thereby, virtually by way of temporal priority, was able to outvote the mass of claimants. However, this ruling led to a race between law firms with incomplete lawsuits being filed just for the reason to pre-empt potential rivals. In the meantime the U.S. abandoned the priority principle. Now the responsiblity lies largely in the judge's hands. The Swedish law contains guidelines as to the group action plaintiff's suitability copied from the (original) American model. Accordingly, the group action plaintiff must with regards to his own financial and other interest in the case be suitable to represent the class members. The purpose of this blanket clause is to have an equally good representation of the group members' interests as if they would sue by themselves. On the other hand the ruling also aims at the protection of the group claimant against impecunious persons. Apart from proper financial interests the group action plaintiff may not have any personal interest conflicting with those of the group (avoidance of conflict of interests).

Despite the negative American experiences there are arguments which speak in favour of giving those plaintiffs or teams of plaintiffs priority over the judge's right to determine the claimant in the admission procedure. As in Europe attorneys do not pre-finance the lawsuit, it is to be expected that none or only limited rival situations arise. However, the situation might be different if insurance companies[9] which are willing to finance the group action show up. Then they might compete with each other, in such situations, the first come first serve rule might turn out to be less efficient.

4.2.3 Group representatives appointed by the court

In the U.S. the court must appoint a group lawyer in the decision granting admission. In England the judge has the right to encourage the group to establish a so-called *'lead committee'*. If the group cannot come to an agreement the English judge will appoint an appropriate leader who he regards capable of being the *lead solicitor* and by this virtually functioning as the group action plaintiff. The details for the appointment as well as a possible removal of the decision are still unclear. Unlike the Spanish, Swedish law allows for a removal. An unsuitable group action plaintiff can be replaced by a new plaintiff. The judge compensates – so to speak *ex officio* – an incorrect decision of the group members and/or their attorneys. In Sweden, the judge remains responsible for a possible removal, in the U.S. and England he is also responsible for the appointment.

4.2.4 Requirements as to the suitability of the group action plaintiff

The judge must examine the suitability of the team of plaintiff and lawyer, also in an excursive way if, contrary to the U.S. law, he does not want to decide about the admission of the team. Even though the potential group

---

9 So far, so-called *Prozessfinanzierer* play a substantive role only in Austria. The required 30% of the total compensation as fee.

action plaintiff should usually appear accompanied by a lawyer, the question remains as to whether the group action plaintiff can be forced to mandate a lawyer. The American model goes beyond the Swedish, as the group lawyer is determined by the judge in the decision granting admission. The English law comes close to the American law as it enables the judge to urge the group to establish a *lead committee* eventually consisting of a *lead solicitor* who at least virtually functions as the group action plaintiff. The Swedish law seems to be a possible alternative, notwithstanding the fact that the introduced obligation to be represented by a lawyer has a different meaning for Sweden than for some continental-European countries.

4.3 Associations as group representatives?

Group action lawsuits focus on the individual plaintiff who seeks for a more effective enforcement of his interests under the realm of a bundling powers. Therefore everybody who is affected by a mass event might at least in theory become a possible plaintiff of a group action lawsuit. This is common opinion in all countries that paved the way for group action suits.

However, it is more difficult to decide whether apart from individual claimants associations, too, should be granted standing to act in the interest or next to the claimants as plaintiff. The extension of association-claims to skimming off procedures with regard to unfair commercial practices and antitrust injuries does not raise problems since the individually affected consumers will generally not go to court for minor damages. This is different if the consumer's individual loss is principally high enough to get active. The Swedish group action law votes under reference to the *American class action* in favour of an extension to non-profit organisations, e. g. in litigations between consumers and merchants.[10] Also Spain enables consumer organisations and associations to file a group action pursuant to the LEC (Spanish Civil Procedure Code). Under Swedish law two agencies, the Consumer Ombudsman and the Bureau of Environmental and Nature Conservation may file a so-called public group action.

If one wants to recognise in addition to individual plaintiffs also associations and/or agencies, that *like to* take action in the interest of the damaged parties, to act as group action plaintiffs, one has to clarify whether apart from public agencies private associations may act, too, quasi in the public interest or whether they must appear as nominal plaintiffs of a precisely described group of individuals – which would be the case under an opt-in solution. Here, difficult questions arise for Austria and Germany, as private associations at least within the scope of the Unfair Commercial Practices Act and the Unfair Contract Terms Act assume duties and responsibilities that in most Member States are managed by public

10 Especially for the field of labour law the problematic issue was not analysed; under the general *class action* associations may probably represent foreign interests pursuant to the general rules concerning representational standing, but this is at least not the rule.

agencies. Regulation no. 2006/2004 on cooperation between national authorities might induce a process under which enforcement powers are shifted away from associations to public bodies.[11] If consumer organisations are granted the right to file group action lawsuits, these non-profit institutions would compete with the Bar that not only in the U.S. regularly organises the plaintiffs.

4.4 The 'managing judge'

The particulars of the group action make it necessary to entrust the judge more than in normal civil procedures with the task to structure the litigation proceedings. This appraisal is confirmed by reference to the American, British and Swedish law. Surprisingly, the Spanish group action rulings are lacking specific competences for the judge. Beyond the traditional duties to subsume the facts and apply the law, the *'managing judge'* has to assume the following tasks:

- all varieties of the *group action* underlie the conviction that the multiplicity of plaintiffs in mass proceedings makes it necessary to choose one or more representatives who, so to speak, *'by proxy'* conduct the case for the others. The judge's task already begins with the question whether and/or who the adequate plaintiff will be. Once the representative is appointed the judge must assure that the group representative does not only pursue his own interests but also the interest of the affected but not participating persons. As the case may be he must be given the authority to exchange the plaintiff;
- the necessity to appoint a group representative entails informational requirements to ensure that the persons who are affected by the process are sufficiently notified about the commencement, the development and the necessary intermediate steps. It complies with the European legal conception to impose such responsible for the flow of information upon the judge;
- the bulk of group action lawsuits in the U.S. ends in a settlement. Whether these experiences will recur in the U.K., in Sweden and in Spain is in view of the relatively young legislation not forseeable, yet. The Dutch regulation aims explicitly at a settlement between the parties. The regulation underlies the assumption that both parties being involved in a collective damage adjustment will call the court to apply for the binding character of the negotiated accord;
- should the group action plaintiff decide to withdraw the lawsuit or to waive the right to sue, such action would require the court's approval;
- besides pure managing activities also social competences are asked for

[11] H.W. Micklitz, *Stellungnahme für den Bund der Versicherten zum Entwurf eines Verbraucherschutzdurchsetzungsgesetzes*, February 2006.

when dealing with the often-difficult conflicts. The judge puts up a form of *social management* to be able to reach the middle-term projected settlement.

4.5 The lawyer-entrepreneur

Equally to the necessity of having a 'different' judge in the group action proceedings, it is also necessary to have a 'different' lawyer. The laws in the Member States that have been adopted so far do not explicitly address the lawyer's role. The U.S. solves the problem, as is generally known, by having the – in Europe mostly criticised – incriminated 'contingency fee'. The lawyer hereby becomes the operation unit of the process. It is probably more in accord with the European conception to strengthen the position of the judge in group action processes.

Nonetheless the – necessary – over-compulsive commitment of the lawyer in the group action process should be beyond any doubt. The lawyer turns, irrespective of the fees, into an entrepreneur. It is his duty to keep the group action plaintiffs together, to organise the process, to keep contact with the judge, to inform the press, in short, just like the judge must be a 'managing judge', also the lawyer must be a 'managing lawyer'. The prototype of the 'managing lawyer' is far away from the professional that still seems to form the self-image of the lawyer. In practice the lawyer-entrepreneur has long been a reality.[12]

5 The objective of the group action

Focussing on the aim of the lawsuit affirmative actions and claims for performance can be differentiated. The latter is focussing on the payment of damages or the rescission of the contract. Another objective to be mentioned is to reach a settlement by means of affirmative action or claim for performance. The interrelation between those lawsuit objectives is difficult. A hierarchy seems to be appropriate under which the action for performance as the furthest reaching claim also sets the highest requirements for group action suits. In the U.S. this is expressed in specific procedural requisites that must additionally be fulfilled under actions for performance.

12 In this regard, the lawyer Mr. Tilp, who represented several so-called Telekom-claimants before the Regional Court Frankurt/Main considered himself at the International Symposium "Collective Legal Enforcement – Chances and Risks" on February 20/21, 2006 in Bamberg, as a businessman; this produced under the attending lawyers, judges and academics not only consent. The results of the conference will be published by the organiser, the Federal Ministry for Nutrition, Agriculture and Consumer Protection.

5.1 Affirmative action

Under German law legal and factual matters that are comparably important for the members of the group cannot be subject to an affirmative action. However, the group should be given the opportunity to name as the lowest common denominator those factual and/or legal matters that shall be overall reviewed under the group action lawsuit. The affirmative action claim to such extent appears as a minus compared with an action for performance.

The American and Swedish legal systems provide criteria for the judge to determine whether the plaintiff's assertion is at all suitable for a group action lawsuit. Implicitly included is an examination of the decision pertaining to the chosen type of action. In practice the question arises whether the judge should not be given review and determination authority with respect to the selection of those factual and legal matters that can be made subject to a principle decision with binding effect as to all members of the group. The Anglo-American law is familiar with such an approach, unlike European continental law, notwithstanding the fact that in the course of growing importance of the preliminary ruling procedure a new court culture begins to develop in Europe, under which plaintiffs, defendants and submitting court collectively formulate the question to be submitted to Luxemburg.

5.2 Action for performance

With an action for performance the plaintiff not only aims at a decision on the basis of liability but also on the amount of damages. The action for performance thus combines best the separately existing individual legal procedures without removing their individual character. While affirmative actions still show a two-tiered legal action mechanism – first the collective decision on the basis of liability, then the individual decision on the amount of damages to be awarded –, the action for performance combines both tiers of the legal action in one single objective.

If one reviews the liability events that became known in the past, it becomes obvious that only a few of the events would have been suitable for an action for performance, by means of which the entire damage and liability complex could have been worked through at once. Ultimately, actions for performance require a certain amount of homogeneity that has only emerged in few social catastrophes. To improve the homogeneity it should be considered to authorize the judge – as it is the case in Sweden and the U.S. – to permit under due discretion to define subgroups. As necessary as it may be to give potential claimants in the event of mass phenomena the opportunity to file an action for performance, even if by way of being divided into subgroups, it is not very likely that the action for performance will in practice play a dominant role. It could be much more significant to resolve individual factual and legal questions by means of an affirmative action.

Given the case that the action for performance was successful and the defendant accordingly ordered, the question arises whether and to what extent the amount of damages granted in the decision can be judicially enforced and how the amount owed, once it is provided by the defendant, is distributed among the plaintiffs. A look into different legal systems immediately verifies that judicial enforcement measures do not attract particular attention whether on a practical level or a legal level. In the U.S., judicial enforcement does not play any role as the proceedings regularly end in a settlement. The Swedish rulings deliberately did not regulate the enforcement of judgments that were decided in group action proceedings. The judgment in a group action lawsuit gives every member of the group a legal title so that the defendant must directly pay the individual group members. It would indeed be adequate, if thoroughly thinking through the problematic issue of association and/or group action lawsuits, to also introduce specific enforcement measures that are orientated towards collective legal redress. These enforcement measures would have to be of such kind to measure up to the problems of a group action lawsuit, i.e. the enforcement measures must eventually ensure a 'fair' distribution of the amount of damages. One could think of a judicial distribution system or the possibility of 'privately' distributing with the possibility for a judicial review in case of a dispute. The Spanish law providing for a subsequent procedure for individual titles could to this extent be an alternative worth considering.

5.3 Order of priority of affirmative action and action for performance

Many argue in favour of committing the group action plaintiff, like under traditional civil procedure law, to file an action for performance. If it turned out during affirmative action proceedings that contrary to the expectations of the plaintiff, his lawyer and the judge, it is nevertheless possible to bring the entire process to an end at once, the affirmative claim would have to be changed to a claim for performance which does not appear impossible but produces additional procedural questions. As the lawyer's fee is bound to the value of the claim and the whole proceedings are not in the least dependent on an adequate remuneration of the lawyer who is conducting the proceedings, it would be simply counterproductive to enable the plaintiff and the group members to lower the value of the claim by means of a newly introduced affirmative action. The lawyer's fee is already minimised as a result of the bundling of the claims.

A decision in favour of an action for performance does not mean that the group action plaintiff cannot change the action for performance to an affirmative action. Exactly this step must be possible and scrutinised in an open legal discussion including the defendant. The judge is thereby given a decisive function.

5.4 Settlement in court

If one reviews the whole spectrum of mass events and their handling in societies that possess collective compensation mechanisms, it should attract attention that settlement consistently dominates. It may be reached under pressure as was the case in Germany in the Contergan (thalidomide) catastrophe, but also in a variety of cases in the U.S. where the *class action* is used as a threat to reach a settlement. The Netherlands chose another way. The out of court settlement is the starting point for having the negotiated accord being declared as generally binding by the court. Here both parties to the conflict approach the court. The aim here is to give the settlement a binding character through judicial confirmation.

Each legislative approach whatever it looks like should pay attention to resolving the dispute by way of a settlement. Settlement negotiations bear the risk for non-involved group members of being disadvantaged by a solution that is primarily useful for the group action plaintiff and his representative in court. According to American experiences it seems to be essential to provide the judge with the necessary competence to supervise the agreement. Under Swedish law the group action plaintiff must not only point out to the group members the possibility of a settlement but even seek their advice as to whether the case can be resolved the way it is proposed. Such a rule, however, does not really provide for an efficient clarification of the factual and legal questions.

6 Procedural requirements

The group action lawsuit is at odds with the procedural law system that is designed for two-party conflicts. In that regard, specific rules are necessary to meet the requirements that the group action lawsuit imposes on the civil procedure law. The central question thereby is what conditions must be fulfilled to obtain a level of homogeneity that is sufficient to permit a group action lawsuit. If the claimants' interests and/or the potential factual and legal questions are, notwithstanding the common starting point, drifting apart too much, there will be no room for a group action lawsuit. It is pivotal to define criteria that enable the judge to review whether those minimum requirements are fulfilled.

6.1 Ensuring a homogeneous group of plaintiffs

Under American law a *class action* is only admissible if it fulfils the requirement imposed by Rule 23 (a) F.R.Civ.P.: *numerosity, commonality* and *typicality*. It is further necessary that the plaintiff represents the class' interest in a fair and adequate way – *fair and adequate representation*. The first two requirements concern the necessary particularities of the group. They ensure that the group action satisfies its economic-procedural justification. The two last-mentioned requirements refer to the character of the appointed plaintiff.

- Numerosity: the amount of plaintiffs must be so numerous that a combination of lawsuits would no longer be practical. There is no fixed benchmark. However, if the number of group members mounts up to hundreds or thousands the combination of lawsuits does apparently not constitute a possible alternative for the group action lawsuit;
- Commonality: the asserted claims must show legal or factual similarities. The judiciary applies rather a qualitative than a quantitative standard. Contrary to the wording, a single common dispute question is sufficient, as far as it is of certain significance (*one significant common question*);
- Typicality: the claim must be typical for the whole group. The prerequisite is closely linked to the *commonality*-requirement. The *typicality*-requirement draws its right to exist from the necessity to avoid having different objectives of the group representative and the group members despite the basic existence of underlying similarities;
- Fair and adequate representation: the most important effect of the *due-process*-principle is that the group is adequately and fairly represented by an appointed plaintiff. It replaces the individual's right to be heard and ensures apart from the group members' informational, participatory and opt-out rights also the constitutionality of the collective legal remedy. This includes the appointment of the adequate group representative and the group lawyer as well as the objective to avoid conflicts of interest between the group representative and the group, but also between the plaintiff's representative in court and the group;
- Superiority test: the group action lawsuit must when compared with an individual lawsuit be the more suitable instrument. This shall prevent the courts from being burdened with time-consuming and complex proceedings despite the fact that other ways exist which are more simple and efficient in dealing with the case.

These requirements must be fulfilled independent of whether the lawsuit pursues an injunction, an affirmation or a performance. The Swedish law is based on 5 criteria with broad reference to U.S. *class actions*: (1) equal and similar circumstances; (2) no substantial differences between the individual claims; (3) superiority of the group action; (4) determinability of the group; (5) suitability of the group action plaintiff.

6.2 Commencement of the procedure

All legal systems that provide for a group action procedure have in common that the case's suitability is determined by the court in a separate procedural step. The main procedure is insofar preceded by an opening or admission procedure. For the judge the specific character of the plaintiffs' demand for relief is only visible if the mass character is indicated to him by the plaintiff. Therefore the group action plaintiff has to file together with the claim an application for the commencement of group action proceedings. By this step a mechanism is to be initiated to ensure that all interested potential plaintiffs are getting in contact.

The recording of the application for the commencement of group action proceedings with the litigation register should under reference to the German Capital Investors' Model Proceeding Act (KapMuG) be in the centre of the information distribution. But the question remains how the potential claimants find out about the process at all. Even under an opt-in solution the publication method is of pivotal importance. Therefore a broad distribution of the publication in the print media is essential. As regards content the publication must contain information about the cause of action, the demand for relief and the group members' rights. To accelerate the process it seems advisable to combine the publication with a deadline for the potential claimants to decide whether they want to participate in the procedure. In addition, it is also possible to enable the judge to permit within a certain time limit subsequently filed applications for participation.

6.3 The group members' position and information during the process

According to the idea of representation, apart from the defendant only the group action plaintiffs that appear by name are deemed to be party to the process. Under the 'opt-in' system it is advisable not to grant any active litigation rights to the other participating claimants, but to assign broad informational rights, whereby in cases of doubt the scope of such rights would be determined by the judge.

The Swedish law, under which the other participants can challenge the judge for bias, can appeal a judicially ordered exchange of the group action plaintiff as well as can appeal the final judgment and the judge's approval of cost distribution agreements, could function as a blueprint. Waiving the right to sue, withdrawing the lawsuit and reaching a settlement in court should anyway require the judge's approval. There are good reasons to generally hear the non-active participants in cases where the right to sue is waived, the lawsuit withdrawn and a settlement in court reached, which should at least in the event of a manageable number of participants be possible.

6.4 Continuation of the proceedings subsequent to successful affirmative action

Under the presumption that affirmative actions could become the prototype of group action suits the following scenario seems possible: By means of affirmative actions a whole bundle of factual and legal issues will be resolved; on the basis of such clarified circumstances individual disputes will, however, be litigated. The action for performance that should basically apply fails, because it is apparently inadequate, the affirmative action does not provide for the intended legal peace. Different ways are possible: The two-tiered procedure, first the affirmative claim then the action for performance could be structured more procedurally. This would lead to the question whether the judge who presides the affirmative action procedure should be given a distinguished role within the second phase, i.e. the individual assessment.

The most important tool given to the judge is Rule 23 (c) (4) F.R.Civ.P. which allows him to subdivide the group in subclasses or to limit the *class action* to certain issues. In many cases it should be possible to build different classes with different levels of homogeneity. But even where an action for performance is not possible it should be considered whether the judge could act as a mediator, a position that the American judge de facto assumes when participating in the settlement and that is performed in Sweden by the *Ombudsman* and in England by the *Office of Fair Trading*.

7 Binding effect

7.1 Binding effect of settlements and decisions

Within group action lawsuits both a settlement between the group action plaintiff and the defendant in court as well as a judicial decision are binding for all (passive) group members. Under the 'opt-in' model the binding effect on everyone who explicitly agreed to participate in the procedure is under the aspect of *due process* unproblematic. In the context of American class actions the binding effect does not pertain to those *group members* who prove that their interests were not adequately represented during the proceedings or that they have not been duly notified as required. Such legal uncertainty should not be imported.

In case of an affirmative decision the group members will be bound by the affirmation. An assessment of the individual damage can then still be reached by way of a settlement. If a peaceful solution fails, the group members will have to conduct their individual process on the basis of the mandatorily ascertained facts. It should be rather rare that a group action lawsuit ends with a mandatory decision for performance.

7.2 The effect of pending group action lawsuits

More difficult to answer is the question about the effects arising from the pendency of group action lawsuits or applications for the admission of such group actions. Two issues arise: How does the group action lawsuit relate to individual lawsuits that were filed simultaneously or later by potential group members? What is the relationship between those actions that were filed by different claimants and, as the case might be, in the name of the same group? One could consider to impose a surcharge on the claimant who is sheering out or to suspend the proceedings until the end of the group action. Both ways lead actually to quasi mandatory participation.

8 Instances, appeal and fees

8.1 Instances and appeal

In view of the complexity of the group action proceedings one should agree on a two instances procedure with a comprehensive factual instance and an opportunity to appeal. It is difficult to assess whether also the other participants of the group action lawsuit should, as it is in Sweden, be entitled to appeal. If they were given such right this would reduce the group action plaintiff's role and function. A type of subsidiary right when the group action plaintiff does not want to continue the proceedings stems to mind.

8.2 Court and lawyer fees

Depending on the value of the claim the court fees may add up to a remarkable sum. If the lawyers fees remain linked to the value of the claim, the question gains importance whether the court could and should be authorized to limit the value of the claim and/or cut it down or whether the court fees, which could be significant, should be lowered by the law.

In all countries that are familiar with group action lawsuits court fees play a minor role. This is due to a specific lawyer's compensation system. If one leaves it with a lawyer's compensation that is dependent on the value of the claim, the conflict centres on how the value of the claim can be adequately assessed. If one uncouples the lawyer's compensation from the assessment of the value of the claim, the decision on the court fees becomes significantly less important. Although contingency fees should not really be considered, lawyers have to be compensated for the additional amount of work that results from group actions. This means that the value of the claim becomes the sole yardstick.

The only way out then is to reduce court fees. A substantial reduction can be justified by arguing that judiciary costs are considerably reduced through the group action. A flat reduction in the amount of 50% is suggested. The introduction of contingency fees for group action lawsuits does not appear obligatory. Conducting a group action lawsuit does however involve substantially higher efforts on the side of the group action plaintiff's lawyer compared to an individual procedure. Such additional efforts should be compensated by additional fees in case the group action lawsuit is resolved by settlement. The group members' share of the costs is evaluated on basis of the amount of the asserted claim which shall be directed at an action for performance.

The group members should only be liable for lawyer and court fees proportionally to their respective share.

9 Association and group action lawsuits in Community law

The European law on all sorts of collective actions is rather underdeveloped. The only well settled collective remedy at EC level is the action for injunction. Member States are under an EC obligation to grant the action for injunction either to public agencies or consumer respectively trader organizations, mainly in the field of unfair commercial practices and unfair contract terms. One might even argue that consumer organizations must be given standing to sue. The ongoing EC debate on private enforcement in antitrust law might lead to a group action meant to skim off ill-gotten gains, probably also in the field of commercial practices. However, the European Commission has not yet published a proposal in the aftermath of the Green Paper.[13] That is why there is ample room for the Member States to develop new regulatory models and to test them with regard to compensation of collective damages. It remains to be seen whether the deviating approaches in the Member States will yield a need for action at the EC level.

13 Green Paper: *Damages actions for breach of the EC antitrust rules*, COM(2005) 672, 19.12.2005.

CHAPTER 3

Public and private transnational enforcement of EU consumer law

Gerrit Betlem*

Summary

This paper examines in some detail the two main EC law instruments containing specific provisions on powers to enforce consumer law: a 1998 Directive and a 2004 Regulation. The focus is on intra-Community infringements, the envisaged enforcers and their powers, and extraterritorial consumer protection, including a comparison with the *Alpine Investments* case. Their combined effect on a number of conceivable transnational enforcement scenarios is analysed. Conclusions are drawn in the light of the 2003 OECD Guidelines on transnational enforcement of consumer law, in order to answer this central question: What progress has been made with the 2004 Regulation and how does it fare when judged by the standards set by the OECD? Despite some shortcomings in the private law sphere (the public law aspects are largely satisfactory), the legislative framework improves on the ECJ's case law by requiring equal protection of consumers based in the home State and abroad.

1 Introduction

It is well-known that the availability of a remedy to uphold a right conferred by Community law, including one under private law, is largely a matter for the applicable national legal systems. This follows from the principle of procedural autonomy, as articulated by the European Court of Justice (ECJ) since the 1976 *Rewe* judgment.[1] This autonomy is not so much a result of a division of legislative powers between the Community and the Member States, as an abstinence of using those powers by the Community legislature. However, on an ad hoc basis EC rules with respect to national procedural law have been adopted.[2] This paper will examine two of those in detail.

Also in *Rewe*, the ECJ formulated two limits to the exercise of this national procedural autonomy – the principles of equivalence and of effectiveness – with a view to ensuring the legal protection of individuals. However, it is likewise well-known that individuals' vigilance to uphold their rights translates as a decentralised (private) enforcement tool in addition to the centralised public enforcement mechanisms of Articles 226-228 EC Treaty (dual vigilance).[3] This general perspective applies to consumer law, which as a creature of EC law is mainly conceived as part of the law of the internal market. As noted by Howells and Weatherill, the substantive consumer law in the books is not automatically able to deliver an effective operation of the internal market; it needs to

---

* Professor of EU Law, University of Southampton. Email: g.betlem@soton.ac.uk; Web: www.eulaw.soton.ac.uk. I am grateful for Dr Renato Nazzini's comments.

1 Case 33/76, [1976] ECR 1989; [1977] 1 C.M.L.R. 533 and Case 45/76 *Comet* [1976] ECR 2043.

2 Anthony Arnull et al., *Wyatt and Dashwood's European Union Law* (London 2006), pp. 232-233.

3 Stephen Weatherill, *Cases and Materials on EU Law* (Oxford 2006), p. 99.

be completed by effective and even (EC-wide) enforcement in all the Member States.[4] As will be seen below, already in 1993 the European Commission identified particular problems with enforcement in cross-border situations in its Green Paper about Access to Justice for Consumers.[5]

The Commission was not the only international body to express awareness of certain legal and practical obstacles to effective enforcement in transnational settings. In 2003, the OECD developed Guidelines for Protecting Consumers from Fraudulent and Deceptive Commercial Practices Across Borders.[6] They are specifically addressed to consumer protection enforcement agencies and seek to improve their cooperation. In terms of facilitating such cooperation the Guidelines include recommendations to States to set up an institutional framework, to provide mutual assistance in particular with evidence gathering and information sharing, the recognition of foreign (judicial) measures, the power of an agency to take action both in favour of foreign consumers and against foreign traders,[7] and the authority to freeze assets of traders located abroad.[8] Without having to explore them in detail, the Guidelines' wish list may serve as a useful benchmark for assessing what has been achieved by the EU during the last ten years or so to overcome barriers to transnational enforcement. At the outset, the following observation by Howells and Weatherill may set the scene: '[...] contributing towards the solution of European transborder consumer problems and complaints seems likely to be a long haul'.[9]

This paper examines in some detail the two main EC law instruments containing specific provisions on powers to enforce consumer law. They contain a mix of public and private enforcement. Crucially, all relevant rules to date are solely concerned with cross-border infringements of EC consumer law not with harmonising public and private enforcement mechanisms as such. Section 2 focuses on the 2004 Regulation, in particular on its definition of intra-Community infringement, the envisaged enforcers and their powers, and extraterritorial consumer protection, including a comparison with the *Alpine Investments* case. In section 3 the 1998 Directive is covered, while section 4 summarizes their combined effect on a number of conceivable transnational enforcement scenarios. Briefly, the cross-border enforcement aspects of the 2005 Unfair Commercial Practices Directive are considered in section 5; section 6 notes possible language problems. Finally, section 7 draws conclusions in the light of the cited OECD Guidelines in order to answer this central question: What progress has

4 Geraint Howells and Stephen Weatherill, *Consumer Protection Law* (Aldershot 2005), p. 484.

5 See fn. 66 below.

6 Available from www.oecd.org. See also the Report on the Implementation of the 2003 Guidelines, July 2006.

7 Guidelines V(B) and (C).

8 Guideline VI.

9 Cited above fn. 4 at p. 488.

been made with the 2004 Regulation and how does it fare when judged by the standards set by the OECD?

2 Regulation on Consumer Protection Cooperation

2.1 Network of watchdogs

The most extensive piece of Community law legislation focusing on the enforcement of consumer law is the 2004 Cooperation Regulation.[10] Its purpose is to create a network of national authorities responsible for enforcing EC consumer law and to oblige them to work together (mutual assistance) and with the Commission (Article 1). The mischief the Regulation seeks to address is the lack of effectiveness of enforcement in cross-border case. Its solution is to require Member States to set up enforcement authorities – where they do not yet exist – and to lay down a minimum of common investigation and enforcement powers for these 'watchdogs' (preamble, recital 6). Like its sister act, the 1998 Consumer Injunctions Directive,[11] the 2004 Regulation is solely concerned with cross-border situations. The Directive does not make this clear at all in its title, but the Regulation states it deals with cooperation between national authorities, which implies transnational scenarios.[12] Although not mentioned as such, the Regulation must be seen as complementary to the Injunctions Directive in that it adds to the remedies made available under the Directive.[13] The Regulation indicates it does not contain any rules of private international law, in particular on jurisdiction and choice of law, nor does it seek to impact on them.[14] This is comparable to the Injunctions Directive[15] and e.g. the Services Directive Proposal.[16] It is clear that the Regulation on Consumer Protection Cooperation only deals with public/private enforcement in transnational scenarios; leaving it up to each Member State how to deal with purely internal situations. This is no surprise as the core provisions of the Regulation concern mutual assistance between the various national watchdogs and cooperation with the European Commission. There is no harmonisation of enforcement

10 Regulation (EC) 2006/2004, O.J. 2004 L 364/1.

11 Directive 98/27/EC, O.J. 1998 L 166/51.

12 See Commission Explanatory Memorandum, COM(2003) 443, No. 3.

13 See the European Parliament's Gebhardt Report of 23 March 2004, A5-0191/2004, p. 37. All the Regulation says is that it is without prejudice to the Directive, Art. 2(5).

14 Art. 2(2), again by using the phrase 'shall be without prejudice to'.

15 Jurisdiction is only mentioned in the preamble, recital 6, not in the substantive provisions.

16 See the Council's Common Position of 24 July 2006, 2004/0001(COD), available from www.consilium.europa.eu, preamble recital 90, Art. 3(2) and Art. 17(15) particularly mentioning choice of law in contract and tort.

powers and administrative, civil and criminal causes of action as such,[17] albeit that the watchdogs will have to posses certain powers in order to combat the transnational infringements.[18] The Regulation also makes it clear that any other form of cooperation between authorities of the Member States remains fully available, notably judicial cooperation in both civil and criminal matters.[19]

The obligation of the watchdogs to engage in mutual assistance, including the possible exercise of investigative and/or enforcement powers, applies when there are intra-Community infringements of the national laws transposing the EC consumer *acquis communautaire* and as listed in the Annex of the Regulation (cumulative requirements). This *acquis* includes fourteen Directives and one Regulation, including the 1985 Doorstep Selling Directive[20] and the 2004 Air Passengers Regulation.[21] As with any list-based system, it must be constantly updated as new legislation is adopted. The 16th instrument has already been added: the important Unfair Commercial Practices Directive (see further section 4 below).[22] The scope of the Cooperation Regulation *ratione materiae* does not extend to national consumer law that goes beyond the norms of EC law as transposed into Member State law[23] and must affect the collective interest of consumers. In borderline cases it may be difficult to assess which is which. These matters will not be further explored here as this paper focuses on transnational issues.

A final point as an introduction to the Consumer Protection Cooperation Regulation is that it is not the first consumer law act requiring the setting up of a network of national authorities who are to cooperate with the European Commission. A separate European enforcement network to remain in place even after the 2004 Regulation was created by the General Product Safety Directive.[24] Its Article 10 speaks of 'administrative cooperation' rather than use the terms 'mutual assistance' as does the 2004 Regulation, although the forms of administrative assistance listed in this provision do amount to similar mechanisms as covered by the Consumer Protection Cooperation Regulation. But the provisions of the 2004 Regulation are far more detailed and more extensive powers for the

[17] By contrast, in the intellectual property law context, there is explicit harmonisation of civil law, civil procedure and some administrative law, see Council Directive 2004/48/EC, O.J. 2004 L 157/45. There is a proposal to also harmonise criminal enforcement, see Amended proposal for a Directive of the European Parliament and of the Council on criminal measures aimed at ensuring the enforcement of intellectual property rights, Brussels, 26.4.2006, COM(2006) 168 final; 2005/0127 (COD).

[18] Regulation (EC) 2006/2004, O.J. 2004 L 364/1, preamble recitals 5-8; Art. 4.

[19] Art. 2(3) '[...] without prejudice [...].'.

[20] Directive 85/577/EEC, O.J. 1985 L 372/31.

[21] Regulation (EC) 261/2004, O.J. 2004 L 46/1.

[22] Directive 2005/29/EC, O.J. 2005 L 149/22, Art. 16 amends the 2004 Regulation to add itself to the list.

[23] Dutch government in Explanatory Memorandum to the Consumer Protection Enforcement Bill, TK 30411, No. 3 at p. 8. Available from www.overheid.nl/op.

[24] Directive 2001/95/EC, O.J. 2002 L 11/4; see Howells/Weatherill, cited above fn. 4, at p. 488.

watchdogs are required. Since this General Product Safety Directive is not one of those listed by the 2004 Regulation, the networks are apparently envisaged to carry on their own separate lives.[25]

2.2 Cross-Border breach

The key concept triggering the use of investigation/ enforcement powers is 'intra-Community infringement'. It is defined as follows:

> ***'Article 3 Definitions.***
> For the Purposes of this Regulation: [...]
> (b) 'intra-Community infringement' means any act or omission contrary to the laws that protect consumers' interests, as defined in (a),[26] that harms, or is likely to harm, the collective interests of *consumers residing* in a Member State or Member States *other than* the Member State where the *act or omission originated or took place; or* where the responsible seller or supplier is *established; or* where *evidence or assets* pertaining to the act or omission *are to be found* [emphasis added];'.

In essence, the provision focuses on the well-known distinction between the so-called *Handlungsort* [place of act/omission] and *Erfolgsort* [place of impact]: only when there is such a dispersal over these two places in two or more Member States does an intra-Community infringement within the meaning of the Regulation occur (the classic so-called *Distanzdelikt*). Having said that, the definition is much wider. For in addition to this main category where a trader acted in State A with ensuing harm in State B, two additional situations are covered. Firstly, State A is the place of establishment of the trader causing harm in State B, even where she acted elsewhere (say State C); secondly, in State A evidence or assets are found while harm occurs in State B (presumably regardless of where the trader had acted: State A or C). In other words: harm to consumers in State B whilst any one (or more) of the following is in State A:

1) trader acted (includes relevant omissions);
2) trader is established;
3) location of evidence or assets.

Please note that the three-pronged notion of intra-Community infringement triggers the exercise of enforcement powers by a watchdog against a trader (details of these powers are below). The scheme of the Regulation seems to

---

[25] See below, third section. Cf. for an appraisal of the functioning of the network of competition watchdogs: Benjamin Perrin, 'Challenges Facing the EU Network of Competition Authorities: Insights from a Comparative Criminal Law Perspective,' (2006) 31 *E.L.Rev.* 540.

[26] I.e.: 'laws that protect consumers' interests' means the Directives as transposed into the internal legal order of the Member States and the Regulations listed in the Annex'.

contemplate only one possible scenario of transnational enforcement: legal action (civil, administrative and/or criminal) by a watchdog against a trader based in its own country – either of its own accord or on request of a watchdog of another Member State – in the interest of protecting consumers based outside its territory.[27] In particular investigation powers to obtain documents and to enter premises are mentioned; powers which cannot be exercised by an authority outside its own territory.[28] This reading is confirmed by the way the Commission has identified barriers to cross-border enforcement by consistently referring to obstacles for the authorities in the Member State of the trader and by the definition of market surveillance activities as these are restricted to the detection of infringements that have taken place within the watchdog's territory, whilst, by definition, the harm occurs outside it.[29]

But are the three listed forms of cross-border breach genuinely confined to traders based in the territory of the watchdog? Only the second one is *prima facie* explicitly concerned with a trader being based in State A and causing harm elsewhere (assume that we are talking about the watchdog of State A here). The first scenario will usually involve traders who are based in State A while acting there; these places (*Handlungsort* and place of establishment/residence) normally coincide but not always.[30] But the third scenario seems to point to situations where it is more likely that the trader is not based in State A, nor in State B given the fact that in these examples the consumers are harmed in what I call State B and by definition the trader and the consumers must be in different States.

The final version of Article 3(b) differs markedly from the original Commission Proposal,[31] which reads as follows:

> 'intra-Community infringement' means any act contrary to the laws that protect consumers' interests that harms, or is likely to harm, the collective interests of consumers residing in a Member State or Member States other than the Member State *where the act originated'* [emphasis added].

This definition only covers the classic *Distanzdelikt* as outlined above: *Handlungsort* differs from *Erfolgsort*. All the elements cited above which effectively constitute connecting factors with the trader's domicile, or where she has assets or where there is evidence, were introduced as amendments by the European Parliament. They first appeared in the Gebhardt Report of the Committee on

27 See also the Dutch government, cited above fn. 23, pp. 5 and 9.

28 Gebhardt Report, cited above fn. 13, p. 36 and Commission Explanatory Memorandum, cited above fn. 12, No. 12.

29 Explanatory Memorandum Dutch Bill, cited above fn. 23, Nos. 12, 21 and 22; see also No. 37; Art. 3(i) of the Regulation.

30 Cf. the famous ECJ ruling in the French potassium mines litigation, Case 21/76, *Bier* v *Mines de Potasse d'Alsace* [1976] ECR 1735 and in particular the Opinion of the Advocate General.

31 COM(2003) 443.

Legal Affairs and the Internal Market[32] and were adopted by the Parliament in its legislative resolution during the first (and only) reading.[33] Remarkably, no justification is given by the EP for the amendment which *prima facie* seems to significantly extend the definition of intra-Community infringement and consequently the scope for enforcement action by the watchdogs.

From the perspective of a private international lawyer, the three listed places closely resemble heads of jurisdiction justifying the competence of a civil court over a defendant. 'Translating' these three *loci* triggering possible enforcement action under the Cooperation Regulation into the language of civil jurisdiction under Brussels I,[34] we get the following picture:

	Cooperation Regulation	***Brussels I***
1.	trader acted (includes relevant omissions);	Art. 5(3): place of the harmful event or *forum delicti*
2.	trader is established	Art. 2 or *forum rei*
3.	location of evidence or assets	Blacklisted head of jurisdiction for EU defendants, Annex I and Arts. 3(2) and 4(2)

No. 1 is unproblematic but does include both traders based in State A (coinciding with No. 2 then) and based elsewhere. In the latter situation, if included in the Cooperation Regulation without more, the watchdog of State A would be acting against a trader based elsewhere. It is unclear to me whether that is what the Cooperation Regulation envisages.

No. 2 is completely unproblematic under both the Cooperation Regulation and Brussels I. Indeed, that is the sole scenario envisaged by the Cooperation Regulation as a whole as it is based on the idea of watchdogs enlisting each other to take action in their territories and not elsewhere. Whereas the domicile of the defendant is of course the main rule of the Brussels I system.[35] However, unlike the Brussels I regime, the Cooperation Regulation says nothing about how to determine where a trader is established. Particularly for legal persons, this may be far from straightforward (e.g. a limited company incorporated and registered in the UK but trading in the Netherlands) and is precisely one of the main changes introduced when the 1968 Brussels Convention was converted

32 Cited above fn. 13.

33 Position of the European Parliament adopted at first reading on 20 April 2004, P5_TC1-COD(2003)0162, O.J. 2004 C 104 E/218.

34 Regulation (EC) 44/2001, O.J. 2001 L 12/1; a consolidated version, including the amendments in the wake of the 2004 EU enlargement, is downloadable here: http://europa.eu.int/eur-lex/en/consleg/main/2001/en_2001R0044_index.html.

35 Indeed, the rule can be considered of universal acceptance, see the Final Report of the International Law Association's Committee on Transnational Enforcement of International Environmental Law, Toronto, June 2006, Gerrit Betlem, Christophe Bernasconi & Maria Gavounelli, Co-Rapporteurs, available online at: http://www.ila-hq.org/html/layout_committee.htm.

into the Brussels Regulation.[36] Again the possibility cannot be excluded that the watchdog of State A takes action against a trader formally established elsewhere but considered equally established in State A.

The third option would be ruled out altogether under the Brussels I regime as the mere presence of assets (the presence of mere evidence would be an even flimsier link) constitutes one of the banned so-called heads of exorbitant fora. Clearly it would be quite conceivable for a trader to be based in State C, causing harm in State B while having assets in State A. An obvious example would be a company operating in various Member States, particularly when electronic commerce over the Internet is concerned.[37] In all these scenarios more than one watchdog will have jurisdiction. Admittedly, the watchdogs will have to coordinate their actions under the Cooperation Regulation (Article 9).[38] But it can still be argued that the definition of intra-Community infringement lacks clarity and that it is inadequate in terms of legal certainty.

2.3 Who are the watchdogs?

So far we spoke of watchdogs as the bodies empowered (and obliged) to take action against traders committing intra-Community infringements. But who precisely are potential enforcers under the Regulation? In addition to public authorities, Member States are empowered, not obliged, to designate non-governmental bodies as enforcers (Article 4). New for a number of Member States (Germany, the Netherlands) is that they must now designate a specific public body responsible for the enforcement of EC consumer law; in others they already exist such as the Office of Fair Trading (UK) or the *Konsumentenverket* (Sweden).[39] But in addition to what was called the watchdog above, other public authorities may be designated as equally empowered (coming within the notion of 'watchdog' then) and, mutatis mutandis, 'bodies having a legitimate interest in the cessation or prohibition of intra-Community infringements in accordance with Article 8(3)'.[40]

---

36 Compare Art. 60 BR I with Art. 53 Brussels Convention; see generally Jonathan Hill, *International Commercial Disputes in English Courts* (Oxford 2005), p. 74.

37 Both the Commission and the EP are referring to e-commerce on numerous occasions, see e.g. COM(2003) 443 at Nos. 1, 10 and 15; Gebhardt Report, at pp. 37 and 40.

38 But see the criticism of the ECOSOC on the Proposal for the 2004 Regulation, O.J. 2004 C 108/86, at No. 3.9, pointing out that the Regulation is too restrictive in that at least three States have to be involved before these rules kick in.

39 Art. 3(c) and No. 31 Commission Explanatory Memorandum, cited above fn. 12. See also Explanatory Memorandum Dutch implementation Bill, cited above fn. 23, p. 14.

40 Art. 4(2) Regulation (EC) 2006/2004, O.J. 2004 L 364/1. Art. 4(1) also requires the establishment of a single liaison office responsible for the cooperation with the relevant bodies in other Member States. This may be the same body as the one designated as (principal) watchdog, see e.g. the Dutch Bill, cited above fn. 23.

Normally these would be non-governmental consumer associations or the like, including business/trade organisations as well as self-regulatory bodies such as those supervising advertising standards or providers of alternative dispute resolution services.[41] Importantly, where they are so designated by a Member State, the cited Article 8(3) of the Regulation contemplates that they may be entrusted with the task of taking action against a trader on behalf of a watchdog, who, in turn, was requested to act by a watchdog of another Member State; the Regulation talks about the requested and the applicant authorities.[42] But they are a kind of second class enforcer as the Regulation makes the exercise of its powers, where the watchdog of, say State A, is the requested authority, subject to approval by the applicant authority of State B.[43] This position of secondary rather than primary enforcer is not the view taken by the Dutch government. On the contrary, it only sees a role for the public enforcers (notably the newly to be established principal watchdog: the *Consumentenautoriteit* [Consumer Authority] as a subsidiary enforcer where self-regulation and civil actions are incapable of thwarting unfair practices by rogue traders.[44]

2.4 Powers

What sort of powers are we talking about here? Article 4 spells out what enforcers must be able to do. Under the Regulation, all watchdogs, i.e. each 'competent authority', 'shall' have all necessary investigation and enforcement powers to apply its provisions properly (Article 4[3]). However, it is up to each Member State to decide whether the watchdog will be able to exercise these powers directly (possibly subject to judicial supervision) or indirectly by applying to competent courts to seek the necessary judicial orders (Article 4[4]). Parenthetically it may be noted that, strictly speaking, this provision could be read as requiring Member States to opt for an either/or system: the watchdogs exercise their powers either directly or via the courts. However, should it not be up to the watchdog to decide which powers to use once so empowered by the national law implementing the Regulation? The norm does not seem to be addressed to the legislature but to the watchdogs who must be given a choice under national law.

A non-exhaustive list of specific powers which the competent authorities (the watchdogs) must be able to exercise is given in Article 4(6) and includes seizure of documents, entry to premises and the right:

---

41 Cf. Commission Explanatory Memorandum, cited above fn. 12, No. 32 and Explanatory Memorandum Dutch implementation Bill, cited above fn. 23, pp. 47-49.

42 Art. 3(f) and (g) Regulation (EC) 2006/2004, O.J. 2004 L 364/1.

43 See the complex procedure included in Art. 8.

44 Explanatory Memorandum Dutch implementation Bill, cited above fn. 23, p. 47. See also Michiel Heldeweg, 'Supervisory governance. The case of the Dutch Consumer Authority,' (2006) *Utrecht Law Review* 67, www.utrechtlawreview.org, at pp. 73, 75 and 83.

'(e) to obtain from the seller or supplier responsible for intra-Community infringements an undertaking to cease the intra-Community infringement; and, where appropriate, to publish the resulting undertaking;
(f) to require the cessation or prohibition of any intra-Community infringement and, where appropriate, to publish resulting decisions;
(g) to require the losing defendant to make payments into the public purse or to any beneficiary designated in or under national legislation, in the event of failure to comply with the decision.'

Although the Regulation somewhat hides this, it is clear that only public authorities, notably the watchdogs, are able to exercise public authority powers.[45] The cited power under (e) is one that is expected to be available only for public enforcers and resembles US and UK practice.[46] Any NGO entrusted with watchdog tasks must seek civil redress.[47] In other words, private enforcers may be able, under national law, to exercise enforcement powers whereas public enforcers must themselves be able to exercise both investigation and enforcement powers under the Regulation. It is therefore important to distinguish between investigation and enforcement powers under the Regulation. The distinction does not coincide with a distinction between public and private law powers/ remedies, however.

The cited power under Article 4(f) for example may be exercised directly by a watchdog under public law or indirectly by an application to a civil court seeking an injunction. The *travaux préparatoires* do not help us with the interpretation of this provision as no detailed explanation is given beyond the expectation that '[i]njunctions are likely to be the main enforcement tool'.[48] Likewise for section (g) which refers to non-compliance with 'the decision'. The term 'decision' presumably refers to both a court order requiring the defendant to discontinue the infringing practices (both a prohibitory and a positive injunction) and a unilateral administrative order by the competent authority. In fact, 'decision' can be construed wider so as to include a trader's undertaking to cease the intra-Community infringement; there must be a sanction for non-compliance with the undertaking. Likewise, making 'payments': covered presumably are both fines and periodic penalty payments either under public or civil law. Such

45 Commission Explanatory Memorandum, cited above fn. 12, No. 34. On NGOs see Art. 8(3) referring to 'enforcement measures available to it [the NGO] under national law [...]'. Please note that this begs the question which national law is the applicable law.

46 See Micklitz et al., 'The Feasibility of a General Legislative Framework on Fair Trading, Vol. 2 UK and US Models of Regulation,' Study for the European Commission by the Institut für Europäisches Wirtschafts- und Verbraucherrecht e.V. (November 2000); available from www.europriv.eu | Unfair Commercial Practices and from ec.europa.eu/consumers/index_en.htm.

47 Except where the relevant legal system allows for private prosecutions.

48 Explanatory Memorandum, cited above fn. 12, No. 39.

a system is being proposed by the Dutch legislature[49] and reflects the public law enforcement powers of competition watchdogs (both national and the European Commission itself) under Regulation 1/2003.[50] Further support for this view may be found in the version of the cited sections of Article 4(6) contained in the 2003 Commission Proposal, which reads as follows:

> '(f) to require the cessation or prohibition of any intra-Community infringement *or to obtain judicial orders* requiring the cessation or prohibition of any intra-Community infringement; and to publish resulting decisions;
> (g) *to obtain judicial orders* against the losing defendant for payments into the public purse or to any beneficiary designated in or under national legislation, in the event of failure to comply with a decision;
> (h) *to obtain judicial orders* requesting the freezing and/or sequestration of assets; [emphasis added]'.[51]

The final version is the one adopted by the European Parliament at first reading as both the Commission and the Council agreed with it.[52] There is no explanation for the reformulation but as the EP clearly agreed with the Commission's approach to add public law powers to civil remedies the better view must be that all such powers/remedies must indeed be made available to the watchdog by the Member States, for under Article 4(3) and (4) all powers necessary for the application of the Regulation are exercised directly by the watchdog (normally under public law) or via the courts (civil law).

It is recalled that no provision of the Cooperation Regulation detracts from investigation and enforcement powers available under other instruments of international, Community or national law; on the contrary, the network of watchdogs and its concomitant powers created by the 2004 Regulation adds to existing public and private law tools.[53] Accordingly, the deletion of the possibility to obtain freezing orders from the list of mandatory powers therefore seems relatively unproblematic as public authorities can be expected to be able to obtain them from the courts under existing national law (begging the question of which courts).

---

49 See the Dutch implementation Bill, cited above fn. 23, which opens up all these routes for the watchdogs; see in particular arts. 2.8 and 2.9 of the Amended Proposal for the Consumer Protection Enforcement Act of 7 July 2006, EK 2005-2006, No. 30411A.

50 Regulation (EC) 1/2003, O.J. 2003 L 1/1, arts. 5, 23-26.

51 COM(2003) 443.

52 See the EP's legislative resolution, cited above fn. 33 and the full legislative history of the Regulation as available from ec.europa.eu/prelex/.

53 Cf. Art. 2(3) and (4) and Art. 18 on cooperation with third countries.

2.5 Which courts?

Which leads us to the next issue: does Regulation 2006/2004 create a right for authorities to apply to the courts of other Member States? Not only as far as freezing orders are concerned but also regarding any application for court orders, notably injunctions, the question arises which courts does Article 4(4)b refer to? It is recalled that under this provision, as an alternative to direct action by the watchdog itself against the trader, the Regulation talks about the exercise of investigation and enforcement powers by the watchdogs 'by application to courts, competent to grant the necessary decision [...]'. As noted, the most likely enforcement tool is an injunction so in practice most relevant will be where the authority will apply for an injunction. The Dutch implementation Bill envisages civil actions by the watchdog as claimant before Dutch courts but presumably only against Dutch based defendants; it underlines that public authorities are already empowered to apply for injunctions in the general interest of, among others, consumer protection law, under regular civil law but will in addition be able to use a new fast track procedure for the same purpose.[54] Both the Dutch Bill and the EU Regulation do not cover the question of international competence of the civil courts so two questions relating to cross-border enforcement, not one, need to be addressed: (i) is the indirect enforcement avenue before civil courts only available where the defendant is based in the home State of the watchdog?; (ii) can the watchdog turn to the courts of another Member State than its own (as said above)?

Regarding the first question, it has already been pointed out above that the Regulation's definition of intra-Community infringement covers more than the only cross-border scenario where the trader is based in State A and the harm occurs in State B and the watchdog of State A takes action against the trader based in its own territory (either on request of another watchdog or on its own initiative). It would seem to follow that defendants based outside the watchdog's State but in another EU Member State can be sued before the courts of the State of the watchdog under the provisions of the Brussels I Regulation[55] because the Cooperation Regulation is without prejudice to it.

The need for the possibility to seek an injunction against a defendant based elsewhere before the courts of the State of the watchdog is confirmed by the experiences with cross-border enforcement of the US Federal Trade Commission (FTC), who, *inter alia*, acts in a capacity similar to the designated competent authorities/watchdogs under the Cooperation Regulation.[56] Also comparably,

[54] See Art. 3:305b Dutch Civil Code and para. 5.3 Explanatory Memorandum, cited above fn. 23. Contrary to the principle of equivalence, in my view, the new procedure will not be available for foreign watchdogs listed under Directive 98/27 (see proposed Art. 3:305d and the unamended Art. 3:305c Dutch Civil Code).

[55] Cited above fn. 34.

[56] See generally Micklitz, cited above fn. 46.

the FTC has concluded cooperation agreements with its neighbouring States, notably Canada, to set up a similar framework of mutual assistance as provided for in the Regulation. A Report containing over 30 cases of civil enforcement over the period 1998-2003 reveals that the US watchdog applied to US courts in all those instances, usually seeking injunctions, while cooperating with Canadian authorities in various respects. This contradicts the assumptions of the Regulation to emphasize watchdog action against traders based within its territory. Rather, the pattern emerging from the US-Canadian experience is one of a mixture of public and private law measures by US and Canadian watchdogs gathering evidence and the like, and acting jointly with US courts granting injunctions against foreign-based defendants.[57]

As for question two, access to foreign courts by a watchdog, again the Brussels I Regulation will cover the question of the jurisdiction of those courts over the defendant. The terms of the Cooperation Regulation cited above, 'courts competent to grant relevant orders,' do not exclude access to courts outside the State of the watchdog, albeit that the whole system seems to assume that a watchdog of State A would then have to ask any other relevant watchdog (State B, C etc.) to apply to the courts in their own State. Unlike the 1998 Consumer Injunctions Directive, the 2004 Cooperation Regulation does not explicitly confer a right on a watchdog to appear before foreign courts. When a Member State has designated a public authority as a so-called qualified entity under that Directive, it must be granted *locus standi* before the courts of other Member States (see further section 3 below). Many of the same authorities are likely now also to be listed under Article 5 of the Cooperation Regulation.

It is regrettable that the Regulation has not covered this scenario explicitly. Although it may not seem such a large obstacle in practice if the watchdog can rely on the provision of the Consumer Injunctions Directive, an explicit recognition of public authorities as claimants before any civil court would do away with the uncertainty surrounding the notion of civil and commercial action under the Brussels I Regulation. It is beyond the scope of this paper to say more than that the case law of the ECJ is not straightforwardly recognizing claims by public authorities as a civil action within the meaning of Brussels I whenever they are perceived to be exercising public authority powers even where they are using tort actions in the same way as any private actor would.[58] By contrast, the Cultural Goods Directive does refer to such a possibility, i.e. State A as claimant in an action against a private defendant before a civil court in State B.[59]

57 'Mass-Marketing Fraud. A Report to the Attorney General of the United States and the Solicitor General of Canada,' Binational Working Group on Cross-Border Mass-Marketing Fraud, May 2003, 'Appendix Selected Cross-Border Mass-Marketing Fraud Enforcement Actions'; available from http://www.ftc.gov/bcp/conline/edcams/crossborder/law.htm.

58 See Gerrit Betlem and Christophe Bernasconi, 'European Private International Law, the Environment and Obstacles for Public Authorities,' (2006) 122 *Law Quarterly Review* 123.

59 Directive 93/7/EC, O.J. 1993 L 74/74, Art. 5.

Article 4(5) is somewhat puzzling where it stipulates that courts 'shall be competent to grant the necessary decisions' insofar as the indirect route is concerned where the watchdog must apply to the courts to obtain any measures against the trader. Just as with Article 4(4)b, the question of which courts may be posed. The watchdog's or the trader's, if different? Presumably this provision does not create a head of jurisdiction for a court outside the framework of Brussels I. Its effect surely cannot be to automatically create jurisdiction over a foreign defendant whenever a watchdog is exercising any powers against it via the court. This does not seem to be a tenable interpretation as grounds for jurisdiction cannot be created out of thin air. So all that Article 4(5) seems to do is to remind Member States to make sure that if watchdogs use the courts, they are sufficiently empowered. But there is little added value in the existence of this provision as all Member States' courts will have the usual judicial powers, one expects.

2.6 Payments for non-compliance

Another transnational enforcement query thrown up by the Regulation concerns the financial penalties under Article 4(6)g (cited above) in the event of non-compliance with a watchdog's decisions, or court orders, as the case may be. As noted, such penalties may come in the form of public law fines and/or periodic penalty payments or in the form of a civil court issued *astreinte* (periodic penalty payment for each day, or each instance of, non-compliance with an injunction). Are such financial sanctions enforceable outside the forum/watchdog State? The answer is undoubtedly yes insofar as the civil law *astreinte* is concerned,[60] but what about fines/penalty payments imposed by the competent authority itself?

To the extent the intra-Community infringement not only constitutes a civil wrong and/or a wrong sanctionable under administrative law but also a criminal offence,[61] a financial penalty imposed by a watchdog may qualify for recognition under the 2005 Council Framework Decision on Mutual Recognition of Financial Penalties.[62] This Framework Decision adopted under the Treaty of European Union (third pillar) extends the principle of mutual recognition beyond the sphere of civil law and applies it to financial penalties imposed by both judicial and administrative authorities. Two forms of recognition of foreign judgments/decisions with no exequatur being required in the executing State are included: without a double criminality requirement for some 35 listed offences and with double criminality check for other offences covered. To the extent a fine imposed

---

60 See Art. 49 in conjunction with arts. 32 and 38 Brussels I Regulation, cited above fn. 34.

61 A definite possibility under Dutch law; the cited implementation Bill includes provisions on the coordination of administrative with criminal proceedings, including the watchdog's obligation to report offences to the public prosecutor, cited above fn. 23, at p. 38.

62 Council Framework Decision 2005/214/JHA, O.J. 2005 L 76/16.

by a watchdog would come within the ambit of the Framework Decision's definitions of 'decision' and 'financial penalty' it would qualify for recognition and enforcement in a State other than that of the watchdog where the defendant has assets or is normally resident (or has a registered seat if a legal person).[63] However, there is a transition period of 5 years until 22 March 2010 within which Member States may limit the recognition to court judgments, excluding decisions by administrative authorities. A declaration to that effect must be notified and published in the Official Journal; any other Member State may invoke the principle of reciprocity regarding decisions of the declaring Member State.[64]

2.7 Protecting foreign consumers

2.7.1 Territorial scope of protection

One of the obstacles to effective cross-border enforcement identified by the Commission is that under certain national legal systems watchdogs can only act on behalf of consumers based in their own State.[65] In other words, the scope of protection of either the norm infringed or the powers or *locus standi* of the relevant enforcer (be it a public authority or an NGO) does not extend to foreign-based consumers. The Commission already documented this problem in the 1993 Green Paper about Access to Justice for Consumers.[66] More particularly, it discussed a case of cross-border misleading advertising, illustrative for private enforcement complexities. A German based company sent misleading advertisements to consumers in France. Both countries had implemented the Misleading Advertising Directive.[67] Germany had adopted civil remedies and France criminal sanctions. The German courts ruled that a tort had not been committed since the German market had not been affected.[68] Neither was there any breach of German criminal law. Even though criminal liability of the trader in France obtained, the French convictions were unenforceable in Germany, as they are not covered by the cited Brussels Convention.[69]

---

[63] Art. 4(1).

[64] Art. 20.

[65] COM(2003) 443, Nos. 12, 21, 37 and 41. See also Norbert Reich, 'Rechtsprobleme grenzüberschreitende irreführender Werbung im Binnenmarkt', (1992) 56 *RabelsZ.* 444 and case note Reich on BGH 26/11/97, I ZR 148/95, 'Grenzüberschreitende Irreführende Werbung, Aktivlegitimation im Verbandsklageverfahren,' *Verbraucher und Recht* 1998/5 (VuR), 171.

[66] Commission of the European Communities, 16 November 1993, Green Paper, *Access of Consumers to Justice and the Settlement of Consumer Disputes in the Single Market*, COM(93) 576 final.

[67] Directive 84/450/EEC, O.J. 1984 L 250/17 amended by Directive 97/55/EC of the European Parliament and of the Council of 6 October 1997 (OJ L 290, 23.10.1997, p. 18); consolidated version at: http://europa.eu.int/eur-lex/en/consleg/main/1984/en_1984L0450_index.html.

[68] See LG München I, 2 April 1992, VuR 1993, 62; LG Aachen 10 December 1993, VuR 1994, 37.

[69] Tribunal de Grande Instance Strasbourg 10 July 1987, IPRax 1989, 47. See for possibilities to start a civil procedure, Tribunal de Grande Instance Nanterre 1 February 1993, VuR 1993, 258.

The Cooperation Regulation ends any doubt about whether a watchdog is able to protect the interests of consumers based outside its own State for it obliges the watchdogs to 'fulfil their obligations under this Regulation as though acting on behalf of consumers in their own country [...]'.[70] It follows that any restrictions to the territorial scope of protection of the national laws may no longer be applied under the Regulation.[71] The gist of this provision settles the issue albeit that the formulation is somewhat cumbersome. Why is it necessary to include the fiction of acting for one's own consumers while the infringement affected consumers elsewhere? There is no need to add this 'as if'; one can simply focus on the wrong of the trader rather than on the rights of the consumers and formulate the rule in positive terms to the effect that the interests of all consumers, wherever they may be based, are protected (this is exactly what happened in the Unfair Commercial Practices Directive, see further below at section 4).[72] Nonetheless, this is an important feature of the Regulation which goes beyond what the ECJ allowed competent authorities to do under primary Community law. To appreciate the significance of the extension of the ambit of protection to consumers based outside the State of the enforcer it is illuminating to examine in some detail how the ECJ dealt with this problem in the *Alpine Investments* case.

2.7.2 *Alpine Investments*

In *Alpine Investments*[73] in the context of the Treaty rules on freedom to provide services (Article 49 EC), the ECJ dealt with the question of whether the Dutch authorities were allowed, under Community law, to ban so-called cold calling by Dutch based traders of potential clients based both inside and outside the Netherlands with a view to concluding securities transactions contracts. Clients based in Germany could be called up lawfully under German law. The firm Alpine Investments was granted a licence to practice brokerage in commodities futures trading in the Netherlands but subject to the condition to comply with the ban. The Dutch authorities' aim was both to protect consumers and to protect the reputation of the Dutch financial services industry. The firm applied for judicial review of this permit condition, invoking Community law.

The most interesting aspect of this case in the present context is the issue of which interests are protected, and are allowed to be protected under Community

---

70 Art. 11(1).

71 This mirrors the protection on non-EU consumers where action at EC level is concerned. See Art. 13(3) of Directive 2001/95/EC, O.J. 2002 L 11/4: export from the Community of dangerous products subject to a ban imposed by the Commission is prohibited. However, the export ban does not apply if the Commission decision provides otherwise.

72 See also the ECOSOC's Opinion on the Proposal for the 2004 Regulation, O.J. 2004 C 108/86, at No. 2.5.3.

73 Case C-384/93, *Alpine Investments* v *Minister van Financiën* [1995] ECR I-1141; [1995] 2 C.M.L.R. 209.

law, by the Dutch Act in question. Because there is an element of extraterritoriality in this administrative law case, *Alpine Investments* is relevant to questions of using private law in an international enforcement context, although the matter was raised in this judgment in the context of considering a possible justification on the grounds of imperative reasons of public interest of a restriction of the freedom to provide services. Alpine Investments argued that the Dutch authorities were prevented by Community law from prohibiting the cold calling of prospective clients in other Member States. In its view, it only had to comply with the law of the State where the prospective client is established and not with Dutch law.

What was the ECJ's view? It examined the justification of the prohibition of cold calling, a hindrance to intra-Community trade in services, in the light of protecting the reputation of the home State's financial industry and not in the light of protecting consumers in the destination State(s). Indeed, to an extent, it seems to agree with the view that the Netherlands is not allowed to protect non-domiciliaries, for it said:

> '[43]. Although the protection of consumers in the other Member States *is not, as such, a matter for the Netherlands authorities*, the nature and extent of that protection does none the less have a direct effect on *the good reputation of Netherlands financial services*. [Emphasis added.]
> [44]. Maintaining the good reputation of the national financial sector may therefore constitute an imperative reason of public interest capable of justifying restrictions on the freedom to provide financial services.'

It would seem to follow that extraterritorial protection of consumers on its own would be an insufficient justification for the ban on cold calling. Only where it is linked to an internal interest is it allowed; the Court stressed that confidence in the competence and trustworthiness of the financial intermediaries are particularly relevant to the type of financial service in issue, the speculative and complex commodities futures contracts.[74] According to Advocate General Jacobs, 'there can be no doubt that the concern to protect consumers *and* the concern to safeguard the reputation of The Netherlands securities markets may justify the imposition of restrictions on the free movement of services'.[75] This could be read as both interests being independently capable of constituting such a justification. However, the Opinion continues by insisting on the link, like the ECJ does, between investor confidence and the integrity of the financial markets.

It should be noted that the national rules in question were not subject to harmonisation. It can be argued that where a Community rule seeks to protect consumers in the internal market – by definition not confined to consumers domiciled in one Member State – in principle a Member State should be allowed

[74] Para. 42 of the judgment.

[75] No. 69 of his Opinion; emphasis added.

to invoke the interest of consumer protection, even where only non-domestic consumers are involved, in order to regulate the conduct of operators established within its territory. The even implementation of such rules justifies, and requires, such an approach, in my view, with or without an explicit clause about protection of foreign consumers such as the one of the Cooperation Regulation cited above. However, the existence of explicit extraterritorial consumer protection is welcome from the point of view of legal certainty.

3 The 1998 Consumer Injunctions Directive

Any powers conferred on watchdogs under the 2004 Cooperation Regulation are in addition to what they can already do under the Consumer Injunctions Directive.[76] According to the preamble, the Consumer Injunctions Directive purports to address the problem of compliance with certain listed consumer protection Directives insofar as infringements of the collective interests of consumers are concerned; the current mechanisms are insufficient (recital 2). The preamble continues by noting that it is where unlawful practices produce effects outside the country they originated from that Community legislative action is required. The Directive seems to focus upon the situation where a trader in country A acts in breach of the implementing laws of a listed Directive but, according to the applicable law, nonetheless commits no tort because the effects of his acts occur outside his State of domicile. Its title (Injunctions for the Protection of Consumers' Interests) is somewhat misleading as it is only dealing with access to the courts by so-called qualified entities from another Member State at the place where persons have acted contrary to listed consumer protection laws. Although the Directive is not entirely clear in this respect, it would seem to follow that it is restricted to cross-border enforcement.

3.1 Envisaged enforcers

What type of claimant does the Directive have in mind? The key term of the Directive is 'qualified entity' as opposed to 'competent authority' under the Cooperation Regulation. The envisaged right of action must be granted to 'any body or organisation which, being properly constituted according to the law of a Member State, has a legitimate interest in ensuring that the provisions referred to in Article 1 [the national implementing laws of listed Direc-

[76] Directive 98/27/EC, O.J. 1998 L 166/51; as amended. The amendments only concern the addition of 4 more Directives to the list of the Annex. A consolidated version is available: http://eur-lex.europa.eu/LexUriServ/site/en/consleg/1998/L/01998L0027-20050612-en.pdf. A Proposal for a codified version was adopted by the Commission on 12 May 2003, see COM(2003) 241; it has so far not been taken further than the EP's first reading on 21 October 2003, O.J. 2004 C 82 E/69.

tives] are complied with' (Article 3). Within the broad category of 'interested enforcer', two types of body are highlighted:

- independent public bodies and
- private consumer protection organizations, in accordance with requirements laid down by their national law.

Compared to the Proposal,[77] and unlike other related Directives such as the Misleading Advertising Directive[78] and the Distance Selling Directive,[79] professional trade organisations are not explicitly mentioned. However, they might of course be included in the concept of the interested enforcer. The same applies under the 2004 Cooperation Regulation: such private actors can be designated by the Member State as a body having a legitimate interest in combating intra-Community infringements.[80] As noted above, both the Regulation and the Directive give rise to lists of watchdogs/qualified entities as designated by the Member States and published in the Official Journal. There is not yet such a list for the Regulation. Under the Directive however, some 175 private and public enforcers have been designated by February 2006.[81] The number and type of organisations varies widely with some Member States listing only one (Sweden: the public *Konsumentverket/Konsumentombudsmannen*; Netherlands: the private *Consumentenbond*) and some up to 71 public and private entities (Greece). Also, some do not designate any private enforcers at all: the UK,[82] whereas others do not designate a public enforcer. As noted above, the latter will no longer be possible under the Cooperation Regulation whereas a system of purely public enforcement already in place under the Directive can of course be carried over to the Regulation regime without more. As will be seen, the legal effect of being on the list is important in that it will guarantee access to courts abroad.

3.2 Scope and protected interests

What issues are covered by the Directive? According to Article 1, the purpose of Directive 98/27 is to approximate the Member States' laws relating to actions for an injunction aimed at the protection of the *collective interests* of consumers. Likewise the Regulation. This potentially broad scope is, however, circumscribed by several restrictions. First, the Directive only applies to

77 Art. 3(1)b: 'organizations with a legitimate interest in protecting consumer interests, as well as organizations representing firms or federations of firms, in accordance with the criteria laid down by their national law', COM(95) 712, O.J. 1996 C 107/3.

78 Cited above fn. 67, Art. 4.

79 Directive 97/7/EC, O.J. 1997 L 144/19, Art. 11.

80 Under Dutch law, self-regulatory supervision bodies will be so designated, Explanatory Memorandum, cited above fn. 23, No. 48.

81 See Commission communication concerning Art. 4(3) of Directive 98/27/EC, O.J. 2006 C 39/2.

82 Next to the OFT there are 10 specialised watchdogs such as the Financial Services Authority.

infringements of Directives listed in an Annex 'as transposed into the internal legal order of the Member States' (Article 1[2]). It follows that enforcement of a Directive which has not been transposed within the required period cannot take place under the terms of the Directive. The same holds true for the Regulation. Second, the list system may be useful from the point of view of legal certainty instead of working with an open criterion such as 'consumer protection legislation'. However, it is questionable whether it is not too restrictive. Neither food law nor product safety law is included.[83] As noted above, the Regulation works with a similar list, which when new Directives are adopted may give a false impression if one is not aware of the new instrument.

Thirdly, no new remedies are to be introduced into the national legal systems on account of the Directive. All the Directive does is prescribe that qualified entities must be able to seek an injunction, publication of the judgment and/or a corrective statement, or *insofar as* the legal system of the Member State concerned so permits, a periodic penalty payment. Under the original proposal the enforcer would have been entitled, as a matter of Community law, to apply for a periodic penalty payment.[84] It follows that legal systems which do not recognize this possibility would have had to introduce it. Already at the stage of the Amended Proposal this interesting form of harmonization of national remedies law was dropped.[85]

Fourthly, a fundamental unclarity of the Proposal was whether the Directive would only be applicable (or rather the implementing legislation) in international disputes or in both purely domestic and cross-border cases. Also the text as finally adopted gives rise to this problem of interpretation. Neither the definition of infringement (cited above) nor the provision prescribing that the qualified entity must be able to seek an injunction to combat that infringement exclude purely internal disputes. In other words, they are capable of covering both cross-border and domestic infringements. However, a systematic interpretation of these provisions of the Directive points in the opposite direction. The preamble, as mentioned, identifies the aim of the Consumer Injunctions Directive in terms of overcoming difficulties in the situation of cross-border

83 Cf. the criticism of the ECOSOC on the Proposal for the 2004 Regulation, O.J. C 2004 108/86, at No. 3.8.

84 Proposal, cited above fn. 77, 'Article 2 Actions for an injunction 1. Member States shall designate the court or authority competent to rule on the proceedings commenced by the qualified entities within the meaning of Article 3, and seeking: [...] (c) an order against the losing party for payment to the plaintiff, in the event of failure to comply with the decision within a time-limit specified by the authority, of a fixed amount for each day's delay or any other amount provided for in national legislation, with a view to ensuring compliance with the decisions.'

85 O.J. 1997 C 80/10 proposed Article 2(1)c. See generally Andreas Schwarztze, 'Enforcement of Private Law: the Missing Link in the Process of European Harmonisation,' (2000) *European Review of Private Law* 135.

unlawful practices, i.e. originating in one Member State while producing effects in another. In addition, Article 2(2) reads:

> 'This Directive shall be without prejudice to the rules of private international law, with respect to the applicable law, thus leading normally to the application of either the law of the Member State where the infringement originated or the law of the Member State where the infringement has its effects.'

As this provision does not say something along the lines of 'in the event of cross-border infringements,' but on the contrary refers to application of the laws of either the country where the act took place or the place of the harmful impact, it assumes that Article 2(1) only operates in transfrontier situations. Against this one might say that Article 4 is headed 'Intra-Community infringements', which is not necessary where the whole Directive is only concerned with intra-Community infringements. However, this provision complements the entitlement to an injunction rather than independently deal with other aspects of enforcement of Community consumer law. This is actually the main Article of the Directive dealing with access to the remedies in the State of origin of unlawful practices by qualified entities from another Member State. This provision seeks to ensure the recognition of the legal capacity to bring proceedings by a claimant from another Member State (mutual recognition), albeit qualified by a possible requirement of prior consultation with either the defendant and/or an 'internal enforcer'.[86]

The presumed factual situations underlying this mutual recognition requirement are apparently limited to extraterritorial harmful effects of acts committed by persons within the jurisdiction. In this respect the factual context, as assumed by this Directive, resembles the one of the *Alpine Investment* case (cited above), where the Dutch authorities took action against a Dutch-based trader for selling activities in connection with German-based consumers. It follows that the Consumer Injunctions Directive addresses but very few of the complex legal questions involved in cross-border litigation with a view to private enforcement of Community law. In fact, on a 'pessimistic' reading, it only prescribes a kind of certification of potentially suitable enforcers seeking legal remedies in the country of the tortfeasor. It says nothing about the mirror image: legal action before the courts of the place where the harmful impact occurred. Also, Article 4(1) stipulates that the list must be accepted as proof of the qualified entity's legal capacity, but 'without prejudice to their right to examine whether the purpose of the qualified entity justifies its taking action in a specific case'. Clearly this is a potential barrier to access to the foreign court, depending on the attitude of the court in question, while any involvement of the ECJ seems doubtful.

---

[86] Art. 5 of the Directive.

[87] Cour d'appel de Bruxelles, 8 December 2005, *Duchesne v. L'Office of Fair Trading*, unreported, R.G.: 2005/KR/38. See OFT Press Releases AR0012585, 208/04, 63/04 and 'Justice 4 you,' available at www.oft.gov.uk.

Finally on the Injunctions Directive, a brief reference to the *Duchesne*[87] case may be made. This is the first case by a qualified entity under the Directive.[88] The English OFT took civil action against a trader in Belgium (domicile trader) to stop him from harming consumers in the UK. The Brussels Court of Appeal upheld a lower court's judgment ordering the Belgian firm to stop sending fraudulent 'You've won a Prize' letters to UK consumers on pain of a periodic penalty payment (reduced on appeal) of € 2,500 per mailing issued contrary to the order with a maximum of € 1m. The Court referred to the list under the Consumer Injunctions Directive cited above as conclusive evidence for the OFT's capacity to bring the claim. While acknowledging the possibility, the OFT opted for an action in Belgium rather than in the UK as it feared enforcement problems.[89] Like in the cited older Franco-German cross-border cases, an obstacle for the Belgian authorities to take action on request of the OFT was the fact that only consumers outside Belgian were targeted. Hence the OFT's own proceedings.[90] In substantive law terms the OFT relied on the Belgian and English transpositions of the Misleading Advertising Directive.[91] But if made clear it was not seeking enforcement of the higher standards provided by Belgian law. There was some disagreement between the first instance and the appeal courts about the applicable law, with the former opting for English law as the *lex causae* and the latter for Belgian law. Both courts accepted that the conduct of the Belgian defendant caused harm to the collective interests of UK consumers. On one count the OFT did not get his way: the costs of translation of various documents into French were not recoverable as the courts did not consider them essential for the proceedings and were not included in the recoverable legal costs under the Belgian Code of Civil Procedure.[92]

The latter point is one of the factors enforcers will take into account when deciding where to bring legal action: before their own courts or abroad. As noted above, the framework for enforcement action laid down in the Regulation and the Directive in my view insufficiently facilitates legal action by enforcers before their own courts against traders based outside the country. Of course that does not mean that in individual cases 'home action' is always the better alternative but the enforcers should be able to decide with as few obstacles to each alternative as possible.

[88] Report from the Commission, 'First Annual Progress Report on European Contract Law and the Acquis Review,' Brussels, 23/9/2005, COM(2005) 456, p. 8.

[89] 'Justice 4 you,' cited above fn. 87, at 15.

[90] Ibid, at 16.

[91] Cited above fn. 67.

[92] Para. 34 of the judgment.

4 Covered transnational enforcement scenarios

What picture emerges from the combined effect of the Directive and the Regulation? The Directive confers a qualified right on the enforcers to take action against a trader who harms consumers in their country by suing her in her country not in the State of the enforcer. However, under general civil law and the Brussels I Regulation the opportunity for 'home State litigation' will usually exist. Somewhat curiously, and as said above, the mainly public authorities in their capacity as Regulation watchdogs are not given this kind of possibility in the 2004 Cooperation Regulation: they always have to 'play the game' by asking their counterparts to take action. At least, under the Regulation. But other provisions may enable them to do so, such as the very 1998 Directive. Of course, when a Member State has no public authority watchdog(s) they cannot be designated under the Directive; but nothing stops them from adding newly created watchdogs under the Regulation to the list of the Directive.

The following Table summarises the result of the analysis from the perspective of the watchdog of the State where harm occurs:

State A: → trader's *Handlungsort*	***State B:*** place of harm to consumers

Harm in State B (*Erfolgsort*) while State A is the *Handlungsort*:	Directive 98/27	Regulation 2006/2004	National law + Brussels I
Enforcer State A v. defendant State A before courts of State A	Not covered	Core scenario: Art. 8	Operates in conjunction with the Regulation; key feature: no harm in State A
Enforcer State B v. defendant State A before courts State B	Not covered	Art. 4 and 3(b)	Brussels I determines jurisdiction
Enforcer State B v. defendant State B before courts State A	Not covered	Not covered	Unlikely scenario
Enforcer State B v. defendant State A before courts State A	Art. 4	Not covered; request to State A enforcers: Art. 8	Example: *Duchesne*

Note that under the Regulation, the whole system focuses on actions by a watchdog in State A against a trader in State A, who caused harm in State B, on request of a watchdog in State B. However, one needs to factor in the scenario where the trader is not based in the country of the watchdog because of the wide definition of intra-Community infringement under the Regulation. Purely internal cases are not covered by any of the instruments.

Confusingly, the main problem both instruments seek to address is close to a purely internal scenario from a jurisdictional perspective in that both claimant and defendant are based in the same State but harm is caused elsewhere; the latter – harm outside the forum State – gives rise to a choice of law question and may be problematic if the protective scope of the governing law does not cover such harm. The Directive, however, does not deal with any of these issues at all whereas the Regulation is almost exclusively limited to contemplate action by the watchdog of State A (place of acting trader) on request of the watchdog of State B (place of harm).

5 The 2005 Unfair Commercial Practices Directive

Only one aspect of the far reaching Unfair Commercial Practice Directive (UCPD)[93] will be mentioned here.[94] That is its explicit inclusion of the recognition in law of the extraterritorial protection of consumers comparable to Article 11 Cooperation Regulation (as noted above). The UCPD contains a rather elaborate provision on enforcement in addition to the usual article requiring Member States to lay down effective, proportionate and dissuasive penalties for breaches of the transposition laws.[95] Comparable to its counterparts under the 1998 Directive and the 2004 Regulation, a list of required remedies is laid down in Article 11 UCPD. However, there are some subtle differences, including the explicit mentioning of competitors of the allegedly misbehaving trader as potential enforcers. Once they, and/or their representative organisations, have been recognised 'under national law as having a legitimate interest in combating unfair commercial practices', competitors must be able to take legal action themselves or, if the Member States so wishes, enlist a watchdog to take action. Perhaps surprisingly, given that the Directive is limited to B2C transactions and Article 11(1) to enforcing compliance with the UCPD 'in the interest of consumers', what one might call B2B litigation is mandatory (where non-public enforcers exist under national law) in that competitor v. competitor legal action is envisaged.[96]

The Directive does not require a Member State to introduce the possibility for direct legal action by 'interested persons' if it has a system of centralised public enforcement. But whatever system applies (with public or private enforce-

[93] Directive 2005/29/EC, O.J. 2005 L 149/22.

[94] See generally Rogier de Vrey, *Towards a European Unfair Competition Law. A Clash Between Legal Families* (Leiden 2005), para. 2.6.2; Christian Handig, 'The Unfair Commercial Practices Directive – A Milestone in the European Unfair Competition Law?,' (2005) *European Business Law Review* 1117 and Stuyck/Terryn/Van Dyck, 'Confidence through Fairness? The New Directive on Unfair Business-To-Consumer Commercial Practices in the Internal Market,' 43 *CMLRev.* 107 (2006).

[95] Art. 13 UCPD.

[96] See also De Vrey, cited above fn. 94 at 61-62.

ment bodies or both): 'these facilities shall be available regardless of whether the consumers affected are in the territory of the Member State where the trader is located or in another Member State'.[97] Importantly, the protection of the interest of foreign consumers extends to all available private law mechanism including the supervision of self-regulatory Codes of Conduct.[98] Like the 2004 Regulation, the UCPD therefore also contributes to the elimination of one of the main obstacles to cross-border enforcement which surfaced in the various cases cited above (including *Duchesne*), namely the perceived inability of a watchdog to take action against traders in their own State on the sole ground that no harm was done within the home State.

6 A *Lingua franca*?

Finally on barriers to effective cross-border enforcement, mention should be made of what is, and probably remains for some time to come, a significant practical complexity: language barriers. In what language are the watchdogs going to communicate with each other? The 2004 Cooperation Regulation deals with this as follows in Article 12(4):

> 'The languages used for requests and for the communication of information shall be agreed by the competent authorities in question before requests have been made. If no agreement can be reached, requests shall be communicated in the official language(s) of the Member State of the applicant authority and responses in the official language(s) of the Member State of the requested authority.'

So if no common language can be agreed upon, each authority uses its own language. Presumably, each Member State is taking care of translation. It seems likely that in practice a *lingua franca* will emerge as that is cheaper, faster and more effective (English being the most likely candidate). In my view, it does not seem feasible to rely on language training of officials of the watchdogs as envisaged by the Regulation.[99] With 25 Member States, mutual cooperation and assistance may be required in any one of the 20 official languages.[100] As some will only have to be used rarely but it is hard to predict when one may nonetheless need them one day, there seems little point in being trained in the various official languages (apart from the *lingua franca*).

---

97 Art. 11(1), last sentence of 4th paragraph.

98 This is because Art. 11(1) refers to Art. 10 dealing with self-regulatory control bodies enforcing Codes of Conduct.

99 See Art. 16(1)a.

100 From 2007, Irish will become the 21st official language. See the Commission's Website: ec.europa.eu/education/policies/lang/languages/index_en.html.

Communication between watchdogs is one thing, contacts between a watchdog and a trader another. Any undertaking to stop a practice[101] or a unilateral administrative order issued to a trader based in a different Member State than the watchdog presumably would have to be in the language of the country of the trader. The Regulation contains no provisions about a language regime for such legally binding acts; the reason probably being that only intra-state measures were envisaged but we have seen above that the definition of intra-Community infringement goes beyond that. Uncertainty rules.

7 Conclusions

The OECD Guidelines refer to a number of obstacles to effective transnational enforcement of consumer law and recommend ways forward. The legal framework in place at EU level, notably the 1998 Consumer Injunctions Directive and the 2004 Cooperation Regulation cover most of the issues identified in these Guidelines. That includes gathering of evidence, sharing of information and coordinating actions against rogue trader traders operating in multiple jurisdictions. But there are some shortcoming compared to the Guidelines particularly insofar as explicit coverage of civil law instruments is concerned. The EU law framework does not impose any obligations on watchdogs to assist individual consumers who litigate against foreign traders, and there is insufficient detail on legal action by watchdogs against traders based in other countries, including the freezing of assets.

Having said that, regarding the protective scope of the norms infringed, both the 2004 Cooperation Regulation and the 2005 Unfair Commercial Practices Directive make a useful contribution by stipulating that watchdogs must protect foreign as well as indigenous consumers. This ends forms of discriminatory enforcement which have occurred in the past. It is also an improvement on the case law of the ECJ.

---

101 See Art. 4(6)e.

CHAPTER 4

Enforcing consumer interests by regulatory agencies – the British experience

A case study of the Office of Fair Trading

Geraint Howells*

1 Introduction

Everybody agrees that consumer laws need to be enforced. The disagreement concerns the manner, means and extent of enforcement. Consumer organisations point to lack of resources in enforcement agencies as causes of under enforcement, while businesses tend to focus on the bureaucracy of regulation that it is claimed unduly burdens businesses, particularly small and medium enterprises. Both claims probably have an element of truth in them. Bad enforcement can needlessly burden businesses, whilst many rogue traders can escape detection or face inadequate sanctions that agencies find difficult to enforce. Governments, at least the United Kingdom Government, are keen to create a competitive economy and take accusations of red tape seriously. In 2004 the Better Regulation Task Force Report *Less is More* advocated adopting the Dutch approach of measuring and then setting targets for reducing the administrative burden and a 'One in, One out' rule whereby new measures have to be matched by deregulation. This approach also lay behind the Chancellor of the Exchequer's announcement in his 2004 Budget speech of a review of regulation which eventually led to the Hampton Report on *Reducing Administrative Burden: Effective Enforcement and Inspections.*[1] Although praising the general competitive climate of UK industry it was critical of some aspects of the way regulators worked which it felt often focussed on process rather than outcomes.[2] It had some particular comments on consumer enforcement. It was keen for enforcement to be more targeted using risk assessment to concentrate on high risk businesses and applying a lighter touch to low risk businesses. It felt more emphasis should be placed on giving advice and there should be less form filling. Interestingly, however, it thought that whilst prosecutions should be restricted to the most severe cases penalties were often inadequate to reflect the costs and should serve as a deterrent. This work has been taken on by the Better Regulation Executive and in particular the work on penalties has been carried forward in the Macrory Report, *Regulatory Justice – Sanctioning in a Post Hampton World.*[3]

This emphasis on less demanding regulation was plainly evident in s.5 of the Deregulation and Contracting Out 1994, which included powers that Government could use to make enforcement more effective and less burdensome on business. However, on coming to power the Labour Government preferred a more consensual approach to improving enforcement and has developed an Enforcement Concordat. S. 5 of the 1994 Act is replaced by a new power for the Secretary of State to make Codes of Practices relating to regulatory require-

* Lancaster Law School. Parts of this paper draw upon work in G. Howells and S. Weatherill, *Consumer Protection Law* (Ashgate, 2005) where the reader will find more detailed analysis of specific topics.

1 Available at http://www.hm-treasury.gov.uk/media/A63/EF/bud05hamptonv1.pdf.

2 Ibid. at p. 20.

3 http://www.cabinetoffice.gov.uk/regulation/documents/pdf/macrory060524.pdf.

ments;[4] but this is viewed as a 'light touch' reserve power.[5] The Enforcement Concordat sets out principles of good enforcement.[6] The Legislative and Regulatory Reform Bill currently before Parliament will require that regulators carry out their activities in a way which is transparent, accountable, proportionate, consistent and targeted only at cases where action is needed. A Code can be established which would supersede the Enforcement Concordat.

Clearly we are at a turning point in consumer law enforcement. At a time when resources are being squeezed, government is demanding a more professional approach to enforcement which focuses resources on high risk activity and prefers advice and prevention to sanction. Parallel to this, substantively the injunction is growing in importance compared to the previous criminal law under the influence of the Injunctions Directive[7] and the Unfair Commercial Practices Directive.[8]

2 Regulators

Consumer protection has a tradition of local enforcement of consumer laws, but a there are a number of layers and sectoral divisions of responsibility for consumer law enforcement. The need for better co-ordination has been recognised, but it is not yet clear whether the necessary amount of coherence and co-ordination can be brought into the present structures.

2.1 Central government

The Office of Fair Trading (OFT) is undoubtedly the best known consumer enforcement regulator. It is also the most important central government agency. The Department of Trade and Industry (DTI) has overall direction of consumer policy and, since the OFT is not a government department, the OFT relies upon the DTI to be its spokesperson within government. However, the DTI has little involvement in the enforcement of consumer laws, apart from some powers in relation to consumer safety, which are used sparingly.

2.2 Local authorities

In fact the bulk of consumer law enforcement is carried out at a local level by Trading Standards Departments. Local authorities are responsible

4 Section 9, Regulatory Reform Act 2001.

5 Explanatory Notes to Regulatory Reform Act 2001, para. 30.

6 Available at http://www.cabinet-office.gov.uk/regulation/publicsector/enforcement/concordat.htm.

7 Directive 98/27/EC, O.J. 1998 L 166/51.

8 Directive 2005/29/EC, O.J. 2005 L 149/22.

for enforcing 80 pieces of legislation and numerous regulation affecting consumer protection. There are 1.2M inspectable premises and in 2002-3 trading standards officers undertook 465,500 inspections.[9] Trading standards officers either take a consumer protection degree and a Diploma in Consumer Protection after 18 months at work or if they have not studied consumer protection they work for three years with release for training blocks.

Much of their work in the past has involved enforcement of criminal law. In 2002-3 there were 3,905 court cases and 9, 000 written warnings.[10] One challenge facing the service is in fact the general policy of switching away from criminal sanctions to injunctions as a remedial tool. Trading standards officers who do not have the same standing in the civil courts as in the criminal courts and are confronted with different rules for collecting evidence in civil and criminal contexts.

Hampton accused the service of not using risk assessment in relation to inspections relating to weights and measures and noted that trading standards officers only inspected 60% of high risk premises and yet inspected 10% of low risk premises.[11] He was also critical of the fact that in 2003-4 there were 510,000 enforcement actions as compared to only 115,000 requests for information; although he concedes that some advice could be given during inspections and in part this is due to the reluctance of industry to seek advice.[12]

Trading Standards Departments are found within local authorities, in all county and unitary authorities. This can cause problems in ensuring adequate trading standards services in smaller authorities that have less resources. The resources devoted to the service are subject to local priorities and Hampton found the ratio between officer and inspectable premises in outer London boroughs varied between 1:219 to 1:748.[13] There have been discussions about whether the system should be restructured on a regional basis. Local enforcement is considered effective because officers are aware of local circumstances and priorities.

There are also problems of inconsistency between authorities. These are sought to be addressed in a number of ways. The Trading Standards Institute[14] tries to promote enforcement standards through training and the development of Codes of Professional Conduct. The Local Authorities Coordinators of Regulatory Services (LACORS)[15] provides an important co-ordinating role. It attempts to address the problem of inconsistent application of the law between Trading Standards Departments. Trading Standards Departments can seek advice on the

---

9 Trading Standards Statistics 2003, (CIPFA, 2003).

10 Ibid.

11 Cited above fn. 1 at p. 29.

12 Ibid. at p. 36.

13 Ibid. at p. 74.

14 http://www.tradingstandards.gov.uk.

15 http://www.lacors.gov.uk.

interpretation of the law from LACORS.[16] Also the Home Authority Principle has been developed,[17] under which the Trading Standards Department where a company has its headquarters will advise and liaise with that company and in particular act as the source for legal interpretation. Though it is not formally binding, the advantages of the Home Authority Principle are such that it is in practice largely, though not uniformly, adhered to. Nevertheless, it poses problems because a few authorities where several major companies are headquartered bear the burden of regulating companies out of all proportion to the size of the authority. As a consequence of the Hampton Report[18] the OFT has been given a role in providing a national voice and strategic leadership to the Trading Standards Service.

2.3 Sectoral regulators

It is a feature of modern consumer law that some areas have become so complex and specialised that they need to be treated as areas of law in their own right. That is why sectors like food and financial services are no longer possible to be treated fully within the confines of a generalist book on consumer protection. Similarly they have their own regulators, the Food Standards Agency[19] and Financial Services Authority.[20] Privacy and freedom of information matters are dealt with by the Information Commissioner.[21]A number of sectors have their own regulators such as the Gas and Electricity Markets Authority ('Ofgem),[22] Director General of Water Services ('Ofwat'),[23] the Office of Communications ('Ofcom'),[24] the Rail Regulator[25] and the Civil Aviation Authority.[26]

There is much work to be done in analysing the regulatory efforts of these bodies. This paper context itself with studying the OFT.

16 http://www.lacors.gov.uk/pages/trade/LACORSAdvice.asp.

17 http://www.lacors.gov.uk.

18 Hampton had favoured a new body being established called the Consumer and Trading Standards Agency.

19 See http://www.foodstandards.gov.uk.

20 See http://www.fsa.gov.uk.

21 See http://www.informationcommissioner.gov.uk.

22 See http://www.ofgem.gov.uk/ofgem/index.jsp.

23 See http://www.ofwat.gov.uk/aptrix/ofwat/publish.nsf/content/navigation-homepage(ofwat).

24 See http://www.ofcom.org.uk.

25 See http://www.rail-reg.gov.uk.

26 See http://www.caa.co.uk/index.asp.

3 OFT[27]

3.1 Background

The OFT is not a government department. Its structures were reformed in the Enterprise Act 2002. It has been the main government body responsible for protecting the consumer interest since it came into existence by the Fair Trading Act 1973. It is both a competition authority and a consumer protection authority. This has both advantages and disadvantages. The Fair Trading Act 1973 established the post of Director-General, but there is no mention in that statute of the Office of Fair Trading. However, the office supporting the Director-General became known as the OFT. The anomaly that the OFT was not officially established is remedied by the Enterprise Act 2002 which in Part I establishes the OFT[28] and simultaneously abolished the office of Director-General.[29] The functions of the Director-General are transferred to the OFT and references in legislation to the Director-General are to be treated as reference to the OFT. The OFT has a board with a chairman and separate Chief Executive. The present Chief Executive is John Fingleton, who previously chaired the Irish Competition Authority.

The OFT has to produce an annual plan setting out its main objectives and priorities for the year.[30] It also has to publish an annual report.[31] Equally it can publish other reports relating to its functions. The OFT has to acquire information relating to its tasks.[32] It also has to make the public aware of how competition may benefit consumers and provide the public with information and advice on its functions, which of course includes consumer protection The OFT has a number of functions. For instance, it provides information to consumers to help them understand their rights and make better choices. It also acts as a co-ordinating body with other regulatory bodies at the national and international level. It is also a regulator of a number of pieces of legislation. By far the largest amount of time is spent on credit matters where its role as credit licensor gives it considerable influence on the market. Many consumer businesses need a credit license to operate. It also has functions as a regulator under numerous other laws. It has broad powers to seek injunctions given to it under the Enterprise Act 2002.

---

27 See http://www/dti.gov.uk.

28 Section 1, Enterprise Act 2002.

29 Section 2, Enterprise Act 2002.

30 Section 3, Enterprise Act 2002.

31 Section 4, Enterprise Act 2002.

32 Section 5, Enterprise Act 2002.

3.2 Licensor – consumer credit

A licence is required to carry on a consumer credit business.[33] The period for which the licence is granted has varied dramatically over the years; initially fixed at three years, it was subsequently increased to ten years in 1979 and to 15 years in 1986. The aim was to reduce the administrative workload of the OFT and to lessen the burden on businesses. It was soon realised, however, that the licence period was too long for the regulators to be able to exercise effective monitoring and control of businesses and in 1991 it was reduced to five years. However, in yet another change of policy the Consumer Credit Act 2006 will allow for the granting of licenses for an indefinite period. This can be seen as part of the general approach of risk assessment allowing the OFT to concentrate on those parties most needing supervision.

There are estimated to be around 215,000 active consumer credit licences. Over half a million licences have been issued since 1976 with 15,855 new standard licences issued in 2002. 15 group licences are in existence.[34] The application fee in 2004 was £100 for a sole trader and £275 for a partnership or limited company The licence application procedure is a positive one, which means that the onus is on the applicant to satisfy the OFT that he or she is a fit person to engage in the activities covered by the licence. the name or names under which he applies to be licensed is or are not misleading or otherwise undesirable[35] When determining a licence application, the OFT can take any relevant circumstances into account, but is particularly directed to consider whether the applicant or his or her past or present employees, agents or associates (or where the applicant is a corporation, the controller of the body corporate or associates) have committed offences of fraud, dishonesty or violence; contravened the Consumer Credit Act 1974 or regulations made under it, or similar provisions in EEA states; carried on discriminatory practices, or engaged in deceitful, oppressive or otherwise improper business practices (whether unlawful or not).[36] The Consumer Credit Act 2006 ensures that irresponsible lending can be treated as a deceitful and oppressive or otherwise unfair or improper practice. The breadth of these powers is quite significant, especially the fact that behaviour can be taken into account even if it is not unlawful. The Financial Services Authority can also notify the OFT where it thinks an application should be refused.[37] In practice the OFT receives much of its information from trading standards officers.

---

33 Sections 21 and 147, Consumer Credit Act 1974.

34 *A Consultation Document on the Licensing Regime under the Consumer Credit Act 1974*, (DTI 2003) at 3.

35 Section 25, Consumer Credit Act 1974; cf. the negative procedure under section. 3, Estate Agents Act 1979 under which the Director-General can make an order prohibiting an unfit person from carrying on estate agency work, but there is no requirement to first obtain a licence. In 2005-5 it made 10 such orders: see Annual Report 2005-6 at p. 31.

36 Section 25(2), Consumer Credit Act 1974.

37 Section 25(1), Consumer Credit Act 1974.

It is perhaps not an overstatement to suggest that the threat of refusal or withdrawal of a credit licence has been the most important weapon in the OFTs fair trading armoury, since almost every trading business needs to obtain a consumer credit licence. This may have changed with the widespread injunction powers in the Enterprise Act 2002. Directors-General have shown themselves willing to use the threat of withdrawing licences to promote general business standards, not necessarily just those related to the credit aspects of the business.[38] It was very noticeable in the *Consumer Credit Deregulation* report (as on other occasions) that the then Director-General frequently drew attention to practices which caused him concern and requested the industry to put its own house in order, with the none too veiled threat that he would invoke his licensing powers should they fail to do so. In one sense licensing is a severe form of regulation, for without it entry to a market is precluded. Nevertheless the Director-General made the point that licensing allows him to exert informal pressures which help avoid the need for excessive regulation of particular practices and also prevent the imposition of sanctions where the problem is incompetence or bad management rather than dishonesty.[39].

On application for a credit licence, the Director-General can grant the licence, grant it subject to conditions, or refuse the application.[40] During its currency he can vary the licence either on application by the licensee[41] or compulsorily if he would subsequently be minded to grant the licence on different conditions.[42] He also has similar powers to suspend or revoke a licence.[43] Where the Director-General is minded to refuse an application, to grant it in different terms from the application, or to vary, suspend or revoke a licence he must inform the applicant of his reasons for that decision and give him or her the opportunity to submit representations in support of his or her application. However, this procedure is not unproblematic for the OFT. As a former Director-General has pointed out, the most difficult 'minded to refuse' notices are those based solely on complaints. By their very nature such complaints are based on only one version of events given to the enforcement authorities by discontented consumers. The specific case may have been less memorable to the trader concerned, who deals with a large number of such matters each day and may be unable to remember clearly the incident complained of, and yet still be able to raise sufficient questions and doubts about the complaints to make it impossible for the OFT to make a finding of fact on the issue raised.[44]

---

38 See for example the action taken against photocopier leasing firms engaged in unfair selling practices, *Bee Line*, 91/4 at p. 12.

39 *Consumer Credit Deregulation*, op. cit. at pp. 98–9.

40 Section 27, Consumer Credit Act 1974.

41 Section 30, Consumer Credit Act 1974.

42 Section 31, Consumer Credit Act 1974.

43 Section 32, Consumer Credit Act 1974.

44 G. Borrie, 'Licensing Practice under the Consumer Credit Act' (1982) *JBL* 91.

In the early 1990s it was estimated around 19,000 licence applications were made each year, with the OFT questioning the fitness of around 900 traders (including existing licensees). Of these 900 cases, 200 would be formally put to adjudicating officers acting on behalf of the Director-General to consider whether their licence should be refused, varied or revoked. For the five years 1989–93, the average number of decisions going against the applicant or licensee was 106.[45] In 2005-6 115 notices to applicants and licences were issued about their fitness to be granted or retain a licence, 229 warning letters were sent, 53 licences refused and 19 licenses revoked.[46] The sanction of revoking a licence is only rarely invoked, particularly against large organisations, because the consequences are so severe. One high profile exception revocation involved the television rental company Colorvision, which ceased trading once they lost their credit licence.[47] The new powers contained in the Consumer Credit Act 2006 allowing the OFT to impose conditions and impose fines for their breach should give the OFT more leverage and fits in with a trend in favour of administrative fines. This trend away from reliance on traditional criminal law is also reflected in the fact the OFT reported that it was notified of 70 successful CCA prosecutions in 2001 resulting in fines of £83,350 and only 18 in 2002 with fines totalling £55,100.[48]

The enactment of the Consumer Credit Act 2006 and the licensing reforms contained therein implemented the White Paper *Fair, Clear and Competitive – The Consumer Credit Market in the 21st Century*.[49] These reforms are in the course of being implemented with and the OFT being in the process of producing guidance based on risk-assessment principles. In the consultation document much was made of the comparison with the more detailed approach of the Financial Services Authority and it is likely that inspiration will be drawn from their practice.[50] Lomnicka makes some unflattering comparisons between the consumer credit licensing regime and the well-resourced and rigorous Financial Services Authority ('FSA') with its modern regime providing strong investigative powers, rule-making ability and flexible enforcement powers.[51] She wonders whether it would not be better to bring consumer credit within the ambit of the FSA, but ultimately believes that more will be gained by having regulatory competition between the two agencies. These comparisons may be harsh as the OFT was always working on a tight budget and dealing with a sprawling sector including many small players. Nevertheless the exclusion of consumer credit

45 Consumer Credit Deregulation, op. cit., at p. 94.

46 Annual Report 2005-6, op cit.

47 However, the OFT was found guilty of maladministration by the Parliamentary Ombudsman and paid nearly £5 million in compensation.

48 Consultation Document, op cit., at pp. 6 and 27.

49 Cm 6040 (DTI, 2003).

50 Consultation Document, op cit., at pp. 15–20.

51 E. Lomnicka, 'The Future of Consumer Credit Regulation' (2003/4)*Contemporary Issues in Law* 184.

from the FSA regime may appear anomalous, especially as consumer credit disputes can now be taken to the Financial Services Ombudsman.

3.3 General regulator

3.3.1 Part II Fair Trading Act 1973

Throughout its history beyond the field of consumer credit the OFT has struggled to find tools to make industry take its seriously. Originally Part II of the Fair Trading Act 1973 was intended to be a mechanism through which the Director-General could exert control over errant businesses, because of the threat of the OFT proposing legislative action against bad practices. However, this procedure soon became recognised as a failure with one former Director-General describing it as 'an example of a bold idea smothered by an excess of nervous caution so that the resulting provisions have inevitable been a disappointment'.[52] Although the procedures became ultimately moribund, nevertheless during the early days of the OFT's existence the fact that it had a route to threaten legislative change was an important factor in causing businesses to take the OFT seriously.

3.3.2 Codes of Practice

The decline of the Part II procedure led to the OFT placing increased emphasis on the development of Codes of Practice. S. 124(3), Fair Trading Act 1973, was something of a legislative after thought, that placed the Director-General under a duty 'to encourage trade associations to prepare and to disseminate to their members, codes of practice for guidance in safeguarding and promoting the interests of consumers in the United Kingdom'. However, during the 1990s the OFT became more sceptical both about the value of the content of some Codes and the effectiveness with which they were enforced. In 1996 in *Voluntary Codes of Practice*[53] the OFT found that codes were not well respected by enforcement authorities and consumer advisers. It considered Codes had achieved 'real, though limited, successes'.[54] Indicators of success were identified as being: the availability of a strong sanction, a plausible threat of statutory regulation, a clear wish by the good players in the industry to distinguish themselves and obvious benefits to consumers, sufficient to affect their choice of trader. Reform was needed. Subsequently, the OFT issued *Raising Standards of Consumer Care*.[55] Its sub-title *Progressing beyond Codes of Practice* indicated the thrust of the report which proposed that British Standards Institu-

52 G. Borrie, *The Development of Consumer Law and Policy*, (Stevens 1984), p. 127.

53 (Office of Fair Trading).

54 Ibid. at 15.

55 (OFT, 1998).

tion (BSI) should develop a core standard and a suite of sectoral standards which businesses would sign up to in order to be able to display a 'better trader' logo. Ultimately, the government stepped back from the standardisation approach and in its White Paper *Modern markets, confident consumers*[56] proposed that the OFT should have the role of developing core principles which the codes should comply with and awarding a seal of approval.

S.8(1) of the Enterprise Act 2002 gives the OFT the function of promoting good consumer practice. As part of that function the OFT can make arrangements for approving consumer codes. As well as approving Codes it can also withdraw approval.[57] This arrangement is known as the Consumer Codes Approval Scheme. This is new as previously it was only possible to encourage codes, but there was no mechanism for officially granting or withdrawing approval. The OFT must specify the criteria to be applied by the OFT and guidance notes have been produced: see *Core Criteria for Consumer Codes of Practice.*[58] It can also provide for a symbol to be used to signify that a code is approved by the OFT and a logo has been developed and is being promoted.

3.3.3 Unfair terms

The OFT was then looking for a vehicle through which to exercise its authority and conveniently found it in the form of the injunctions powers in the Unfair Terms in Consumer Contracts Regulations 1999 (originally 1994 Regulations). The enthusiasm with which the OFT threw resources and energy into this project matched its need for a potent weapon to raise its stock and authority amongst the business community.

The OFT challenged literally thousands of contract terms and between May 1992 to September 2004 published 29 Unfair Contract Terms Bulletins covering concluded unfair terms cases. The very act of publishing in a series of bulletins seemed to illustrate the OFT's desire to reinforce its virility in this area. Since 2004 the cases are reported on the Consumer Regulations website.[59] It seems that the rate of enforcement has slackened off no doubt due to the worst offenders having been addressed and also education of the business community. The OFT has produced both introductory guidance on Unfair Standard Terms and more detailed Unfair Contract Terms Guidance (OFT311) as well as sectoral work on *Calculating fair default charges in credit card contracts; Guidance on unfair terms in holiday caravan agreements; Guidance on unfair terms in package holiday contracts; Guidance on unfair terms in consumer entertainment contracts; Guidance on unfair terms in tenancy agreements; Guidance on unfair terms in health and fitness club agreements; Guidance on unfair terms in care home contracts; Guidance on unfair terms in home improvements contracts and Guidance on IT consumer contracts made at a distance.*

---

56 Cm 4410 (1999).

57 Section 8(2), Enterprise Act 2002.

58 (Office of Fair Trading, 2002).

3.3.4 Rogue traders

Another reason why the OFT felt the need to make full use of its powers under the Unfair Terms in Consumer Contract Regulations was because its other powers in Part III of the Fair Trading Act 1973 had proven to be hopelessly ineffective. The powers could only be exercised where there had been a breach of the criminal or civil law[60] and there were practical problems in showing that the trader had 'persisted in a course of conduct'. The OFT had long recognised that its powers to deal with rogue traders was inadequate. An ambitious discussion paper was put out in 1986 entitled *A General Duty to Trade Fairly* and this was followed by the more pragmatic *Trading Malpractices* report in 1990. The legacy of these eventually ill fated policy initiatives explains in part why the United Kingdom was so supportive of the general clause approach of the Unfair Commercial Practices Directive.[61]

3.3.5 Part 8 Enterprise Act 2002

The reform of Part III of the Fair Trading Act 1973 was heavily influenced by the injunctions approach favoured by EC law which culminated in Directive 98/27/EC on injunctions for the protection of consumers' interests.[62] This extended the injunction procedure to a wider range of EC Directives. It also sought to tackle the problem of companies using the internal market as a means of evading enforcement by locating in one Member State and directing unfair practices at consumers in a different state.[63] Bodies qualified in a Member State to protect the consumer interest must be allowed to take action in the courts or before administrative authorities in other member states. This was implemented in the United Kingdom by the Stop Now Orders (E.C. Directive) Regulations 2001.[64] These have now been repealed together with Part III of the Fair Trading A ct 1973 and replaced by Part 8 of the Enterprise Act 2002. The OFT has produced substantial guidance notes, *Enforcement of Consumer Protection Legislation.*[65] ('OFT Guidance')

Part 8 introduces separate rules for breaches of domestic and Community law. Before any enforcement powers arise there must be harm caused to the collective interest of consumers. Part 8 of the Enterprise Act 2002 provides

---

59 http://www.crw.gov.uk.

60 This contrasts with his credit licensing powers where he could act against any conduct he considered to be 'unfair'.

61 Directive 2005/29/EC, O.J. 2005 L 149/22.

62 Directive 98/27/EC, O.J. 1998 L 166/51.

63 See H.W. Micklitz, 'Cross-Border Consumer Conflicts – A French-German Experience' (1993) 16 *Journal of Consumer Policy* 411.

64 S.I. 2001/1422.

65 Hereafter, 'OFT Guidance'.

for three categories of enforcers: general enforcers, designated enforcers and community enforcers. General enforcers are the OFT, every local weights and measures authority i.e. Trading Standards Departments and the Department of Enterprise, Trade and Investment in Northern Ireland.[66] A general enforcer may make an application for an enforcement order in respect of any infringement. Designated enforcers are those the Secretary of State thinks has as one of its purposes the protection of the collective interests of consumers and has so designated by order. They can be either public or private bodies. Public bodies must be independent,[67] but their designation is conclusive evidence that they are indeed public bodies.[68] The Civil Aviation Authority, Director General of Electricity Supply for Northern Ireland, Director General of Gas for Northern Ireland, Director General of Telecommunications, Director General of Water Services, the Gas and Electricity Markets Authority, Information Commissioner and Rail Regulator have all been made designated public bodies.[69] They can make applications in respect of any infringement to which their designation relates, but in fact they have all been designated for all infringements.[70] Private bodies must satisfy criteria specified by the Secretary of State.[71] These relate to matters such as independence, impartiality, experience, competence, expertise, ability, capability, readiness to follow best practice and to co-operate with the OFT, other enforcers and regulators. The DTI has published guidance for private bodies seeking designation.[72] To-date no private bodies have been designated, but the Consumers' Association continues to have standing to seek injunctions under the Unfair Terms in Consumer Contracts Regulations 1999. Community enforcers are qualified entities specified in the Official Journal.[73] Community enforcers can bring applications in respect of Community infringements. The Court can refuse the application if it thinks the purpose of the Community enforcer does not justify its making the application.[74]

When the matter goes to court and an infringement is found the Court has a discretion to make an enforcement order.[75] However, court action is the last step and an enforcer who could make an application can also accept an undertaking. It is still too early to discern how widely these powers are being used.

---

66 Section 213(1), Enterprise Act 2002.

67 Section 213(3), Enterprise Act 2002.

68 Section 213(8), Enterprise Act 2002.

69 The Enterprise Act 2002 (Part 8 Designated Enforces: criteria foe Designation, Designation of Public Bodies as Designated Enforcers and Transitional Provisions) Order 2003, S.I. 2003/1399, Reg. 5 and Schedule.

70 Ibid. Reg. 5.

71 Ibid. Reg. 3.

72 Designation as an Enforcer for Part 8 of the Enterprise Act 2002 (DTI, 2003)

73 Section 213(5), Enterprise Act 2002.

74 Section 215(7), Enterprise Act 2002.

75 Where expedient it is possible for an interim order to be made: section 218.

During the discussions surrounding reform of Part III of the Fair Trading Act 1973 one of the issues was whether the power should be retained by the OFT or shared with trading standards. As trading standards are general enforcers the political decision seems to have been made that it is better to share out the power. Indeed the OFT Guidance states that when there is a local or sectoral problem it should be dealt with by the local or sectoral enforcer.[76] The OFT Guidance also makes it clear that it will expect the Home Authority Principle and Enforcement Concordat to be adhered to.[77]

However, the OFT has a number of mechanisms for controlling how the new powers are used. It must be consulted where enforcers believe an infringement has occurred and can direct which enforcer should make an application, taking over the case itself where it considers that appropriate. It is clear that it will favour referring matters to sectoral regulators, even self-regulatory bodies like the ASA.[78] It also provides guidance and has powers to make the system run effectively. For instance, it can seek information, not only for itself but also for Community enforcers and private designated enforcers. It can step into monitor compliance with undertakings and orders, notwithstanding which enforcer had previously been involved. These powers fit well with the new role of the OFT as responsible for co-ordinating trading standards services. The OFT is also the co-ordinator at the international level.[79]

4 Conclusions

4.1 General approach to enforcement

The prevailing enforcement philosophy is certainly against the heavy handed practices that sometimes occurred in the past. Particularly at local level it was possible for local trading standards officers to bring criminal proceedings for what could appear minor offences.[80] This should no longer be possible and indeed the Court of Appeal has thrown out a prosecution as an abuse of process when it was not in accordance with its own prosecution protocol.[81] As regards the OFT its willingness to bring legal action has been seen to vary depending on the inclinations of the organisation's leadership. The present hierarchy certainly stress the desire to educate and achieve market based solutions by working with business.[82] Equally there is a realisation that enforcement

76 Guidance, para. 3.76.

77 Guidance, para. 3.80.

78 Guidance, paras. 3.77-78.

79 Guidance, paras. 3.87-89.

80 Case *Smedleys v Breed*, [1974] A.C. 839 [1974] 2 W.L.R. 575.

81 Case *R. v Adaway (Glen)*, [2004] EWCA Crim 2831 (2004) 168 J.P. 645 (2004) 168 J.P. N. 956 Times, November 22, 2004.

82 See Objective 2 Action Plan 2006-7.

may be necessary where this does not work. In a change from the past there has been signalled a move away from a reactive enforcement approach based on complaints to an intelligence based approach based on information on how the market functions.[83] This is part of the desire to yield greater benefits from public enforcement resources. It is important that enforcement remains a last resort, but one that is available to the regulators. Risk assessment, more emphasis on advice etc. are fine so long as business knows that it also has a responsibility to comply with the rules and there is a sanction if it fails to do so.[84] In this respect moves towards higher and more easily imposed administrative fines are to be welcomed.

4.2 Going all the way to court

It must be possible for regulators to take matters to court. In recent times there has seemed to be an increased readiness to take matters to court where traders do not accept the OFTs line. It is well known that the OFT lost its challenge under the Unfair Terms in Consumer Contracts Regulations to a clause which allowed interest to be charged on outstanding debt in *Director General of Fair Trading v First National Bank.*[85] The latest OFT Annual Report however highlighted two significant victories in the English High Court and Scottish Court of Sessions. In *Office of Fair Trading v The Officer's Club*[86] an undertaking was accepted that a High Street retailer would not permanently advertise 70% off everything. This was an important authority in establishing what was appropriate own price comparisons. In *Office of Fair Trading v. MB Designs (Scotland) Ltd*[87] Part 8 of the Enterprise Act was invoked against a double glazing company for consistently supplying poor quality goods. This is also an important decision, because it was thought it would be difficult to apply the injunction procedure where what was in question was compliance with general quality standards. The effect is that continued breach of such standards can now amount to contempt of court with a wide range of punitive sanctions available.

A key element of the OFT enforcement strategy has been to tackle scams. This is important given the fraudulent nature of many of these business practices and because they frequently prey on the most gullible and vulnerable. Home work, pyramid selling, bogus prize draw, premium rate scams and internet spamming scams were all targeted. Some of these highlight the OFT's enforcement work has involved cross border practices. Undertakings were taken from two Dutch companies in relation to bogus prize draw mailings.[88] Moreover

83 Annual Report 2005-6 p. 4; Action Plan 2006-7 p. 11.

84 This fits in with the philosophy of I. Ayres and J. Braithwaite, *Responsive Regulation*, (Oxford 1992).

85 [2002] 1 AC 481.

86 [2005] EWHC 1080 (Ch).

87 2005 S.L.T. 691.

88 DC Direct Communications Venk BV and Fitanova BV, see Annual Report 2005-6.

the OFT pursued the Belgium company D Duchesne SA to the Brussels Court of Appeal[89] and may have to go even higher in the Belgium courts.

There may be understandable reluctance sometimes on the part of trading standards officers to go to court. Particularly small authorities can be reluctant to enter into contested litigation; especially where it requires that products be tested so the costs involved can make a big dent into small budgets. We have already speculated about the uncertain impact on litigation arising out of the move towards civil court actions for injunctions where trading standards officer do not have the same rights of audience as they enjoy in the magistrates' court.

4.3 Organisation

Traditionally local enforcement was seen as a strength of the United Kingdom system. However, increasingly the system is coming under pressure, partly as the nature of local authorities has changed with the growth of smaller unitary authorities. There is a need for more co-ordination. There are roughly four and half thousand trading standards officers employed in the United Kingdom, but the numbers are reducing (and ageing) and they are dispersed amongst many authorities varying greatly in size. The average staff number is 51 in the counties, 17 in London boroughs and 14 in unitary authorities. The OFT has been given a leadership and co-ordinating role and it remains to be seen if this is sufficient. There would seem to be more scope for creating umbrella services across a number of authorities as happens in West Yorkshire.

The OFT itself has issues it needs to address. Fundamentally of course there is its dual function as consumer protector and competition authority, which has synergies but also poses the risk of consumer protection being viewed as the 'Cinderella' service. It also has had at times an uneasy relationship with the DTI , who it has to rely upon to sponsor its cause within Government and to find space for and steer its desired legislative measures through Parliament. Now the DTI is itself more pro-active in consumer affairs there is a degree of parallel energy that needs to be co-ordinated. The OFT also has to work with the sectoral regulators like the two FSAs (Food Standards Agency and Financial Services Authority) and OFCOM. The problems of co-ordination are at least now being recognised and it remains to be seen how well the different links work or whether at some point there will be a need to revisit Hampton's idea of a general enforcement authority of consumer protection.

---

89 See M. Haley, 'Stop Now-Injunctions Protecting the Interest of European Consumers' at Austrian Presidency Conference on Effective Legal Redress available at http://eu2006.bmsg.gv.at/cms/eu2006EN/attachments/2/0/9/CH0604/CMS1133512397104/haley.pdf.

4.4 Final remarks

It should not be forgotten that the regulatory state is a relatively new post war phenomenon. The OFT is itself only just over 30 years old. It would not be surprising if some mistakes had not been made along the way given the young agency's needed to experiment with enforcement strategies. The study of regulation is itself relatively new.[90] The interesting academic work on regulation is now feeding into policy work and practice of enforcement agencies. It is important the baby is not however thrown out with the bath water. In particular the tight financial constraints on consumer enforcement authorities (even compared to many other public regulators) need to be taken into account. The link between substantive law and enforcement has also to be drawn. This supports calls for laws that are self-enforcing or which can be easily enforced because of their clarity. The move away from criminal law to prospective civil law injunctions should help this enforcement process so long as the legal costs of using the civil law are taken into account.

90 *Inter alia* one might mention I. Ayres and J. Braithwaite, *Responsive Regulation* (Oxford 1992); A. Ogus, *Regulation: Legal Form and Economic Theory* (Clarendon 1994), R. Baldwin and M. Cave, *Understanding Regulation* (Oxford 1999) and in the consumer context P. Cartwright, *Consumer Protection and the Criminal* Law (Cambridge 2001).

CHAPTER 5

Enforcement of consumers' collective interests by regulatory agencies in the Nordic countries

Klaus Viitanen

1 Introduction

The Nordic countries started building their national systems of consumer protection from the beginning of 1970s. In spite of the fact, that there are differences amongst these systems, there are also clear and fundamental similarities, which justify us clubbing it together as the Nordic model of consumer protection.

The most typical features for the Nordic system of consumer protection, in the area of substantive law, are the following ones:

1) *regulation of marketing and unfair contract terms by general clauses which have a very wide scope of application;*
2) *possibility to adjust unfair contract terms – including the price of the goods or services – in already concluded contracts;*
3) *quite comprehensive use of mandatory contract law provisions.*

Perhaps the biggest difference between Finland and the other Nordic countries may be found in the field of substantive law. In Finland almost all relevant regulation has been codified into one single act, to the Consumer Protection Act 1978 instead of adapting several separate acts as in other Nordic countries.

In enforcement/access to justice questions the typical features of the Nordic system are the following ones:

1) *special state authorities, Consumer Ombudsmen, have been established for the supervision of marketing and unfair contract terms;*[1]
2) *frequent use of preventive actions in the supervision of marketing and standard contract terms;*
3) *special courts – often called Market Court or Council – are used in cases which concern consumers' collective interests;*[2]
4) *consumer organisations have always had a rather limited role, especially in the enforcement;*
5) *public out-of-court bodies for the settlement of individual consumer disputes are widely used instead of private bodies.* The protection of consumers' individual rights is in most Nordic countries based on two-stair system of out-of-court procedures for the settlement of individual consumer disputes. Consumer advisors exist at the municipal level in Finland and Sweden while in Norway, consumer centres are found at the district level. Their competence is limited to advice and mediation. Besides that, all four countries have a special centralised body – often referred to as the Consumer Complaint Board – with a general jurisdiction to settle all kinds of consumer-to-business disputes. Their decisions are, however, only recommendations, except in Norway;[3]

---

1 For more details, see ch. 2.1. of this article.

2 For more details, see ch. 2.2. of this article.

3 For more details of the Nordic Public Complaint Boards, see K. Viitanen, 'The Scandinavian Public Complaint Boards: the Aims, Present Situation and the Future' (1996) *Consumer Law Journal*, pp. 118-126.

6) *small claims procedure in ordinary courts.* The new Norwegian Act on Civil Procedure (tvisteloven), which will enter into force in year 2007, establishes a separate small claims procedure for disputes, where the monetary interest do not exceed a certain sum of money. In Denmark, where a major reform of Danish court system and procedural rules was adopted in summer 2006, small claims procedure in minor disputes will be available from the beginning of year 2008. Also in Sweden a separate small claims procedure was available between the years 1973-1987;[4]
7) *group action for compensation.* The Swedish Group Action Act entered into force in 2003. In Norway group action for compensation will be possible from the beginning of year 2007. In Denmark and Finland, proposals for the adoption of this court action exist;[5]
8) *the minimal role of criminal law in the enforcement.* In spite of the fact, that it is possible to impose criminal sanctions to those persons who have intentionally or by negligence infringed the rules concerning marketing, these sanctions are in practice very seldom used.

Access to justice-questions are often divided into two main groups: to the protection of consumers' collective interests and to the protection of consumers' individual rights. In the protection of consumers' collective interests, it is question of protecting consumers as a group. The group may consist of all consumers, or may be more limited. Often the aim in the protection of consumers' collective interests is to prevent economic and physical damages caused by unfair marketing practices, unfair standard contract terms, or unsafe or poor-quality products. This prevention usually takes place by supervision which is carried out by state authorities and/or different kinds of trade and consumer organisations. However, supervision often fails on the consequence that illegal activities cause similar kinds of damages to a large group of consumers. For such problems other means of protection are required for consumers' collective interests. One of the most promising means of protecting consumers interests in mass consumer disputes is group action for compensation.

The purpose of this article is to shortly present, how consumers' collective interests are protected in four Nordic countries: Denmark, Finland, Norway and Sweden. In section 2 the Nordic system of supervision of marketing and standard contract terms will be presented. In section 3 the focus will be on collective actions for compensation in the Nordic countries, mainly on the group action

4 For more details of small claims procedure in Norway, see *Ot.prp.nr. 51(2004-2005)* Om lov om mekling og rettergang i sivile tvister (tvisteloven), pp. 193-202 and *NOU 2001:32*, Rett på sak. Lov om tvisteløsning (tvisteloven). Bind A. (Oslo 2001), pp. 317-344. For Denmark, see *Reform af den civile retspleje III. Adgang til domstolene*, Betænkning nr. 1436 (København 2004), pp. 425-462. For Sweden, see B. Demeulenaere, *Sweden's System to Resolve Consumer Disputes. Especially the Public Complaints Board and the Small Claims Procedure* (Stockholm 1983), pp. 53-83.

5 For more details, see ch. 3.3. of this article.

for compensation. Due to the active law drafting during the recent years in these countries, this action is at this moment a very topical issue in the Nordic countries.

2 Supervision of marketing and standard contract terms

2.1 The Nordic Consumer Ombudsmen

2.1.1 General

The enforcement of consumers' collective interests in the Nordic countries is taken care of by a special state authority, called the Consumer Ombudsman. His task is to supervise marketing practices and the use of standard contract terms, but also to promote consumer interests in general. These authorities were established in all four countries between years 1973-1978. The activities of the Consumer Ombudsman are in the many Nordic countries connected to the activities the National Consumer Agency. In Finland and Sweden the Consumer Ombudsman is the head of the National Consumer Agency.

The most relevant acts which regulate the activities of the Consumer Ombudsman offices, are the following ones: in Denmark *Markedsføringsloven* 2005 (hereinafter the Danish Marketing Act), in Finland *Kuluttajansuojalaki* 1978 (hereinafter the Finnish Consumer Protection Act), in Norway *Markedsføringsloven* 1972 (hereinafter the Norwegian Marketing Act) and in Sweden *Marknadsföringlag* 1995 (hereinafter the Swedish Marketing Act). Especially those acts, which have entered into force already in 1970s, have been amended several times later on. The English translations of these acts are available on the home pages of the Nordic national consumer agencies or ombudsman offices.[6]

2.1.2 Preventive measures

An extremely typical feature for the Nordic system of consumer protection is the frequent use of preventive measures in the supervision of marketing and standard contract terms: advance opinions, marketing guidelines and negotiations with the trade organisations concerning standard contract terms. The aim is to prevent any infringements of law by informing the traders and by negotiating with them. Often these preventive measures are not based on the law, but have been created in practice during the years.

---

6 For the Danish National Consumer Agency, see http://www.forbrug.dk; for the Finnish National Consumer Agency, see http://www.kuluttajavirasto.fi; for the Norwegian Consumer Ombudsman, see http://www.forbrukerombudet.no and for the Swedish National Consumer Agency, see http: //www.konsumentverket.se.

Advance opinion is an opportunity for an individual advertiser to check beforehand whether a planned marketing campaign is infringing the marketing law or not. The Danish Marketing Act contains a special provision on this topic. On request, the Danish Consumer Ombudsman will give a statement regarding his view of the lawfulness of the planned marketing arrangement. Once the Consumer Ombudsman has shown 'green light', he cannot interfere on his own initiative with an arrangement covered by the advance opinion and implemented within a reasonable time of its delivery.[7] In the other Nordic countries the system is more informal. This means that in principle an advance opinion does not bind the Consumer Ombudsman. However, in practice this has never been a problem. For example, the Finnish Consumer Ombudsman gave altogether 107 advance opinions in year 2004.[8]

The offices of the Nordic Consumer Ombudsman have issued during the years *marketing guidelines* in several sectors of marketing. These guidelines are mainly based on the existing case law and their purpose is to inform traders what kind of marketing practices are infringing the law. For example, in the year 2004 the Finnish Consumer Ombudsman issued three new guidelines: Marketing error situations; Minors, marketing and purchases and Changes in contract terms. In addition, the Finnish National Consumer Agency and the National Board of Education prepared principles concerning marketing and sponsorship in schools.

The third preventive method used by the Nordic Consumer Ombudsmen are *negotiations with trade organisations concerning standard contract terms* in several branches of business.[9] In Finland a good example of these negotiated standard contract terms are the Package Travel Contract Terms, which are used in practice by almost all Finnish travel agencies. The results of these negotiations do not necessarily mean that the Consumer Ombudsman approves of all the contract terms used in the negotiated standard contract terms, but he approves of most of them.

There are many benefits connected to these negotiations. From the point of view of traders the probability that Consumer Ombudsman would take actions against negotiated contract terms is in practice quite minimal. From consumers' point of view one benefit is that consumer law prohibits only the use of unfair contract terms. By these negotiations it is possible to add new terms to the standard contracts which improve consumers' contractual position compared to the earlier used standard contract terms, or even compared to the mandatory consumer contract law provisions. This fact clearly shows the task of the

7 The Danish Marketing Act, Art. 25.

8 Consumer Agency/Ombudsman. Annual report 2004, p. 22.

9 See, e.g., T. Wilhelmsson, 'The Implementation of the EC Directive on Unfair Contract Terms – An Assessment from a Nordic Point of View', in: Francoise Maniet ja Beata Dunaj (eds.), *The Implementation Process of EC Directives on Product Safety, Product Liability and Unfair Contract Terms* (Louvain-la-Neuve 1994), p. 34.

Consumer Ombudsmen to promote consumers' collective interests, and not only to supervise, whether the legislation in force is violated or not.

2.1.3 Repressive actions

In case infringements of law are observed, the supervisory systems in the Nordic countries are still given priority to the use of soft law methods. The Consumer Ombudsmen have an obligation to persuade the trader in question to abandon unfair marketing practices or the use of unfair contract terms in voluntarily.[10] The trader is asked to sign a written engagement in which he promises not to continue unfair marketing practice or the use of unfair contract terms.

The use of soft law methods has shown to be extremely effective during the years. The great majority of clear infringements of law are solved in this manner without the need to use any legal sanctions. Even in more principal cases traders often prefer to change their marketing practices instead of letting the Consumer Ombudsman take the case to the court.

In cases where persuasion fails, hard law sanctions are available. The Consumer Ombudsman may take legal action against the trader in a special court, which in most Nordic countries is called as the Market Court or Council. However, in clear cases or in cases of minor importance, the Consumer Ombudsman is entitled in his own right to impose an injunction order together with conditional fines. In case a trader resists, the systems in the Nordic countries differ from each other. In Denmark, Finland and Sweden, the injunction becomes void if the trader resists within a certain time limit and the Consumer Ombudsman has to take the case to the court. In Norway the decision of the Consumer Ombudsman has a stronger legal position. In Norway, the trader who is not satisfied with the decision made by the Consumer Ombudsman, has to appeal to a court in case he wants to reverse it.[11] In all four countries the Consumer Ombudsman may impose a temporary injunction order in urgent cases. It is valid until the courts start to try the case.

2.2 The Nordic Market Courts

2.2.1 General

The final decision-making power when assessing whether marketing practice or standard contract terms may be regarded as unfair or not, has in the Nordic countries been given to special courts. In Finland and Sweden these courts are called the Market Courts. Their jurisdiction is limited to the following areas of law: consumer law (only marketing and standard contract

---

10 See, e.g., the Finnish Consumer Agency Act (1056/1998), Art. 5.

11 The Norwegian Marketing Act, Art. 14.

terms), unfair competition and competition law. In Norway the similar court is called the Market Council. All these three courts were established in the 1970s. In Denmark the competent court is, however, the Maritime and Commercial Court of Copenhagen, which was established already in 1862. It is a special court for commercial disputes, including marketing and unfair contract terms cases. All courts consist of professional judges, and expert members, who in practice may be also representatives of different interests groups. For example, in the main hearing the Finnish Market Court normally consists of three professional judges and from one to three expert members, everybody with an individual right to vote.[12]

2.2.2 Right of action

In consumer matters a court procedure in the Nordic Market Courts is initiated by a petition of the Consumer Ombudsman. In Finland and in Sweden the right of action has been formally restricted to the Consumer Ombudsman only. However, if the Consumer Ombudsman refuses to file a petition with the court for the hearing of cases concerning advertising measures or contract terms, the petition may be filed by a registered association looking after the interests of traders, consumers or employees. In Norway also individual traders or consumers who have been affected by the marketing practice, have a secondary right of action, and may submit the case to the court. The situation is most liberal in Denmark, where anyone with a legal interest, may bring a case to the court.[13]

In practice competitors often take legal actions against each others in the Nordic Market Courts, but on the basis of unfair competition law, which provide to them more than only a secondary right of action. However, individual consumers, or even consumer organisations, have not shown interest to use their right of action in the Nordic countries. For example, in Finland in spite of the fact that the secondary right to institute proceedings in the Market Court has been available since year 1978, it has never been used.

The right to take legal action against traders in the Nordic countries used to be reserved only to the consumer authorities and consumer/trade organisations of the same country where the defendant was domiciled. Due to the Directive 98/27/EC on injunctions for the protection of consumers' interests[14], so called *injunction directive*, the legislation was amended also in the Nordic countries so, that in cross-border matters a case may also be initiated by petition of a foreign

[12] The Finnish Market Court Act (1527/2001), Art. 9.2.

[13] The Danish Marketing Act, Art. 27.

[14] Directive 98/27/EC O.J. 1998 L 166/51. For more details of this directive, see, e.g., C.E. Côté, 'Injunction Actions for the Protection of Collective Interests of Consumers', in: Jean-Paul Pritchard (ed.), *Access to Justice and Alternative Dispute Resolution Systems in Central and Eastern Europe* (Louvain-la-Neuve 2001), pp. 18-28.

authority or organisation. However, at least in Finland, so far there have been no cases in the Finnish Market Court which would have been initiated by foreign organisations or authorities. Neither has the Finnish Consumer Ombudsman used the benefits of the injunction Directive 98/27/EC in other Member States. It is more than probable, that the situation is similar in other Nordic countries.

However, it might be worth mentioning in this context, that for example, the Finnish Market Court solved its first case concerning cross-border marketing already in the year 1987. In that case a big multinational company was marketing its products via satellite television from Britain to Finland. The Finnish Consumer Ombudsman took legal action in the Finnish Market Court against the Finnish subsidiary company of the multinational company in question. The court stated, that the Finnish Consumer Protection Act was applicable in the case due to the fact that marketing was intentionally targeted also to the Finnish consumers. Perhaps the most interesting point in this case was the fact, the injunction order with a conditional fine was imposed to the Finnish subsidiary company.[15]

2.2.3 Sanctions

In case the Nordic Market Court considers a marketing practice as unfair, the following sanctions are available:

1) *injunction order.* The purpose of this order is to prohibit the trader to carry on his illegal activities. In most Nordic countries an injunction order is strengthened with a conditional fine. Conditional fine is a fine which the trader has to pay in case he does not comply with the court order. However, in Denmark criminal sanctions are used instead of conditional fines. Non-observance of an injunction imposed by the court, or even imposed by the Danish Consumer Ombudsman in clear cases, is punishable by fine or imprisonment of up to four months;[16]
2) *corrective advertising.* This means an obligation to correct, normally by a totally new advertisement, the information given in unfair marketing.[17] In practice the significance of corrective advertising has been rather small. The reason for this is the simple fact, that marketing campaigns have in practice ended a long ago before the judgment is given;
3) *market disruption fee.* In Sweden a special sanction, called market disruption fee, has been available since the year 1996. A trader may be ordered to pay a market disruption fee, if he or a person acting on his behalf intentionally or by carelessness violates the substantive rules of the Swedish Market Act. However, it is not possible to impose a fee in case a trader has infringed only the general clause in Article 4. The ordered fee has to be

[15] The case number 1987:13 of Finnish Market Court.

[16] The Danish Marketing Act, Art. 30.1.

[17] See, e.g., The Finnish Consumer Protection Act, ch. 2, Art. 9.

at least SEK 5 000 and it may not exceed SEK 5 000 000 (approximately EUR 500 000) and ten percent of the trader's annual turnover. Market disruption fee is an alternative sanction to an injunction order with conditional fines, and the intention was, that it would be used only in serious cases. In most cases the court should still impose only an injunction order together with conditional fines.[18]

2.2.4 Criminal sanctions

In Sweden the possibility to use criminal sanctions was abolished when the market disruption fee was adopted. However, in other Nordic countries criminal sanctions are still in principle available, but the criminal procedure takes place in general courts, which also impose the sanctions. In practice criminal sanctions have very seldom been used. For example, in Finland the Consumer Ombudsman tried to use criminal sanctions against unscrupulous traders, but the criminal charges were dismissed or the punishments were so low, that there was no sense in bringing new criminal cases to the courts.[19]

2.2.5 Compensation of damages

Neither do the Nordic Market Courts have jurisdiction to order compensation of damages in individual cases. This means that individual consumers, who want to claim compensation for their economic damages caused by unfair marketing practices or the use of unfair standard contract terms, have to take legal action in a general court in case out-of-court procedures turn out to be useless. Due to the risk of high costs of litigation, this possibility is at this moment often more theoretical than practical. However, the new Nordic group actions for compensation, where the Consumer Ombudsmen may act as plaintiffs on behalf of a group of consumers, may change this pattern in the future.

2.2.6 Right to appeal

Right to appeal differs between the Nordic countries. In Sweden the judgment of the Market Court is final. No one has a right to appeal to the Court of Appeal or directly to the Supreme Court. This was also the situation in Finland until the year 2002. However, since year 2002 the parties have had right to appeal to the Supreme Court provided that the Supreme Court grants a leave to appeal.[20] In Denmark the decisions of the Maritime and

---

[18] The Swedish Marketing Act, Art. 22-25; *SOU 1993:59*, Ny marknadsföringslag. Slutbetänkande av Marknadsföringsutredningen. (Stockholm 1993), pp. 410-424.

[19] See, e.g., T. Wilhelmsson, 'Administrative Procedures for the Control of Marketing Practices – Theoretical Rationale and Perspectives', in: Tuuli Junkkari (ed.), *Twelwe Essays on Consumer Law and Policy* (Helsinki 1996), p. 149.

[20] The Finnish Act on Certain Proceedings before the Market Court (1528/2001), Art. 21.

Commercial Court may be appealed to the Supreme Court. Also in Norway the parties may appeal to a general court.

In Finland the parties have been quite active to use their new right to appeal. In fact, it has been used in most cases and the Supreme Court has been so far quite liberal when granting its leave to appeal. In its final decisions, the Supreme Court has confirmed the judgement made by the Market Court. The changes have been minor.[21]

2.2.7 Legal expenses

In consumer law cases the no-cost rule is applied in the Market Court in all Nordic countries. This means that both parties have to carry their own legal expenses in spite of the outcome of the case. In spite of the no-cost rule, the lack of sufficient resources has probably been one reason for the unwillingness of consumer organisations to initiate cases in the Nordic Market Courts.[22]

3 Collective actions for compensation

3.1 General

In modern society it is not uncommon that many consumers suffer economic damages due to problems which are more or less similar to other consumers. The reason for this is the increasing mass production of consumer goods and the mass supply of consumer services, e.g., package travels and insurances. However, the dispute settlement systems in most western countries are at present unable to solve these mass consumer disputes. The traditional civil procedure is still only aimed at solving disputes between individual litigants.[23] However, the same problem may also be seen in most out-of-court procedures which have been created during the last few decades. They are forceless in front of the mass consumer disputes.

In the discussion concerning the settlement of mass consumer disputes most attention over the last few decades has without doubt been paid to group action for compensation. Group action for compensation can be briefly defined as a court action in which a plaintiff – either a member or a non-member of a specified group – brings a suit for the benefit of a specified group without the

---

21 See, e.g., J. Bärlund, 'Om högsta domstolen som besvärsinstans i vissa marknadsrättsliga ärenden' (2005) *Tidskrift utgiven av Juridiska Föreningen i Finland*, pp. 424-427.

22 See, e.g., K. Viitanen, 'The Crisis of the Welfare State, Privatisation and Consumers' Access to Justice', in: Thomas Wilhelmsson and Samuli Hurri (eds.), *From Dissonance to Sense: Welfare State Expectations, Privatisation and Private Law* (Aldershot 1999), p. 552.

23 See, e.g., M. Cappelletti, *The Judicial Process in Comparative Perspective* (Oxford 1989), pp. 268-287.

express permission of the group members, and this results in a judgement that is binding both for and against all the members of the group.[24]

Based on who the plaintiff is group actions can be divided into three types. Firstly, we may identify a proper *class action*, where the plaintiff is a member of the group and seeks, e.g., redress also for his own damages which he has suffered. A second possibility is that the plaintiff is not a member of the group, but a public authority responsible for the supervision of collective rights of a certain group. This kind of actions has been called *public action*. Thirdly, there are actions where the plaintiff is a private group, e.g., a consumer organisation, which has received legal standing. These actions have been called *actions by organizations*.[25]

The settlement of mass consumer disputes is in principle possible also in the traditional civil procedure. If there are several plaintiffs against the same defendant, the court may join these actions in one proceeding if that contributes to a quicker and proper trial of the case.[26] This is called *consolidation of actions*. In spite of the fact that all these cases are handled in the same trial, it is basically a question of several individual claims which for economic reasons have been consolidated. This means also that all the members of the group who want to have compensation must be involved in the trial as plaintiffs. In case a consumer organisation or another third party is representing the members of a group, it must have a proxy from each of them. In consolidated cases the same principle is applied as in most other countries concerning legal expenses. It is the loser who has to pay his own trial costs and those of the other party.[27] This means that all the members of the group who are plaintiffs in the trial have to bear their part of the legal expenses if the case is lost.

The second alternative in the settlement of mass consumer disputes is the so-called *pilot case*. This means that only one case is taken to a court and in the other cases parties comply with the court's judgement made in the pilot case. In most pilot cases this happens without any prior agreement between the plaintiff and defendant.

In Finland the Consumer Ombudsman can assist consumers in a court in an individual dispute if a case has significance for consumers' general interests and a preliminary ruling is desired. The Consumer Ombudsman can also decide that the National Consumer Agency will pay for consumer's all legal expenses, including those which he has to pay to the other party if the case is lost.[28]

---

[24] See, e.g., P.H. Lindblom, *Grupptalan*. (Göteborg 1989), p. 19.

[25] See, e.g., T. Bourgoignie, *Foreword. Group Actions and Consumer Protection*. Edited by Thierry Bourgoignie. (Bruxelles 1992), pp. v-vi.

[26] See, e.g., The Finnish Code of Procedure, ch.18, Art. 1-8.

[27] In Finland, see the Finnish Code of Procedure, ch. 21, Art. 1.

[28] See the Finnish Consumer Agency Act (1056/1998), Art. 9.

In practice the Finnish Consumer Ombudsman makes from 2 to 6 decisions to provide aid of this kind each year. For example, at this moment, the Finnish Consumer Ombudsman is assisting a consumer in the Supreme Court in a case where the consumer had bought consumer goods from USA via internet and paid by using his VISA credit card. He never received the ordered goods, but anyway got the bill from VISA. He refused to pay on the ground of connected lender liability. Now the Finnish Supreme Court is deciding, whether the connected lender liability, as implemented in the Finnish Consumer Protection Act, ch. 7, sets obligations also to credit card companies such as VISA.

The main problem in the use of pilot cases is that from procedural law viewpoint the court's judgement does not differ in any way from judgements given in normal individual cases. It does not have res judicata-effect in other similar cases. This means that the defendant who has lost his case, does not have any legal obligation to comply with the judgment in other identical disputes. The effects of pilot cases are only based on defendant's fear that a preliminary ruling may encourage other consumers to take legal actions in similar cases. Creating a precedent is only helpful in situations where a company is willing to comply with the ruling in all other cases, too.

In Finland pilot cases have shown to be useful in some situations, but there are also a lot of examples in which traders have been unwilling to comply with decisions made in pilot cases. In the latter cases time limits on claims have caused problems to those consumers who have waited for the results of a pilot case. If a pilot case is under consideration for years, other claims with a similar basis can lapse. Preventing this may require individual measures on the part of each consumer, which conflict with the main idea of a pilot case.

In most European countries the possibility of bringing a group action for compensation does not yet exist. Group action for compensation has been much more popular in common law countries outside the Europe. The most well-known examples may be found in the United States, Canada and Australia.[29] The lack of group action for compensation in Europe has been a problem, because it is expressly this type of court action which could be very useful in the settlement of mass consumer disputes. Group action for compensation is an important weapon when making justice more accessible in mass disputes.

[29] See, e.g., P.H. Lindblom, *Progressiv process* (Uppsala 2000), pp. 427-439; Access of Consumers to Justice and the Settlement of Consumer Disputes in the Single Market, COM(93) 576, pp. 63-64; M. Eisenstein, *Consumer Protection in the United States* (Stockholm 1982), pp. 30-53; N. L'Heureux, 'Effective Consumer Access to Justice: Class Actions' (1992) *Journal of Consumer Policy*, pp. 445-461; D. Harland, 'Group Actions: A Discussion of the Australian Proposals, with Some Other Perspectives from Asia and the Pasific', in: Thierry Bourgoignie (ed.), *Group Actions and Consumer Protection* (Bruxelles 1992), pp. 126-139.

3.2 Nordic group actions for compensation

However, now it seems that the Nordic countries may once again show example in the field of consumer protection by adopting new procedural legislation which makes group action for compensation possible in mass consumer disputes.

In Finland and Sweden law drafting procedure for group action for compensation, started in the beginning of 1990s. In Sweden this procedure led to the Government's Proposal to Parliament concerning Group Action Act, which was adopted by the Parliament in May 2002. The new act entered into force on January 1, 2003.[30]

In Finland the law drafting stopped in the year 1999 for political reasons temporarily, after two committee reports. The preparation work continued in this decade and in March 2006 a new committee report was published. It contained a proposal on group action for compensation, which scope of application was, however, much more restricted when compared to the other Nordic countries. Government's proposal on group action was given to the Parliament in September 2006.[31]

However, it is good to remember, that group action for compensation has been a very sensitive political question in Finland since 1995, when the first committee report was published. Several proposals have been made during the years without any further legislative progress. The resistance from the business lobby organisations has been very hard and successful.

In Norway, the new Act on Civil Procedure, its chapter 35, which will enter into force in the year 2007, will introduce group action for compensation to the Norwegian procedural system. In Denmark a committee report was published in December 2005. It suggested that the Danish Act on Procedure should be amended in a way which would make group action for compensation possible also in Denmark in the near future.[32]

The *scope of application* would in most Nordic group actions be general. This means that group action will be possible in all kinds of disputes on the condition that they fulfil the general requirements of group actions, e.g., it is a question of disputes where the facts are identical or at least identical to each others, and it is sensible to handle these disputes together in one trial.

However, in this respect the Finnish proposal differs clearly from the other Nordic countries. According to the newest committee report, the scope of application was planned to be restricted to two types of disputes: to mass consumer

---

30 *Prop. 2001/02:107*, Regeringens proposition. Lag om grupprättegång; *The Group Action Act* (SFS 2002: 599).

31 *OLJ 4/2006*, Ehdotus laiksi ryhmäkanteesta. Oikeusministeriön työryhmämietintö 2006:4 (Helsinki 2006); *HE 154/2006*, Hallituksen esitys eduskunnalle ryhmäkannelaiksi ja laiksi Kuluttajavirastosta annetun lain muuttamisesta.

32 See *Reform af den civile retspleje IV.Gruppesøgsmåls mv*, Betænkning nr. 1468 (København 2005).

disputes and to environmental damage issues. The government's proposal is even more strict: group action will be possible in mass consumer disputes only.[33]

There is also a clear difference between other Nordic countries and Finland concerning the question *who may act as a plaintiff* in a group action for compensation. In other Nordic countries all previous mentioned types of group action are possible. So, in Denmark, Norway and Sweden the plaintiff may be a member of the group (class action), an organisation, who is protecting the interests of a certain group of citizens (action by organisation), or state authority, as the Consumer Ombudsman (public action).[34]

In Finland only a public action would be possible. The Finnish Consumer Ombudsman would have a right to take legal action on behalf of a specified group of consumers. This means that consumer organisations or individual consumers would not have even a secondary right of action in cases where the Consumer Ombudsman have decided not to start legal proceedings. According to the latest committee report, in environmental damage issues the environmental organisations would have had a right of action, but only a secondary one.[35]

In group actions judgements have a legal effect on all members of the group, although they are not parties to the case. However, there are in principle two opposite ways how the group may be formed. Firstly, all persons who fill certain requirements will automatically become members of the group. Those who do not want to be members of the group have to use their right to *opt out*. The opposite alternative is the *opt in* model. In this alternative only those persons, who have joined the group by registration, will be members of the group and will be covered by the judgement.

In Sweden and Finland only the opt in alternative is available. This is also the main rule in Norway and Denmark. However, in these two last-mentioned countries the opt out alternative is also possible in mass disputes, where individual court actions are not sensible, e.g., due to the fact that the monetary interest of individual cases is so low. This possibility increases usefulness of group action, especially in mass consumer disputes. However, in Denmark the opt out alternative would be available in public actions only.[36]

Otherwise the procedure to be used would primarily correspond to ordinary legal procedure in civil cases in all four countries. Moreover the same civil law remedies are available in normal traditional individual cases, e.g, compensation of damages, price reduction.

In all Nordic countries the main rule in the civil procedure is that *the loser is obliged to pay the legal expenses of his own and those of the other party*. This cost rule is also applied in the Nordic group actions for compensation. In

---

33 *OLJ 4/2006*, cited above fn. 31, pp. 53-56; *HE 154/2006*, cited above fn. 31 at pp. 16-17.

34 See, e.g., the Norwegian Act on Civil Procedure, ch. 35, Art.3.

35 *HE 154/2006* cited above fn. 33 at p. 20; *OLJ 4/2006*, cited above fn. 33 at pp. 61-67.

36 See the Norwegian Act on Civil Procedure, ch. 35, Art. 7; Betænkning nr. 1468, cited above fn. 32 at pp. 275-276.

Finland and Sweden only the parties to the case are responsible for the costs. Since the members of the group are not parties to the proceedings, they will not be responsible for the costs. On the contrary, in Denmark and Norway the members may become partly responsible of the legal expenses. The ceiling of members' liability will, however, be decided by the court already at the beginning of the trial.[37] In case the ceiling is individual, but not collective, it becomes possible for the potential members of the group to assess, whether it is economically sensible to opt in or not.

3.3 The question of legal expenses

The most essential question when evaluating the practical significance of group action for compensation is, how the actions will be financed. Group actions entail much higher costs than individual cases in a normal civil procedure, albeit that in individual cases too the costs of litigation are the biggest obstacle to the use of courts in consumer disputes.[38] In group actions the plaintiff takes a great financial risk, which in practice is too big for individual consumers or small and medium-sized consumer organisations. So, if group action is wanted to serve as a serious alternative in the settlement of mass consumer disputes, which would also work in practice, the problem of high litigation costs, has to be solved first.

When assessing the Nordic group actions – acts or proposals – from this viewpoint, one has to admit, that the situation is far from satisfactory. All Nordic group actions are based on the so called English rule: the loser has to pay the expenses of his own and those of the other party. Besides in Denmark and Norway the courts have a right to decide that also the members of the group have to pay a certain amount of the expenses. These kinds of rules create barriers for access to justice. Who is willing and able to start a group action for compensation, or join the group as a member, if he has to pay the expenses from his own pocket? The Finnish proposal, which limits the right of action to public authorities only, do not solve the financial problem, because also public authorities, including the Consumer Ombudsman, have to work with limited economic resources.

In Sweden group action for compensation, with a general scope of application, has been possible since the year 2003. So far the number of actions in Sweden has been only six. One of them has been started by the Swedish Consumer Ombudsman.[39] It is obvious that the risk of high legal expenses has

[37] See the Norwegian Act on Civil Procedure, ch. 35, Art. 14 and Betænkning nr. 1468, cited above fn. 32 at pp. 276-277.

[38] See, e.g., M. Cappelletti, 'Alternative Dispute Resolution Processes within the Framework of the World-Wide Access-to-Justice Movement' (1993) *Modern Law Review*, p. 285.

[39] See, e.g., P.H. Lindblom, 'Lagen om grupprättegång – bakgrund och framtid.' (2005) *Svensk Juristtidning*, pp. 152-161.

been the main reason for the small number of group action for compensation in Sweden.

However, the legislator may use different methods to lower the economic threshold in group actions, in case there is enough political will to use them. Firstly, by using *the no-cost rule and contingency fee or conditional fee-payment systems* it would be possible to transfer the financial risk from the parties to the law offices. In this system both parties would cover only their own expenses and attorneys would be paid only in the event of a successful outcome. Law offices may accept this kind of payment system, because if they win the case, they are able to charge much higher fees than in normal cases and they will also receive good publicity, which will increase goodwill towards the office and bring new clients to the firm in the future. This system has been a very popular way to finance class actions in the United States.

However, this system does not fit very well in the Nordic legal system and would probably be strange in many other European countries, too. As mentioned before, in the Nordic countries the main rule is that the loser has an obligation to pay all legal expenses for the winner. No-cost rule in group action for compensation would mean a clear exception from this main rule. Contingency fee and conditional fee payment systems are in principle possible, but are not used in the Nordic countries in practice. The amount of attorneys in these countries is still quite reasonable, which means that there is no need to attract new customers by using payment systems where the risk would be transferred to law firms. Attorneys prefer to work on hourly wages, which means that their income does not depend on the outcome of the case at all. That is why, it is also probable that the use of conditional fees would not become popular in Sweden, in spite of the fact that this possibility is expressly mentioned in the Swedish Group Action Act.[40]

Secondly, it is possible to use *different kinds of funding systems.* A public or private fund could financially support the plaintiff who brings a group action. These funds could receive state subsidies, but also a certain percentage of the money won by group actions could be channelled into these funds to be used as capital for future cases. These kinds of funding systems are already used at least in Canada.[41]

The first Finnish committee, which published its report in year 1995, also drew special attention to the financing of potential group actions. It proposed the establishment of a special State Group Action Board. This board would have received its funding mainly from the state budget. Potential plaintiffs could apply for economic support which would also have covered the legal expenses that the plaintiff would have had to pay to the other party in cases which were lost. Naturally, the Board would have had to consider whether there were good

---

40 The Swedish Group Action Act, Art. 38-41.

41 *N. L'Heureux,* cited above fn. 29 at pp. 456-457 and Lindblom 2000, cited above fn. 29 at pp. 429.

enough grounds to bring a group action or not.[42] In practice, this Board would have decided in which cases group action is brought and in which not.

However, the second Finnish committee, which published its report in June 1997, abandoned this idea. The willingness to public savings was the main reason. According to the instructions which were given to the committee when it started its work, the new legislation should not cause any extra expenses to the state.[43]

Unfortunately, the second committee did not propose any alternative models how the problem of financing could be solved. As mentioned above, it would be possible to establish a special fund which could finance group actions without continuous state aid. A certain percentage of the money received by successful group actions could be channelled into this fund. Instead of using public resources the fund would collect its capital mainly from private sources. In this system only the basic capital would normally be needed from the state.

3.4 Group complaints in the Public Consumer Complaint Board

The traditional court procedure in most countries has been criticised because it is not applicable to the settlement of mass disputes, including consumer mass disputes. The same criticism – the inability to solve mass disputes – may also be directed against the Nordic Public Complaint Boards. However, concerning this matter an interesting experiment started in the Swedish board already in year 1991. It is now a permanent system based on the law.

The Swedish Consumer Ombudsman is entitled to bring to the Swedish Consumer Complaint Board a special group complaint against an individual trader. The Board may – if it considers the complaint justified – recommend that the trader should give the recommended remedy to all consumers who have similar demands against the same trader, but who have not personally complained to the Board. If the Ombudsman is not interested in bringing a group complaint, consumer and labour organisations are entitled to do so. For some reason, the right to complain has not been given to individual consumers. So, a procedure comparable with a class action is not possible in the Board.

The Swedish Consumer Ombudsman has brought approximately one or two group complaints to the board every year. Most of the Board's decisions given in these cases are said to be complied with.[44] However, it is unclear how

---

42 *OLJ 1/1995*, Ehdotus ryhmäkannelaiksi. Työryhmän mietintö. Oikeusministeriön lainvalmisteluosaston julkaisu. (Helsinki 1995), pp. 21-23, 60-65, 103-105 and 115-117.

43 *OLJ 3/1997*, Ryhmäkannelaki. Työryhmän 1996 mietintö. Oikeusministeriön lainvalmisteluosaston julkaisu. (Helsinki 1997), pp. 2, 97-98 and 131-133.

44 *ECLG 2005*, The need for group action for consumer redress. The opinion of the ECLG. ECLG/033/05. February 2005, pp. 5-6. Available in address: http://www.europeanconsumerlawgroup.org; R. Ljungqvist, 'Konsumenters access to justice i Sverige och i det nya Europa.' (1993/94) *Allmänna rekla-*

the compliance has been controlled in these cases when most of the consumers involved are not known by the consumer officials. The optin-system is not applied in group complaints.

In Finland a committee, which published its report in January 2006, proposed that a similar system should be adopted also in Finland. According to this proposal, the Finnish Consumer Ombudsman could bring a group complaint to the Finnish Consumer Complaint Board in consumer disputes, where several consumers have similar kinds of claims against the same trader, and it would be possible to solve all of them by a single decision. In the Finnish proposal the right to complain, not even a secondary one, would not be given to single consumers or consumer organisations. The decisions of the Board in group complaints would be recommendations just like in other issues handled by the Board. The Government's Proposal on group complaints was left to the Parliament in September 2006.[45]

4 The Nordic enforcement system: a success story or something else?

4.1 Supervision of marketing and contract terms

May the Nordic enforcement system be called as a success story or something else? It is clear, that the Nordic system contains many positive elements from the viewpoint of consumer protection. *First of all*, it is of tremendous importance that from the very beginning of the establishment of the system for consumer protection, serious attention was paid, not only to the content of the substantive consumer law, but also to the access to justice questions: enforcement of consumers' collective interests and individual rights.

Secondly, a special, independent supervisory body, called the Consumer Ombudsman, was established in each of these four countries. It is also essential to notice in this context, that enforcement of consumer protection was the sole task of these ombudsmen. Supervisory tasks were not given to some already existing authority, for example, to the competition authorities. This has meant that the Consumer Ombudsmen have been able to focus all their available resources to the supervision of marketing and standard contract terms without a fear that the fulfilment of other tasks, for example, enforcement of competition law, would have started to dominate their activities.

---

mationsnändens årsbok, pp. 20-21; *TemaNord 1998:572*, Nye utfordringer i klagesaksbehandlingen. Fra et nordisk seminar på Lillehammer den 5.-7. mars 1997. (København 1998), pp. 56-65.

45 *OLJ 1/2006*, Kuluttajavalituslautakunnan toimivallan laajentaminen ja ryhmävalitusmenettely. Oikeusministeriön työryhmämietintö 2006:1. (Helsinki 2006), pp. 9-10, 15; *HE 115/2006*, Hallituksen esitys eduskunnalle laeiksi kuluttajariitalautakunnasta ja Kuluttajavirastosta annetun lain muuttamisesta.

One example from Finland may illustrate this risk. In the year 2002 the Finnish Market Court's jurisdiction was enlarged to also cover the competition law issues, which soon started to dominate the activities of the Court. Nowadays, more than 95 percent of the all cases dealt by the Court concerns public procurement. The growing amount of competition law cases have caused delays also to the duration of consumer law cases.

Thirdly, it was extremely important to establish special courts as decision-making bodies instead of channeling consumers' collective interests cases to already existing general courts. As mentioned before, in the Nordic countries criminal sanctions may, even in consumer cases, be imposed by general courts only. However, the use of criminal sanctions in consumer law cases has in practice been very rare in the Nordic countries. The main reasons have been the dismissive attitudes of public prosecutors and judges in general courts concerning the importance of the protection of consumers' collective interests. That is why it is more than probable that the leading marketing law principles, which were created by the case law of the Nordic Market Courts since 1970s, would be rather different than what they are now if the Consumer Ombudsmen would have had to take legal actions in general courts instead of these special courts.

Fourthly, one clear benefit in the Nordic system has been the wide use of preventive actions. The Nordic Consumer Ombudsmen use significant part of their resources in trying to prevent any violation of law. They give advance opinions on request, draw marketing guidelines and negotiate with trade organisations concerning standard contract terms in several branches of business. It is interesting to notice that these preventive actions are mainly not based on any law. On the contrary, they have been created in practice during the years when the Nordic Consumer Ombudsmen have carried out their supervisory duties.

Also in cases, where infringements of law have been observed, persuasion effort instead of sanctions has been normally the first reaction of the supervisory authorities. These preventive and persuasive methods have turned out to be very successful due to the fact that most traders are in practice more than willing to co-operate. The main reason for this willingness is the possibility to use hard law sanctions in case persuasion fails. That is why it is important to remember the close connection between soft law methods and hard law sanctions. Without the possibility of using hard law sanctions if necessary, the persuasive methods would not be quite as successful as they have so far been.

However, there are also clear defects in the Nordic enforcement system. Perhaps the biggest problem is that the traditional sanction system does not pay enough attention to the unscrupulous traders who intentionally and repeatedly violate the law in order to increase their sale numbers and profits. Against these traders, sanction systems in which the hardest sanction is an injunction order is in practice rather toothless. These traders are not worried about the potential bad publicity connected to these cases, because they anyway have to change their trade name once a year in order to get rid of dissatisfied and complaining consumers. Because criminal law sanctions enforced by public prosecutors and general courts have turned out to be very rare in practice, more attention has to be paid to the development of the market law sanctions. In Sweden it has been possible to impose a market disruption fee since the year 1995. The ceiling for this sanction is ten percent of the trader's annual turnover or EUR 500 000. It is obvious, that also the other Nordic countries have to adopt more or less similar financial sanctions in the future.

4.2 Group action for compensation

Also in the Nordic countries one great problem has been the lack of access to justice in mass consumer disputes. In many of these cases the damages are caused by the use of unfair standard contract terms or unfair marketing which have tempted consumers to buy something they would not otherwise have bought. Traditionally the court system in the European countries has been inapplicable for the settlement of mass consumer disputes. In the discussion concerning the settlement of mass consumer disputes most attention over the last few decades has without doubt been paid to group action for compensation.

Group action for injunction in consumer matters is nowadays possible in all EC Member States. Group action for compensation is, however, still quite rare outside common law countries. The EC is at this moment not preparing any directive on group action for compensation. The directive on injunctions for the protection of consumers' interests (98/27/EC) entitles supervisory bodies to take legal action in other Member States only in order to impose an injunction order.

The passivity of the EC concerning group action for compensation was, for example, used in the Finnish legal debate at the end of 1990s. It was argued that the adoption of group action for compensation before other Member States do so, would cause serious problems to Finnish enterprises in the internal market. This so called 'EC card' has also been used in the legal debate in Finland before. Thus, in matters concerning product liability it was possible to delay the adoption of strict liability for more than a decade.[46]

However, the argument that more advanced legislation would cause serious problems to domestic enterprises is questionable. It seems that it is based on an exaggerated conception of the effects of legal regulation on business activities. In Canada, for example, group action for compensation is possible only in three provinces, British Columbia, Ontario and Quebec Ontario. So far there has been

46 K. Viitanen, *Implementation of the EC directive on Product Liability in Finland. In The Implementation Process of EC Directives on Product Safety, Product Liability and Unfair Contract Terms.* Edited by Francoise Maniet ja Beata Dunaj. (Louvain-la-Neuve 1994), pp. 165-167.

47 See, e.g., Lindblom 2000, cited above fn. 29 at pp. 428-429.

no alarming news that group action has caused serious damage to enterprises in these provinces.[47]

Due to the active law drafting during the recent years, it seems that situation is slowly changing in Europe. Especially the Nordic countries have been quite active. Group action for compensation has been possible in Sweden since the year 2003. The Norwegian legislation on group action will enter into force in the year 2007. A recent committee report in Denmark and a government's proposal in Finland already exist. They both propose the adoption of group action for compensation to these countries. It is obvious, that in the near future group action for compensation belongs to the typical features of Nordic consumer protection.

However, it is probable, that in consumer disputes group action for compensation will be used quite rarely in practice. The major obstacle to the use of group action is the cost of litigation. In all four Nordic countries public action, where plaintiff is a public authority, is or will be possible. This means that in mass consumer disputes the Nordic Consumer Ombudsmen may bring group actions for compensation on behalf of a group of consumers. However, the use of the Consumer Ombudsmen as plaintiffs instead of single consumer or consumer organisations does not solve the problem of financing. Also the state authorities have to work with limited yearly resources.

For example, the yearly budget which the Finnish National Consumer Agency may use for its own expenses is approximately EUR 6 000 000. The great majority of these monetary resources are, however, aimed at certain purposes: salaries for the permanent employees, rents, etc. This means that without extra resources the Finnish Consumer Ombudsman has to select the cases for which he could initiate group actions for compensation extremely carefully. As mentioned before, so far the Swedish Consumer Ombudsman has started only one group action in three and a half years. So, one of the most important questions concerning the practical functioning of group action for compensation would without doubt be the financing of these actions. Who can afford group actions for compensation?

In case these financial problems are solved, group action for compensation may become an important instrument when making justice more accessible in mass consumer disputes. Group action for compensation can, by its mere existence among other legal procedures, promote the opportunities to reach an agreement with the trader in question in mass consumer disputes, without needing to bring a suit to court.

One argument which is often used on behalf of group action for compensation is that it brings savings both to the disputing parties and to the court system because several individual disputes may be settled in one single court case. However, this argument is based on the assumption that there really would be several individual court cases if the group action for compensation were not recognised by procedural law. This is probable in cases in which the economic interest exceeds the costs of litigation and it also makes an individual court case feasible. However, in other cases – including most consumer disputes – only the possibility of collecting individual interests together makes it sensible to take legal action. Thus, in practice, in most cases group action for compensation actually increases expenses incurred by the court system, because it makes legal actions possible which would not otherwise be raised as individual actions. But at the same time it makes justice more accessible in mass disputes where access to justice is still a great problem today.

If group action for compensation will be possible in some Member States, but not in the others, it would be interesting to see how the enforcement problems will be solved in cross-border group actions. The Brussels Regulation is applicable in individual cross-border consumer disputes, but group actions for compensation have also clear collective elements. That is why it is not clear whether judgments will in practice be enforceable also in those Members States which have not adopted this type of court action in their procedural law.

CHAPTER 6

The Dutch Consumer Authority: an introduction

Sjoerd Ammerlaan and Dirk Janssen[1]

1 January 2007 will see the Consumer authority, the newest member of the family of market and other supervisory authorities, open its doors for business. The Consumer authority will be operating in a busy playing field already occupied by other supervisory authorities, civil society organisations and various self-regulation initiatives.

Administrative law enforcement of predominantly consumer law regulations under private law is to some extent virgin territory in the Netherlands. This is why we are taking this opportunity to outline the various features of the Consumer authority and the basic principles that will underlie our supervisory and enforcement activities in practice.[2]

1 Why the Consumer Authority?

Briefly, the main reasons for setting up the Consumer authority are firstly that we have witnessed a lack of compliance with regulations in consumer markets, and second, the expansion of the internal market. The reasoning behind the decision to set up the Consumer authority is therefore twofold and can be traced back to the cabinet policy stemming from a Strategic Action Programme for consumer policy[3] and to Regulation 2006/2004 on consumer protection cooperation (hereafter: the Regulation).[4]

1.1 Cabinet policy – strategic action programme for consumer policy

The reasons for the formulation of the strategic action programme for consumer policy were the Dutch Cabinet's view of the way in which consumer and other markets were working, along with research into a number of 'blank spaces' in the consumer protection system[5] and developments at a European level. The strategic action programme outlines the consumer policy and the protection of the economic interests of the consumer. In order to

1 Whose positions at the Consumer Authority (which organisation is in the process of being formed) are respectively Senior Staff Member of Strategy and International Affairs and Head of Supervision.

2 This statement is based on the bill for the Consumer Protection Enforcement Act ('Wet handhaving consumentenbescherming') in the form it was in at the time that this article was written. See the Senate of the Dutch Parliament, parliamentary year 2005-2006, Parliamentary Document ('Kamerstuk') 30 411, A.

3 House of Representatives of the Dutch Parliament, parliamentary year 2003-2004, Parliamentary Document 27879 nrs. 9 and 10.

4 Regulation (EC) 2006/2004, O.J. 2004 L 364/47.

5 Including 'Investigation into the handling of individual consumer complaints' (Onderzoek naar afhandeling van individuele consumentenklachten), Twijnstra Gudde, April 2004 and 'Consumer complaints and collective actions' (Consumentenklachten en collective acties), EIM, April 2004.

strengthen the position of the consumer, the strategic action programme sets itself the following objectives:

- knowledge: increasing consumers' and suppliers' knowledge of their rights and obligations and options for obtaining legal redress;
- individual handling of complaints and disputes: improving the way consumer complaints are dealt with and simplifying the options available to consumers for obtaining legal redress;
- collective infringements: Reducing the number of infringements of consumer law by extending the enforcement of legislation to protect the economic interests of the consumer.

The Consumer Authority will focus on the first and third of these objectives. One measure already taken to help realise the first objective is the setting up of a consumer helpdesk known as ConsuWijzer, the purpose of which is to inform consumers about their rights and obligations. ConsuWijzer has been set up in collaboration with OPTA (the Dutch Independent Post and Telecommunications Authority) and the NMa (the Netherlands Competition Authority), and should already be 'on air' by the time you read this (see www.consuwijzer.nl).

1.2 Regulation 2006/2004

The second reason for the foundation of the Consumer authority is an official one, namely Regulation 2006/2004 (hereafter: the Regulation). This regulation is intended to improve cooperation between authorities charged with monitoring compliance with the consumer protection regulations in the event of cross-border infringements. This cooperation needs to be improved because a lack of enforcement by national authorities in the event of intra-Community infringements can lead to disruption of competition and to a loss of consumer confidence in respect of cross-border transactions, something that could hinder the development of the EU internal market.

The Regulation sets out the reciprocal rights and obligations of national authorities regarding the provision of mutual assistance. The Regulation also sets out conditions for cooperation between national authorities and the European Commission.

The key aspect of the Regulation is that the competent authorities in the various member states are to assist each other in combating cross-border infringements of fourteen directives (and one regulation) that are listed in the annex to the Regulation and that form part of the so-called 'consumer acquis [i.e. legislation]'. This relates to such matters as the directives on misleading advertising, unfair contract terms, guarantees and distance selling. The scope of application of the Regulation is to be extended even further in 2007 by the recently approved directive on unfair commercial practices.

Each member state must designate one or more 'competent authorities' for each of the fourteen directives (and one regulation) that is/are charged with monitoring compliance with these directives and who consequently have to have certain powers to investigate and enforce. Each member state also has to designate a single liaison office that is charged with coordinating the application of the Regulation in that member state.

Competent authorities in the different member states can submit 'requests for mutual assistance' to each other, consisting of a request for the exchange of information or a request to take enforcement measures. In principle, the recipient authority is obliged to comply with a request for mutual assistance.

The competent authorities are also obliged to report possible cross-border infringements to the network whose members include all the competent authorities.

2 Consumer Protection Enforcement Act

The above Regulation is being implemented in the Netherlands by means of the Consumer Protection Enforcement Act ('Wet handhaving consumentenbescherming', hereinafter Whc). At the time this article was being written, the bill to this end had been passed by the House of Representatives and lay before the Senate.[6]

The Whc satisfies such requirements as the need to designate 'competent authorities' in the Netherlands within the meaning of the Regulation. At that time, there was no public supervisory authority in the Netherlands that was charged with monitoring compliance with regulations of *generic* consumer law[7]. This has now been rectified by the provisions made in the Whc for the foundation of the Consumer authority. The Consumer authority has been designated as the 'competent authority' for the majority of the directives. The Consumer authority has also been designated the Single Liaison Office for the Netherlands. Under the Regulation, the AFM (Netherlands Authority for the Financial Markets), the Dutch Media Authority, the Transport and Water Management Inspectorate, the Health Care Inspection Agency, and the VWA (Food and Consumer Product Safety Authority) have been designated as a 'competent authority' for one or more of the directives, as has the Consumer authority.

6 Senate of the Dutch Parliament, parliamentary year 2005-2006, Parliamentary Document 30 411, A.

7 In addition to the generic consumer law regulations laid down in the Netherlands Civil Code, consumer law regulations have been laid down in certain sector-specific laws such as the Telecommunications Act and the Electricity Act, which are enforced by sector-specific supervisory authorities.

3 Basic principles for the Consumer Authority's work

3.1 Positioning

The Consumer authority is established within the Minister for Economic Affairs. Those powers relating to monitoring and enforcement have been assigned directly to the Consumer authority, which emphasizes the independent decision-making abilities of the Consumer authority in these areas. Nevertheless, the Minister remains fully responsible for the Consumer authority's actions. For instance, it is the Minister who prepares the annual report and sends it to both Houses. The Minister can also issue instructions, both general instructions – in the form of policy regulations – and instructions in a particular case.

Initially, the Consumer authority will be staffed by 25 FTEs, of which 8.5 FTEs will be performing supervisory tasks.

3.2 Mission, tasks and objectives

The Consumer authority's Mission is: *To promote fair trade between businesses and consumers, based on the economic interests of consumers.*

The Consumer authority bears this mission in mind when it carries out its tasks, which may be described as follows:

1) monitoring compliance with the consumer law regulations, and if necessary taking action to enforce them;
2) coordination of cross-border requests for mutual assistance on the basis of the Regulation (as Single Liaison Office), and
3) providing information to consumers and suppliers via a helpdesk (called ConsuWijzer).

The first two tasks relate to statutory tasks arising from the Regulation and the Whc, with the third task supporting the first two tasks and being a consequence of the strategic action programme for consumer policy.

The Consumer authority's mission can be translated into two objectives:

1) *to promote compliance with the consumer law regulations;*
2) *to improve consumers' and suppliers' knowledge of consumer laws and obligations and of the options for obtaining legal redress.*

Both objectives aim to restore and/or improve consumer confidence in the markets. After all, collective infringements prevent consumers from making informed and efficient choices, which leads to imperfect operation of a market, in which fraudulent suppliers would be able to unfairly take sales away from bona fide suppliers. The Consumer authority's mission and the two objectives that stem from it are designed to combat this.

The above-mentioned objectives are inextricably bound to each other and support each other. After all, the Consumer authority receives information from

ConsuWijzer that it can use to monitor infringements of consumer laws, and conversely the Consumer authority can inform consumers via ConsuWijzer for instance that an investigation has been completed into a supplier's unfair contract terms. The Consumer authority also believes that keeping consumers better informed about their rights and obligations will make the market more likely to play by the rules. If consumers tackle businesses about infringements themselves then businesses will be quicker to comply with the rules and regulations. Furthermore, keeping suppliers better informed about their rights and obligations should help to reduce the number of infringements.

3.3 What will the Consumer authority be supervising?

The Consumer authority is authorised to take action against national and cross-border infringements of consumer law provisions in the fields of:

Provision	*Article(s) of the law*
Misleading advertising	Articles 194a up to and including Article 196 of Book 6 of the Civil Code
Package tours, including holiday packages and roundtrip packages	The provisions from or by virtue of Articles 500 up to and including 513 of Book 7 of the Civil Code.
Unfair contract terms in consumer agreements	Articles 231 up to and including 247 of Book 6 of the Civil Code
Timesharing	The provisions from or by virtue of Articles 48a up to and including 48g of Book 7 of the Civil Code
Distance selling	Articles 46a up to and including 46j of Book 7 of the Civil Code and Articles 11.7 and 11.8 of the Telecommunications Act.
Certain aspects of the sale of and guarantees for consumer goods	Articles 5 up to and including 6a, Articles 17 up to and including 19, Articles 21 up to and including 23 and Article 25 of Book 7 of the Civil Code
E-commerce	Articles 15a up to and including 15f of Book 3, Article 196c and Articles 227a up to and including 227c of Book 6 of the Civil Code
Agreements entered into away from business premises (i.e. doorstep selling)	The provisions from or by virtue of the Door-to-Door Sales Act, insofar as they do not relate to a financial service or activity.
Quoting of prices for products offered to the consumer	The provisions from or by virtue of Articles 2b and 3, insofar as they relate to Article 2b of the Prices Act.

Figure: Overview of the Consumerauthority's supervisory domains

Note that the Consumer authority is not authorised to take action in the financial sector, which remains the exclusive supervisory domain of the AFM.

3.4 Collective consumer interests

The Consumer authority cannot take action against every violation (whether cross-border or national) – it can only act when the *collective* interests of consumers are affected. This requirement is set by Article 3 paragraph b of the Regulation as well as in Article 1.1 under f of the Whc. Article 3 paragraph k of the Regulation defines the term 'collective interests of consumers' as *'the interests of a number of consumers that have been harmed or are likely to be harmed by an infringement.'* The Regulation does not define the circumstances under which the interests of a number of consumers could be harmed. Nevertheless, a number of general conclusions relating to the interpretation of the term 'collective interests of consumers' can be made from the tenor and wording of the Regulation.

In the first place, the Consumer authority cannot take action if just a single consumer feels that he has been affected by a violation. In other words: the Consumer authority will not intervene in disputes between a single consumer and a supplier of a product or service. If other consumers have not been affected by the deliberate violation or if the violation was not followed or preceded by similar violations then the violation will not affect consumers 'collectively' and thus the Consumer authority cannot take action against it.

In the second place, the number of complaints that the Consumer authority receives about a particular supplier will not be the deciding factor in any assessment of whether there has been a violation of the collective interests of consumers. After all, these complaints may all relate to individual, standalone cases that do not constitute a collective infringement. All the same, a single complaint may be sufficient grounds for the Consumer authority to start an investigation, if it suspects that the supplier's conduct is such that more consumers have been or could be affected in the same way.

The above leaves many possible scenarios unresolved – for instance, conduct by a local supplier will affect fewer consumers than conduct by a national supplier. The Consumer authority will use the above general basic principles to define the term 'collective interests' in respect of its day-to-day supervisory activities in practice. Furthermore, agreement may be reached within Europe on a definition of the term 'collective interests'. After all, this would help to ensure that this term is interpreted in the same way in each member state.

Note too that the Consumerauthority is less interested in finding the 'lower intervention threshold'; instead, it will endeavour to deploy its resources and funds in those areas and for that conduct where there is the greatest need for consumer protection (see also Section 3.7).

3.5 Supervisory powers

In order for the Consumer authority to be able to fulfil the supervisory tasks and duties assigned to it, those of its officials designated as supervisors have been given the powers set out in Articles 5.15 up to and including 5.19 of the General Administrative Law Act (the 'Awb'). This relates to the following powers:

1) *The right to carry out on-site inspections* (Article 5:15 Awb);
   Consumer authority supervisors are entitled to enter any site and may call for police assistance in this respect. Officials of the Consumer authority may be accompanied by other persons, such as IT and forensic experts;
2) *The right to demand information* (Article 5:16 Awb).
   Consumer authority supervisors are authorised to demand information. The interviewee must answer truthfully.
3) *The right to demand personal identification* (Article 5:16a Awb);
   A supervisor is authorised to demand that persons show him/her personal identification as referred to in Article 1 of the Compulsory Identification Act.
4) *The right to inspect information and documents* (Article 5:17 Awb);
   The officials are authorised to insist that they be permitted to view commercial information and documents and to make copies of them. If necessary, this information may be removed for copying purposes. An exception is made for those documents exchanged between an offender and a lawyer that are kept at the offices of the lawyer (pursuant to 5:20 Awb) or offender (pursuant to Article 2.4 para. 2 Whc).
5) *The right to investigate, record and take samples* (Article 5:18 Awb);
   Consumer authority supervisors are authorised to investigate items, to record them and to take samples of them.
6) *The right to investigate vehicles* (Article 5:19 Awb);
   Officials are authorised to investigate cars and other vehicles.

Pursuant to Article 5:20 Awb, all parties are obliged to cooperate with the Consumer authority's supervisors. The Consumer authority can compel the person or company in question to cooperate, by means of the imposition of a fine in the event of non-compliance (Article 2.10 para. 2 Whc).

3.6 Powers of enforcement

The Consumer authority has various powers of enforcement that it can use to enforce compliance. The powers it will have in a particular case depend on the regulation that has been violated.

3.6.1 Powers of enforcement under civil law

The Consumer Authority may enforce under civil law those provisions whose enforcement has been entrusted to it and which have been implemented in the Civil Code by means of 'open standards'.

In order to end an infringement 'without delay', as required by the Regulation, a special application procedure for the Consumer authority has been put in place at the Court in The Hague ('Gerechtshof Den Haag'). The Court in The Hague has to hear applications by the Consumer authority 'without delay' (Article 3:305d CC (Civil Code)). At the Consumer authority's request, the Court in The Hague can order that an infringement be ended, and may also impose a fine in the event of non-compliance. The Consumer authority can also ask the Court in The Hague to order the infringer to have the ruling on the application made public, at the infringer's expense.

The Consumer authority may use information obtained from supervisory activities in its application procedure. Note too that pursuant to Article 2.5 Whc the Consumer authority will give the offender the opportunity to end the infringement before it submits an application to the court. The Consumer authority will also allow the offender to view the information on which the intention to initiate an application procedure was based, this information being contained in the investigation report (the 'onderzoeksrapport').

Apart from the opportunity afforded by the above-mentioned special application procedure, the Consumer authority is also authorised to start a 'standard' collective action *qualitate qua*, on the basis of Article 3:305b CC. In such a proceedings commenced by a summons, an injunction, ban or declaratory judgement may be requested. This power will be used less often, given the available option of using the above-mentioned special accelerated application procedure.

3.6.2 Powers of enforcement under administrative law

The Consumer authority may enforce under administrative law those provisions of the Civil Code whose enforcement it has been entrusted with and that are embodied in the so-called 'closed standards' (such as the 'blacklist' ['zwarte lijst'] referred to in Article 6:236 CC) and the provisions of the Doorstep Selling Act and the Price Indication Act. It is likely that these will be supplemented by 'closed' provisions from the directive on unfair commercial practices.

If the Consumer authority is of the opinion that that there has been an infringement of one of the provisions that is/are being enforced under administrative law then it is authorised to:

1) impose a fine in the event of non-compliance;
2) impose an administrative fine.

The administrative fine and the fine in the event of non-compliance can be imposed in combination. A fine in the event of non-compliance can be imposed as soon as it is evident that the violation could occur (a 'preventive fine' ['preventieve last'], Article 2.16, para. 3 Whc). The administrative fine and the fine in the event of non-compliance may be imposed on a natural person or legal entity, as well as on the actual manager or mandator in question. The administrative fine is a maximum of EUR 45,000.00 per violation (equivalent to the fine for the fifth category as referred to in Article 23 of the Dutch Penal Code).

3.6.3 Disclosure

In addition to the imposition of an administrative fine or fine in the event of non-compliance, the Consumer Authority is authorised to disclose the following:

- a decision that no fine in the event of non-compliance or administrative fine is to be imposed;
- a decision concerning the imposition of an administrative fine or fine in the event of non-compliance;
- an undertaking from the offender that the violation shall be ended.

The authority to disclosure does not come from the Awb but from the Regulation. The Consumer authority sees its authority to accept an undertaking from an offender and then to make this public as an alternative to having to follow the entire process through to the imposition of an administrative fine or fine in the event of non-compliance. After all, it has been agreed with the offender that he will end his infringement and that the Consumer authority will not take any (further) enforcement measures as long as the offender keeps his promise. Disclosure means that consumers are informed about this undertaking.

For a civil law case too, the Consumer authority may – as an alternative to going to court – accept an undertaking from the violating company that will then be made public.

3.6.4 Class settlement

Pursuant to Article 2.6 Whc, the Consumer authority is authorised to enter into an agreement with a party that has violated one or more provisions whose enforcement the Consumer authority is charged with, under which agreement the infringing party undertakes to pay compensation for the loss arising from the violation. At the parties' request, the court may declare such an agreement binding on persons who have suffered loss as a result.

However, the Consumer authority will deploy this power with restraint, also in the light of the remarks on this subject in the Explanatory Memorandum ('Memorie van Toelichting') for the Whc. The Consumer authority is of the opinion that the market (e.g. consumer organisations) should take the lead with such initiatives. After all, deploying this power means that the Consumer authority would become a party to a civil law or other settlement agreement, something that should be reserved for exceptional circumstances.

3.7 Prioritisation

The Consumer authority aims to take action effectively and decisively. One aspect of this is having a policy of systematic enforcement, under which transparent, well-reasoned decisions are taken about the question which cases to take up by the Consumer authority. It is important to note that this freedom of choice in decision-making is limited to 'national' cases. After all, the Consumer authority is in principle obliged to heed requests for assistance submitted from other EU member states. We expect a significant part of the Consumer authority's capacity to be taken up by these international cases.

In contrast to the 'ad hoc' taking up of national cases, the Consumer authority will endeavour to pursue a policy of systematic enforcement. Briefly, this means devoting our limited capacity and resources to those areas/cases that require the most attention, which have been identified beforehand as satisfying certain criteria ('priorities'). After all, if we simply tried to take up every case presented to us, our limited capacity would soon be spread in a fragmented way, something that would make it more difficult to achieve the desired structural changes in behaviour.

Each year, the Consumer authority will consult with stakeholders as to possible priorities, which will then be decided on and set out in an Agenda. A 'priority' could for instance be a particular industry or a particular type of infringement. When a priority has been identified then a 'programme' will be developed that will set out in detail the chosen approach to the problem in question (such as changing behaviour in a particular market), along with the suitable resources and instruments to be used to combat this problem. The primary objective behind this approach is to reduce the overall number of infringements of consumer protection regulations.

Prioritisation criteria

The Consumer authority will use the following criteria to select its priorities. Each year, stakeholders will be consulted about this selection, after which the priorities will be set down in detail in an annual Agenda.

The key criterion when making this selection will be the *impact* of non-compliance with the regulations: which legal and other interests would be harmed and to what degree? The criteria that play a role in this decision are:

1) the *extent of the loss suffered by consumers*: what is the actual, estimated or potential total economic loss suffered by consumers (i.e. how many consumers were actually or could potentially be harmed and what is the average loss per consumer?);
2) impact on *consumer confidence*: is a particular issue relevant with a view to restoring or improving consumer confidence?

3) the *impact on market forces* in a particular sector, which refers to the impact that a particular type of conduct (e.g. misleading advertising) could have on the level of competition and fairness in a particular sector.

4 Cooperation

When carrying out its tasks, the Consumer authority will be cooperating with a number of different organisations, both nationally and internationally, such as other supervisory authorities and civil society organisations. In the preceding section, we looked briefly at international cooperation under the Regulation; we will now do the same in the context of cooperation with other organisations within the Netherlands.

4.1 Relationship with existing 'private sector initiatives'

The basic principle is that it will be consumers and businesses themselves who will be primarily responsible for solving consumer rights disputes. The existing private sector initiatives, including the existing self-regulation initiatives such as consumer organisations, the Dutch Advertising Code Commission, the Complaints Boards, the general discussion of contract terms in the SER-CCA (Socio-Economic Council/Commission for Consumer Affairs) context, industry-wide codes of conduct, certifications and so on, all belong in this basic principle. The arrival of the Consumer Authority will not affect this basic principle or these private sector initiatives.

It follows from this that in principle the Consumer authority will only take action if a problem cannot be effectively rectified within the above-mentioned system or if the Consumer authority has an additional role to play. The Consumer authority will decide on a case-by-case basis whether this is so. The following factors will play a role in this decision:

a) if the Consumer authority expects the market players in question to be able to rectify an infringement efficiently and effectively themselves then rectification will in principle be left to these parties;
b) 'rectifying an infringement efficiently and effectively' is defined as the finding of a solution that ends a structural infringement and that is not (just) a solution in an individual dispute. In other words, the fact that a supplier reaches a settlement with an individual consumer (or consumer organisation) in an individual case does not automatically mean that the supplier has made a systematic change to his conduct. In such a case, this may be grounds for the Consumer authority to take action (after all);
c) the above-mentioned basic principle does not imply any passivity on the part of the Consumer authority. For instance, it does not mean that the Consumer authority will only take action if all legal remedies open to consumers and consumer organisations have been exhausted. If it does

not look like the market players will be able to rectify the infringement quickly and efficiently themselves then this may be reason enough for the Consumer authority to take the lead directly, for example if the infringement (and the resulting loss for the consumer) means that we cannot wait a long time for the infringement to be rectified or if it is a repeated offence. Considerations in the decision to take action, even though consumers and/or consumer organisations still have legal remedies open to them, include the fact that any action taken by the Consumer authority as a supervisory authority would have a certain deterring effect and/or that it has certain supervisory and enforcement instruments not available to parties in the private sector;

d) finally, it is not the case that the Consumer authority will always take action in situations where the market players are unable to solve the dispute themselves: the Consumer authority's decision whether to take action will be based on the criteria that it uses to decide whether or not it should take up a case (i.e. its prioritisation criteria).

4.1.1 The SRC

The SRC (the Dutch Advertising Code Commission) has set itself the objective of acting as a body that rules quickly and effectively on private sector complaints about advertisements, including those from consumers. To this end, the SRC has drawn up regulations that advertising must comply with, namely the NRC (the Dutch Advertising Code). In addition, the Advertising Code Committee, an independent body, has been set up, whose job it is to assess whether the advertisement being complained about violates the NRC. Articles 12, 15 and 16 of the Television Without Frontiers directive, one of the directives under the Regulation, have been implemented in the Netherlands in the NRC. In line with the basic principle that the Consumer authority will leave the existing private sector initiatives intact, the Consumer authority will in principle leave it to the SRC to handle any infringements in the field of misleading advertising that fall within the latter's jurisdiction. The Consumer authority can take action (after all) in cases where a supplier does not comply with the SRC's ruling, as well as in cases where the NRC does not apply. The above will be worked out in more detail in a cooperation protocol between the SRC and the Consumer authority.

4.1.2 Consumer organisations

Dutch consumer organisations such as the Consumentenbond and the Ombudsman Foundation play an important role in representing the collective interests of consumers. It is important for the Consumer authority to cooperate well with these organisations, in order to be able to operate effectively. To this end, agreements are being made with them on procedures such as the reporting of the latest developments regarding compliance with consumer regulations.

In addition, consumer organisations can take advantage of their right to take collective action and to use the new application procedure set down in the Whc. Consumer organisations and the Consumer authority must always properly coordinate their enforcement measures in this regard. Procedures for this too will be agreed with the consumer organisations.

4.1.3 Social consultation

We have already noted above that the Consumer authority will dovetail its activities with those of the private sector initiatives that already exist in the form of self-regulation, consumer organisations, centralised employers' associations and the similar. In order to facilitate consultation with these players, the Whc provides for a social consultation process. The purpose of the social consultation process is firstly to ensure that the Consumer authority's work to implement the Whc dovetails as far as possible with private initiatives that are designed to protect the consumer, and secondly to allow the government to obtain feedback from civil society organisations as to the effects and effectiveness of the Whc's implementation.

The social consultation process will take place every quarter.

4.2 Relationship with other supervisory authorities

The other supervisory authorities that the Consumer authority will be working with when carrying out its tasks may be divided into three categories, namely:

a) other competent authorities under the Regulation within the Netherlands;
b) supervisory authorities where there is a concurrence of statutory powers, and
c) other supervisory authorities.

Special mention must be made of the relationship with the OM (the Public Prosecution Office).

a) Cooperation with the other competent authorities under Regulation 2006/2004 within the Netherlands

In addition to the Consumer Authority, there are a number of other Dutch supervisory authorities who have been designated a 'competent authority' ('bevoegde autoriteit') under the Regulation. These are the (already mentioned) AFM (Netherlands Authority for the Financial Markets), the Dutch Media Authority, the Transport, Public Works and Water Management Inspectorate, the Health Care Protection Inspection, and the VWA (Food and Consumer Product Safety Authority).

In principle, there is no overlap between the tasks allotted to these supervisory authorities and to those of the Consumer authority. Each of these supervisory authorities has been designated an independent competent authority for one of the directives, or provisions contained therein, under the Regulation. In the case of the AFM, the Whc specifically stipulates that the Consumer Authority will not supervise the financial markets, as this financial supervision is to remain the exclusive jurisdiction of the AFM.

Accordingly, the Consumer authority's relationship with these competent authorities will mainly be informed by its role as Single Liaison Office for the Netherlands. Cooperation protocols will be signed with the above-mentioned competent authorities.

b) Cooperation with those supervisory authorities where there is a concurrence of statutory powers

Apart from the above competent authorities, the Consumerauthority also works with a number of supervisory authorities whose powers overlap to some extent with those of the Consumerauthority. These supervisory authorities are:

- the NZa (the Dutch Healthcare Authority);
- the OPTA (Dutch Independent Post and Telecommunications Authority) and
- the NMa/DTe (Netherlands Competition Authority/Office of Energy Regulation) as supervisory authority for the energy markets.

In the terminology of the Regulation and the Whc, these supervisory authorities are designated as 'other public bodies'. In certain cases, these other public bodies can take action against an infringement of consumer protection regulations that are actually enforced by the Consumer authority, by virtue of their 'own' sector-specific legislation and regulations. In this case, their statutory powers overlap with those of the Consumer authority. If in a particular case both the Consumer authority and another public body are authorised to enforce or supervise, then in principle the Consumer authority will not utilise its powers unless the other government agency asks it to. This basic principle is regulated in Article 4.2 para. 1 of the Whc and applies to both national and cross-border cases. The reason for this arrangement is that in many cases the special standards in the sector-specific regulations go beyond the more general standards laid down in the Civil Code. This arrangement also prevents the practice of so-called 'forum shopping', and also prevents 'double supervision'.

Nevertheless, the Consumer authority could still work together with one of the above-mentioned other authorities, should this be the most effective approach for a particular case.

Procedures for cooperation with the above-mentioned other government agencies will be set down in cooperation protocols, along with agreed interpretations of terms.

c) Cooperation with other supervisory authorities

The Consumer authority may work together with other supervisory authorities, for example to exchange reports about possible violations.

Worth noting in this respect is the NMa – the generic supervisory authority for competition matters. After all, a certain market may be imperfect from both consumer protection and competition points of view. In such a case, it makes sense to carry out joint market analyses or perform joint enforcement measures. We might also find such common ground with other supervisory authorities (such as the VWA). The Consumer authority will actively investigate such common ground and will take joint action where this is appropriate.

d) The OM (Public Prosecution Service)

A particular infringement of consumer law regulations may be coupled with conduct deemed to be a criminal offence, such as fraud or deception. In such a case, there is an overlap with the jurisdiction held by the OM under criminal law. In short, the Whc stipulates that in such a case the Consumer authority must submit the case to the OM. If the OM then declares that it will not be initiating criminal proceedings, or should a period of 13 weeks have elapsed since the Consumer authority submitted the case to the OM, then the Consumer Authority may act to enforce the law, administrative or otherwise.

The above will be set out in more detail in cooperation agreements with the OM, in which the Consumer authority will endeavour to agree on joint action with the OM in cases of conduct where there is an overlap between the respective supervisory jurisdictions, such as in the case of misleading lotteries, sweepstakes and prize draws.

5 Conclusion

The Consumer authority will commence its supervisory and enforcement activities on 1 January 2007. This article has endeavoured to shed some light on the way in which the Consumer authority will operate, and on the general basic principles it will follow in the process. This policy will be formulated in more detail and fine-tuned in the light of our experiences in practice and our improved knowledge of consumer markets over time.

CHAPTER 7

Enforcement of collective consumer interests: a competition law perspective

Kati J. Cseres

1 Introduction

Law and policy making consists of a number of essential ingredients that are all interdependent. Law consists of substantive rules whose impact and eventual effect on the market depend on the procedural and institutional setup they are placed in and on the actual policy they are part of. In order to create competitive markets and an effective legal or regulatory system credible enforcement and adequate remedies are essential. The choice of enforcement methods and appropriate remedies is just as significant as the prohibition of the rules.

The focus of discussion in both European and international market regulation has been shifted from substantive issues to enforcement and institutional matters. There seems to be internationally a common understanding of what kind of practices should be disciplined or even prohibited, however, opinions largely differ on what would be the optimal enforcement method to enforce the law. It is being recognised that mere prohibition of certain behaviours is not sufficient to discipline corporations, private individuals or even state bodies. The discussion, therefore, focuses on which enforcement methods are the most effective, which remedies and sanctions have the best deterrent effect and what would be an ideal institutional setting for enforcing the law. The choice for one or another set of enforcement tools has to take into consideration the economic incentives behind these practices, the strategic behaviour of firms and consumers to legislation, the actions of public authorities and last but not least the social and economic setting they operate in. The impact of the law and the effectiveness of the different enforcement models on business and consumers have to be assessed in order to make new suggestions for improvements and future policy choices.

This paper will discuss the competition law[1] implications of finding effective means for the enforcement of consumer interests. It will deal with three main issues. First, it will map out the legal possibilities consumers have (will have) in order to enforce their rights by making use of competition rules. Second, it will set out the competition law perspectives of enforcing consumer interests by applying consumer protection rules. The available system of remedies and sanctions will be also reviewed. Third, it will study the institutional side of this discussion. On the one hand, it will address the question whether public agencies or private organizations are better placed to enforce the law. On the other, it will address the question how competition authorities, consumer organizations and courts can or should cooperate in order to make enforcement of collective consumer interests a success.

1 In this paper the term competition law will be referred to as the legal rules prohibiting anti-competitive conduct of undertakings in the form of collusive practices and unilateral behaviour (abuse of dominant position).

This paper will show parallels, cross-references and points for cross-fertilization between the enforcement methods of consumer law and competition law.

This paper will have as a starting point the recent developments in both European competition law and European consumer law. These developments are strongly focusing on the question how the enforcement of European and national rules can be improved. In European and national competition laws new methods of detection and control, new forms of sanctions and remedies are being explored and various institutional settings including the individual incentives to enforce the laws are analysed in order to increase deterrence and achieve compliance with the laws. Among these developments one of the main policy issues is private enforcement of competition law. Perhaps for the first time in the history of European competition law consumers are in the frontline of the discussion. This discussion concentrates on how to enhance the incentives of consumers and how to provide them with the necessary tools to bring damages claims in competition cases before national courts. Collective consumer actions seem to provide a realistic solution both with regard to compensation for consumers and the efficiency of competition law enforcement.

Similarly in European consumer law the shift from substantive rights to procedural rights has been gaining more weight. Previously Directives in the consumer protection field have left enforcement of the law entirely to the Member States. It is obvious, however, that effective legal redress for consumers constitutes a corollary of the substantive rights conferred by any legal order. If consumers are granted substantive rights without providing mechanisms to ensure their effective exercise, these rights have no practical value. The development of European law that has evolved along the lines of the Injunctions Directive and the Enforcement Cooperation Regulation has led the discussion on the one hand, to finding effective means of collective consumer redress providing an efficient supplement to individual redress schemes such as small claims procedures and ADR. On the other, the deterrent effect of currently available remedies and sanctions are being reviewed. The question is whether the present arsenal of remedies and sanctions (mainly consisting of injunctive relief and fines) should be extended to recovery of damages. With regard to providing consumers with meaningful compensation for damages suffered as a consequence of 'anti-consumer' practices the discussion taking place in competition law can provide useful insights.

An effective institutional framework is equally important to achieve an efficient redress system. Whether it is public authorities or private organizations who take consumers by their hands can make a difference not only for consumers but for business, too. The role of competition authorities is perhaps more obvious in cases where consumers enforce their rights on the basis of competition law. Whether they could assist consumers in other ways, for example, by enforcing fair trading rules requires a more careful consideration.

These legal developments at European level have been triggered by problems in the Member States. And these developments have already induced certain discussions and changes in these countries. These national solutions will be occasionally referred to. Experience and expected problems in the new Member States brings into the discussion difficulties, which are specific to these jurisdictions of these countries and which call for a more proactive approach. The role of the EU institutions in the overall process is, however, limited to stimulating discussion and providing some guidance.

It seems that these enforcement issues in competition law and consumer law have placed the interplay between competition law and consumer protection on the forefront of both European and national policy agendas. This development is to be welcomed. It is time that lessons from the demand side and the supply side are brought together and are mutually considered. The idea that consumers can discipline producers does not work when the demand side lacks the tools and the incentives to do so. Similarly any regulation that aims to improve the legal and economic position of consumers is deemed to fail if the interests and incentives of business and the process of competition is neglected.

2 A preliminary remark

Any discussion on access to justice and designing effective and efficient ways to resolve disputes and seek redress needs to take account of the inherent nature of procedural rules. Procedural rules address actual consumer activity on the market. Their application and effectiveness directly depend on consumer and business behaviour. Whether consumers make complaints and seek redress by making use of the procedural possibilities offered by the law does not merely depend on well designed legal rules. The actual realization of consumer redress depends on individual economic incentives, on simple practical and technical circumstances and on psychological factors.

While insights from economic theory have been gradually introduced into the general discussion of consumer law, lawyers and economists have considered the cognitive aspects of consumer actions and transactions until now to a limited extent. However, we need to know more about consumers' general attitude towards redress in order to accurately predict their behaviour and in order to adopt those legal tools or other kind of measures that consumers in fact are going to apply to enforce their rights and resolve their disputes. Basic practical and technical problems can render any procedural rules and the enforcement of consumer rights ineffective. We need empirical evidence to answer questions like what do consumers want when they seek redress and how do they seek redress. Such evidence provides relevant insights on the incentives of consumers to take action and therefore can accommodate the selection of policy tools and enforcement methods.

Consumer complaints are influenced by consumers' general attitude toward seeking redress and situational variables.[2] Psychologists have shown that attitude has some, though limited influence on behaviour and that general attitude can be changed. If indeed consumers' attitude can be changed then policy makers should make use of these psychological insights in order to encourage consumers' self-protection and increase consumer complaints by providing effective redress routes. The general attitude is at the moment aversion and reluctance to take action.

Consumer redress also depends on situational variables. These are variables which describe the situation in which the behaviour takes place.[3] These situational variables may have greater impact on complaint making than general attitudes. Some of these variables are under control of firms and government and can be effectively addressed by policy makers.[4]

The success of consumer redress also depends on and needs to take account of business behaviour.

The impact of the enforcement of consumer interests on business cannot be neglected. The influence of regulation or the threat of regulation for example on roaming prices of mobile phone operators is a topical example. When the European Commission proposed a regulation to establish a price cap on the charges that mobile operators apply to one another for handling international roaming calls, mobile phone operators announced that they would start bringing down roaming charges to anticipate the effects of possible legislative intervention by the EU. European mobile operators have announced major price cuts reducing the roaming tariffs paid by more than 70% of travellers by an average of over 40%.[5]

In order to draft problem oriented policy options and implement effectively working corrective measures it is not enough to assume the problems and needs of consumers on the marketplace. It is key to obtain empirical evidence about the actual market failures that consumers face, about the economic incentives and the psychological capacity of consumers to fight these problems. It is equally important to be familiar with the perceptions of the problems by business, with their economic incentives behind creating market failures and with their strategic behaviour to the various corrective measures. Consumer law and policy and especially consumer redress is 'contextual'[6] and presupposes a solid understanding of the role of legal rules and other consumer oriented measures in the

---

2 M.L. Richins, B.J. Verhage, 'Seeking redress for consumer dissatisfaction: The role of attitudes and situational factors' (1985) *Journal of Consumer Policy*, p. 30.

3 Ibid at p. 30.

4 Ibid at p. 31.

5 GSM Association Press Release 14 June, 2006, Commission's latest proposal to regulate roaming is flawed.

6 I. Ramsay, 'Consumer redress and access to justice' in: Rickett, C.E.F., Telfer, T.G.W. (eds.), *International perspectives of consumers' access to justice* (Cambridge 2003), p. 26-27. see also I. Ramsay, OECD Workshop on Consumer Dispute Resolution 19-20 April 2005, Washington D.C.

marketplace. For such an understanding the interests, the incentives and the actual behaviour of both the demand and supply side is indispensable.

For the above mentioned reasons policy makers and legislators should be encouraged to go beyond legal rules and economic theories and make use of a multiple toolbox, where legal measures are supported by economic insights and behavioural economics and cognitive science play a role as well.

3 The barriers to consumer redress

The barriers to consumers' access to justice are well-known. Litigation before courts takes excessive time and money when compared to the small value of the dispute at stake. Moreover, the individual nature of civil procedure has to be taken into account. Traditional procedure is simply not geared to the institution of mass procedures. It can also be argued that in the courts adjudication rather than mediation or conciliation is arrived at. Besides these factors, there are also barriers of a psychological nature due to the complexity and formalism associated with court procedures. Consumers are often reluctant to sue because of their unfamiliarity with legal language and the hermetic rituals characteristic of judicial proceedings. In these circumstances many consumers do not even try to assert their rights and simply allow them to be infringed.

The relationship between consumer dissatisfaction and the actual number of actions consumers take before courts can be demonstrated by a pyramid. The 'complaints pyramid' (see figure I) is a graphical demonstration of consumer dissatisfaction. The lowest base of the pyramid shows the number of dissatisfied consumers. When consumers experience dissatisfaction not all of them take action. The problem this pyramid wants to demonstrate is how many of the dissatisfied consumers take action. The upper layers of the pyramid shows the number of dissatisfied consumers who do take action and the pinnacle of the pyramid shows the number of those dissatisfied consumers who turn to a court or a neutral third party with their complaint in order to get redress. Between the base and the pinnacle of the pyramid those dissatisfied consumers are situated who take some form of action which can vary from negative rumours to complaining to the suppliers.

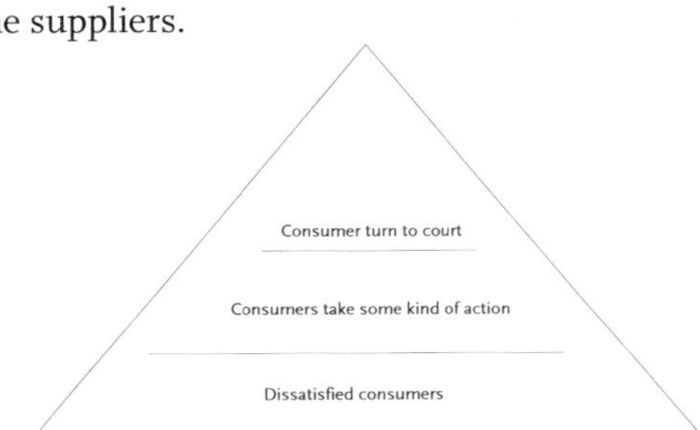

Figure I: Complaints pyramid; Source: Jacobs (1997)

Empirical evidence shows that a large number of consumers who directly make a complaint to the traders and try to resolve the dispute through direct negotiation instead of turning to a third party. This shows that consumers are in the first place interested in actual solutions such as apology, delivery, repair replacement or refund for the products or services. Consumer complaints are the most frequent and most important means of problem solving and they seek resolution of their disputes rather than legal redress.[7] This form of direct, two-party solution of consumer problems is an important starting point for discussing redress schemes.

Two major ways to increase the number of consumers placed in the upper part of the pyramid are alternative dispute resolution and some kind of aggregate, collective consumer actions. In order to get to know in which way this could be achieved one should analyse consumers' complaint behaviour. The question why the course of consumer complaints has the form of a pyramid, can be explained by the reasons why consumers refrain from complaining. First, consumers are under the impression that it is not worth the cost involved and second, consumers often think that it does not make any difference whether they complain or not.[8]

4 The objectives of consumer redress

As has been mentioned in the previous section consumers want to have a direct and concrete solution to their problems. Therefore dispute settlement rather than litigation is their goal. In the second place consumer redress is aimed at providing access to justice. Consumers will more often and more frequently make use of redress schemes where procedural rules are relaxed and where both the time and the costs incurred are reasonable and predictable for consumers. Furthermore, consumer redress is aimed at deterring firms from transgressing the law and modifying their behaviour in a way that they will comply with the law and thus operate in a pro-consumer manner. Besides actual solutions, optimal deterrence, and behaviour modification consumer redress also seeks meaningful compensation for consumer harms.[9]

The ultimate goal of consumer redress should be to implement redress schemes that can provide effective means of dispute resolution in a way that increases the confidence of both consumers and business in the market. Needless to say consumers and consumer organizations play a significant role in well

7 More than 50% of the European consumers at least once already made complaints about a product or a service and how they addressed their complaint to the sales person, retailer or service provider. Eurobaromater, European Union citizens and access to justice, October 2004, p. 9.

8 W.A. Jacobs, *ADR en consument, Een rechtvergelijkende studie naar mogelijkheden van alternatieve geschillenoplossing* (Deventer 1998), p. 374.

9 Cited above fn. 6.

functioning markets and in creating a competitive business environment. Confident consumers activate competition and consumer rules should also provide certainty for business and the least disruptive means of redress for the market. It is a difficult task to establish such an efficient balance, but it is the key to realizing effective competition and maximized consumer welfare on the market.

5 The impact of the consumer redress on business and competition

Consumer redress in principle should regulate and discipline the marketplace. Does it indeed? Can consumers vote with their feet?

Businesses are rational and profit-oriented organizations. Therefore, it could be argued that the economic incentives of the supply side can be more precisely predicted and controlled with the help of the law than for example consumer behaviour. However, even though business will value consumer complaints and seeking redress as a feedback mechanism, they 'can be insensitive to legal influences when they are estimated to be economically advantageous.'[10] Business organizations operate on the basis of cost-benefit analysis and they give preference to the benefits of commercial success over the costs of obeying the law. Violations of consumer rights might be seen as the price of doing business, where a degree of wrongdoing is incidental to continue marketing and promotional practice.[11]

This insight raises two questions. On the one hand, how can compliance of business with consumer-oriented rules be achieved? On the other, how to avoid the risk of over-deterrence and over-enforcement, which would disrupt market transactions to an unnecessary degree and discourage business activities.

The first question directly relates to the selection of enforcement methods and in particular to optimal sanctions. Sanctions need to be designed by considering the fact that businesses know that few consumers make complaints and even fewer consumers take any kind of action and even fewer consumers are successful with their claims or they settle with business. Sanctions will be effective when they bite into business profits. Sanctions and remedies will be discussed in the section below.

In the following the enforcement of consumer interests on the basis of competition rules will be discussed. This discussion will be restricted to procedural issues and the evaluation of these rules.

---

10 R. Cranston, *Consumer and the law* (London 1984), p. 140.

11 Ibid. at p. 140.

6 Enforcement of consumer interests through EC competition rules

The question how competition law can serve consumer interests can be answered by referring to substantive and procedural rules. Substantive competition rules can in the first place take care of economic interests of consumers expressed in terms of price, quality and variety of products and services. However, substantive competition rules are often unable to provide direct and explicit protection of consumer interests.[12] Procedural rules can provide more explicit ways for the participation of consumers in competition proceedings and for enforcing their rights.

Consumers play a double role in competition law enforcement: they can bring complaints before competition authorities and they can claim damages before national courts. In the first case they can encourage public authorities to enforce competition rules, in the second situation private individuals can enforce the competition rules that safeguard their interests. In other words, consumers can considerably contribute to both the public enforcement as well as the private enforcement of competition rules. The way consumers can exercise these procedural rules will be examined against the backdrop of EC law.

It could be argued that while the substantive rights of consumers are underdeveloped and rather enforced in an indirect way in EC competition law, the procedural rights of consumers in EC competition law have been fairly well developed. In the past Article 3 of Regulation 17 was the legal basis for lodging a complaint with the Commission. The interest for lodging a complaint was interpreted in a broad way by the Commission and by the European Courts, which allowed individual consumers who could prove to have been personally affected by anti-competitive practices as well as consumer organizations to file complaints. BEUC[13] has made active and successful use of these rights in the past.[14] Moreover, the modernization of competition law further strengthened the procedural rights of consumers in the framework of both public and private enforcement of competition law.

---

[12] For a detailed discussion on the protection of consumer interests through substantive competition rules see K.J. Cseres, *Competition law and consumer protection*(The Hague 2005); K.J. Cseres, 'The interplay between consumer protection and competition law in the EC', *Revue européenne de droit de la consommation (R.E.D.C.)* 2005/2.

[13] The Bureau Européen des Unions de Consommateurs ('BEUC') is an international association established under Belgian law which represents at Community level the national consumer organizations established in the Member States and other European countries.

[14] Case T-256/97 *BEUC v. Commission* [1999] ECR II-169.

7 A new framework of competition law enforcement

The new procedural framework of EC competition law as established by Regulation 1/2003 has brought about major developments for private market actors. Briefly, the essence of Regulation 1/2003 lies in the direct application of Article 81(3)[15] and the decentralisation of the Commission's enforcement powers. The notification system has been abolished and agreements that fulfil the criteria under Article 81(3) are enforceable without prior administrative decision of the Commission. Regulation 1/2003 abolishes the Commission's monopoly in granting exceptions under Article 81 (3) EC and it devolves enforcement in new areas to national competition authorities (NCA), to national courts and to private individuals.[16] Accordingly, national authorities apply Articles 81 and 82 EC when a restrictive practice as understood under these provisions restricts trade between Member States and they apply national laws to these situations where the conduct does not affect trade between Member States. The new procedural framework of EC competition law forms a system of decentralised enforcement and parallel competences.[17]

8 Public enforcement of consumer interests

Consumers and consumer organizations can bring complaints regarding anti-competitive practices to the NCAs or the European Commission. Given their knowledge of the day-to-day functioning of markets, in particular those in mass-market consumer goods, consumers can provide the competition authorities with relevant information on undertakings. Such information may enable the enforcement agencies to initiate investigation proceedings. Competition authorities may start an investigation on the basis of such a complaint and can require the undertaking to end the infringement, however, they are not obliged to do so.[18] Moreover, competition authorities might be limited by their

15 Arts. 81 (1) and 82 were directly applicable even before 1 May 2004 and the Commission has shared enforcement competences with the NCAs under these provisions.

16 Regulation (EC) 1/2003, O.J. 2004 L. 1/1, Arts. 5 and 6.

17 In the new system the European Commission shares its competence with the national authorities. The NCAs and the Commission form a network of public authorities co-operating closely together. This so-called European Competition Network (hereinafter ECN) provides a focus for regular contact and consultation on enforcement policy. The Commission has a central role in the network in order to ensure consistent application of the rules.

18 The refusal to act upon a complaint can be subject to judicial review. In its Automec II judgement the Court of First Instance has recognized the Commission's right to priorities and to reject a complaint when it is not in the Community's interest to devote its scarce resources to it. Case T-24/90 *Automec v. Commission* [1992] ECR II-2223. The Commission may reject a complaint pursuant to Art. 7 of Regulation (EC) 1/2003 without initiating proceedings.

resources and might pursue different priorities and thus refuse to act upon the complaint.

This role has been further strengthened in Regulation 773/2004 relating to the conduct of proceedings by the Commission pursuant to Articles 81 and 82 EC. Recital 11 declares that '[P]rovision should also be made for the hearing of persons who have not submitted a complaint as referred to in Article 7 of Regulation (EC) No. 1/2003 and who are not parties to whom a statement of objections has been addressed but who can nevertheless show a sufficient interest. Consumer associations that apply to be heard should generally be regarded as having a sufficient interest, where the proceedings concern products or services used by the end-consumer or products or services that constitute a direct input into such products or services.' Recital 37 of the same Regulation says that '[C]onsumer associations can equally lodge complaints with the Commission. The Commission moreover holds the view that individual consumers whose economic interests are directly and adversely affected insofar as they are the buyers of goods or services that are the object of an infringement can be in a position to show a legitimate interest.'[19]

A recent judgment of the Court of First Instance (CFI) reaffirmed that competition law and competition policy have an indisputable influence on the economic interests of consumers and that consumers contribute to the realization of the objectives of competition law. The CFI recognized that consumers have a legitimate interest in securing a finding of an infringement of the competition rules by the European Commission.

The judgment of the CFI in *Österreichische Postsparkasse*[20] concerned the so-called Lombard club decision of the European Commission from 2002.[21] In this decision the Commission found that eight Austrian banks had participated, over a number of years, in a cartel known as the 'Lombard Club' covering almost the whole of Austria. The eight Austrian banks within that cartel referred to had, *inter alia*, jointly fixed the interest rates for certain investments and loans. The Commission found an infringement of Article 81 EC and imposed fines totaling 124.26 million euros on those banks. The case before the CFI concerned the question whether an Austrian political party, the *Freiheitliche Partei Österreichs* (FPÖ), who maintained that its members had suffered substantial financial damage as a result of the anti-competitive practices could be regarded as a complainant with a 'legitimate interest' within the meaning of Article 3(2) of Regulation 17.

In this case the CFI discussed important aspects connected to the participation of consumers in competition proceedings. The CFI has interpreted the notion of 'applicant or complainant who has shown a legitimate interest' broad

19 Commission Notice on the handling of complaints by the Commission under Arts. 81 and 82 of the EC Treaty, OJ C 101/65, 27.04.2004.

20 Joined cases T-213/01 and T-214/01 *Österreichische Postsparkasse v. Commission* [2006] ECR-II-3993.

21 11 June 2002 in Case COMP/36.571/D-1 – *Austrian banks ('Lombard Club')*.

enough in order to allow the participation of natural or legal persons in competition proceedings other than the undertakings in respect of which the Commission has adopted objections. The CFI observed that the Community legislature has established a scale according to which the degree of participation in such proceedings is determined by the intensity of the harm caused to the interests of the person concerned, a distinction being drawn between an 'applicant or complainant who has shown a legitimate interest', a 'third party showing sufficient interest' and 'other third parties'. The Court noted that any applicant or complainant who has shown a legitimate interest is entitled to receive a non-confidential version of the statement of objections of the undertakings who are under investigation of the Commission.[22]

The Court considered that a final customer who shows that he has sustained or is likely to sustain harm to his economic interests owing to the restriction of competition in question has a legitimate interest for the purposes of Article 3 of Regulation No 17 in lodging an application or a complaint with the aim of securing a finding by the Commission that there has been an infringement of Articles 81 EC and 82 EC.[23] The Court has emphasized that the ultimate purpose of the rules which seek to ensure that competition is not distorted in the internal market is to enhance the welfare of consumers, the recognition that such final customers who purchase goods or services have a legitimate interest in securing a finding by the Commission that there has been an infringement of Articles 81 EC while 82 EC helps to achieve the objectives of competition law.

'Insoweit ist daran zu erinnern, dass mit den Bestimmungen, die einen unverfälschten Wettbewerb im Binnenmarkt gewährleisten sollen, letztlich der Zweck verfolgt wird, das Wohlergehen des Verbrauchers zu erhöhen. Dieser Zweck ergibt sich insbesondere aus dem Wortlaut des Artikels 81 EG. Auch wenn nämlich von dem in Artikel 81 Absatz 1 EG festgelegten Verbot Vereinbarungen ausgenommen werden können, die zur Verbesserung der Warenerzeugung oder -verteilung oder zur Förderung des technischen oder wirtschaftlichen Fortschritts beitragen, ist diese in Artikel 81 Absatz 3 EG vorgesehene Möglichkeit doch namentlich an die Voraussetzung geknüpft, dass die Verbraucher der in Frage stehenden Waren an dem entstehenden Gewinn angemessen beteiligt werden. Das Wettbewerbsrecht und die Wettbewerbspolitik haben damit auf die konkreten wirtschaftlichen Interessen der Endabnehmer von Waren oder Dienstleistungen unbestreitbar bestimmte Auswirkungen. Dass diesen Endkunden – die geltend machen, sie hätten infolge eines Vertrages oder einer Verhaltensweise, die möglicherweise den Wettbewerb beschränken oder verfälschen, einen Vermögensschaden erlitten – ein berechtigtes Interesse an der Feststellung einer Zuwiderhandlung gegen die Artikel 81 EG und 82 EG durch die Kommission zuerkannt wird, trägt jedoch zur Verwirklichung der Ziele des Wettbewerbsrechts bei.'[24]

---

[22] Cited above fn. 20 at para. 106.

[23] Cited above fn. 20 at paras. 113-114.

[24] Cited above fn. 20 at para. 115.

The participation of consumers in national competition law proceedings can vary considerably. While for example in the Netherlands consumers are not recognized as having a legitimate interest and therefore, their participation in competition proceedings is limited to bringing complaints without further rights in the proceedings[25] in other countries like in Germany consumers are recognized as parties in the proceedings before the *Bundeskartellamt* (Article 54 (3) GWB). In many countries, however, the consumers have no claims against the cartel members. The reason for this mainly lies in the view that only undertakings, but not consumers, will be seen as falling within the protection of competition law. This is the view for example in Austria, Finland, France, Poland and Portugal. In these countries it is assumed that the interests of the consumer are already protected by the intervention of the competition authority on the public law level.[26] Heineman and Moellers argue that it is paradoxical that competition law is intended to bring consumers the best results in the market, however, when undertakings violate the competition rules consumers often have no own rights in the proceedings. They rather have to rely on the activities of others, in particular the competition authorities. Consumers have merely the possibility to call for action on the part of the authorities, however, in the field of competition law the opportunity principle is dominant and widespread. The consumer has in effect no claim to the intervention of the competition authority.[27]

---

25 For an individual consumer to be able to file a complaint with the NMa, he has to qualify as an interested party under the rules of the General Administrative Law Act of the Netherlands (Art. 1: 2 *Algemene Wet Bestuursrecht*). In case the four conditions as defined by the Administrative Act are not met by the consumer, he can file a complaint but he has no further procedural rights to order the NMa to issue a decision. The most difficult condition to be met by the individual consumer is that the complaint must concern an actual and personal interest, which should have a direct link to the requested ruling. Furthermore it has to concern the party's 'own' interest, which is objectively determined. This was also the central issue in the *Essers* case (Zaaknummer 130 – *Essers vs N.V. TeleKabel*). A cable subscriber wanted to file a complaint against increase of the cable tariffs, which he considered to be an abuse of dominant position. The NMa did not recognise him as an interested party, because he did not distinguish himself from the other subscribers of the cable, who also had to pay higher tariffs. The NMa has considered in several cases that it was insufficient to qualify as an interested party when the consumer was part of an indefinite group, like clients of a supermarket (Besluit van 26 mei 1998, zaaknr.377 (*X/Albert Heijn*)), cable subscribers in a municipality, customers of a post office box service (Besluit op bezwaar van 5 juli, 1999, zaaknr. 13 (Meuters/ PTT Post inzake introductie vergoeding postbus) or users of an air service (Besluit van 8 november 2000, zaaknr. 906 (*Swart/KLM*) See also R.J.M. Van Den Tweel, 'Vindt de consument gehoor bij de NMa?', (2001) *SEW* 5, p. 173; B.M.J. Van der Meulen, 'Klagers onder de Mededingingswet', in: O.J.D.M.L. Jansen, B.M.J. Van der Meulen, R.J.G.M. Widdershoven (eindreds.), *Handhaving van de Mededingingswet* (Deventer 2001).

26 A. Heineman, T. Möllers, *Remedies in Competition Law* (2006) (forthcoming), p. 556.

27 Ibid at p. 559.

Besides recognizing the participation of consumer in competition law proceedings other ways of public enforcement can pursue consumers interests. Public authorities may act in the interest of consumers. For example, in Germany and in Hungary public authorities can initiate competition proceedings in the interest of consumers. In Germany, Section 34 GWB (*Vorteilsabschöpfung durch die Kartellbehörde*) allows the German *Bundeskartellamt* to skim off the economic benefits that an undertaking has earned by violating the competition rules. In other words the *Bundeskartellamt* can order the undertaking that infringed the competition rules to pay an amount which corresponds with the profits made as a result of the antitrust infringement.

Section 92 of the HCA can be applied when a wide range of consumers have been put at a substantial disadvantage by infringing the rules of the HCA. The Hungarian Competition Authority (*Gazdasági Versenyhivatal*, GVH), in cases falling into its competence, if it established an infringement by its decision; the chambers of commerce in respect of their members; or consumer protection organisations may file an action against persons who have put consumers at a substantial disadvantage or have disadvantaged a wide range of consumers by their activities infringing the HCA even if the identity of the consumers suffering damage cannot be established.

Public enforcement arguably has a number of disadvantages when compared to private enforcement. Public enforcement has structural, financial and other operational limits. Public agencies might lack the financial and informational resources to detect anti-competitive practices and can be vulnerable to political and personal conflicts of interest, to bureaucratic slack and inefficiency. Nevertheless, for consumers the advantage of public enforcement is that they do not have to incur any enforcement costs in order to bring a complaint. They, however, can neither claim damages nor be certain that the alleged infringement will be brought to an end.

In the following sections the private enforcement of competition rules and the relevance of private enforcement for consumers will be discussed.

9 Private enforcement of competition law: compensation for indirect purchasers

Regulation 1/2003 and the ECJ's judgment in *Courage*[28] signals the beginning of a new way of enforcing competition law on the European continent: empowering private individuals to bring suits and recover damages and thereby increase the effectiveness of overall competition law enforcement. While Article 81 (2) EC is the statutory provision providing for the right to invoke the nullity of a prohibited agreement, however, no further statement on private law remedies are present in the EC Treaty. The practical significance of private

[28] Case C-453/99 *Courage v. Crehan* [2001] ECR I-6297.

claims has been limited and there have been no cases claiming damages before the European courts until *Courage*.[29]

A legal basis does exist in European law for the application of EC competition rules in civil disputes before national courts, however, there are no Community rules and the European courts have no jurisdiction in the matter. It is, therefore, for the Member States to provide for remedies to effectuate damages actions and it is for the national courts to hear cases.[30] A 2004 study published by the Commission found an 'astonishing diversity and total underdevelopment' of private damages actions in the EU.[31] There have been very few damages claims before courts of the Member States for breach of the competition rules. The Commission argued that such low levels of private enforcement means there is less incentive for companies to comply with the EC competition rules. In order to stimulate private enforcement the Commission has published a Green Paper on how to facilitate actions for damages caused by violations of EC competition rules in December 2005.[32]

The purpose of the present development is part of the Commission's efforts to increase its effectiveness in enforcing competition rules. Private enforcement is expected to deter transgressors from violating the competition rules. Private enforcement is believed to present a credible threat through court judgments awarding damages claims and it is argued to have similar effects as the monetary sanctions of NCAs that further deliver an educational and moral message to the business community. Greater involvement of private individuals is believed to result in greater public awareness of competition rules and thus build and stimulate a competition culture. The explicit recognition of national courts' competence to decide disputes between private individuals and to protect their subjective rights under Community law by awarding damages to victims of infringements has relevant implications for consumers as well.[33] The corrective justice goal of the private enforcement system is aimed at compensating victims who suffered monetary damages as a consequence of anti-competitive conducts of undertakings.

Private enforcement of EC competition law is expected to encourage the direct participation of consumers in the enforcement of competition law in Europe.[34] Both Mario Monti and Neelie Kroes have emphasized that private enforcement was among others meant to bring the competition rules closer to

---

29 Ibid at paras. 26-27.

30 Green Paper: Damages actions for breach of the EC anti-trust rules, COM (2005) 672, 19.12.2005 final, p. 4.

31 D.F. Waelbroeck, E. Clark, *Study on the conditions of claims for damages in case of infringement of EC competition rules* (Brussels 2004).

32 Green Paper: Damages actions for breach of the EC anti-trust rules, COM (2005) 672 final.

33 Art. 6 and Recital 7 of Regulation 1/2003, cited above fn. 16.

34 Point 7 Commission Staff Working paper, Annex to the Green Paper on damages, SEC (2005) 1732, p. 7.

the citizen.[35] Private enforcement is expected to address anticompetitive conduct where public authorities lack sufficient resources to investigate and initiate proceedings.

These developments in European competition law delineate a double role for consumers and consumer organizations in the future enforcement of EC competition law. On the one hand, their role to bring complaints and participate in the public enforcement of competition law has been strengthened by the Courts and, on the other, a new role to bring damages claims before national courts for loss suffered as a consequence of the violation of competition rules is to evolve. This double role is expected to be key to ensure that competition law is complied with. The recent initiatives taken are meant to provide consumers and consumer organizations adequate economic and legal tools to exercise their double role in competition law enforcement. Moreover, together with the Commission and the national authorities, consumer associations are believed to have an important role to play in competition advocacy.[36] Consumers allegedly also contribute to greater compliance by asserting their right to compensation for harm suffered as a result of an infringement before the national courts.

The application of national procedures in EC competition cases should encourage and make it easier for consumers and consumer organizations to bring complaints and damages claims before national authorities. However, the obstacles to introduce private damages claims are numerous and involve complicated and complex legal and economic issues as the Green Paper and the debate it has launched show. One of the main contiguous issues of how private enforcement should actually take shape is closely related to consumers. Although former Commissioner Monti and the present Commissioner Neelie Kroes in accordance with the spirit of the Green Paper have on several occasions emphasized that consumers should have more access to remedial action in order to protect their rights and obtain damages, serious practical problems exist in allowing consumers to bring damages actions for violations of European or national competition rules. Compensating individuals stands in contrast with the lack of legal and economic incentives of consumers, the costs of identifying injured parties, estimating damages, the present rules on access to evidence and the high standard of proof demanded in competition law cases. The possible solutions for these complicated and complex economic and legal issues will inevitably make trade-offs between corrective justice and efficiency. However, finding effective remedies for final consumers will benefit the overall competition enforcement efforts. A balanced approach taking account of both efficiency and equity arguments is critical to make the private enforcement of competition

35 See latest the speech of Neelie Kroes on damages claims by consumers: Competition Policy and Consumers General Assembly of Bureau Européen des Unions de Consommateurs (BEUC), Brussels, 16th November 2006.

36 Ibid.

law a success. In the following the obstacles consumers face when bringing damages claims will be briefly discussed.

10 Barriers of bringing damages claims by consumers

The picture on private damages claims in the European Member States and on the possibilities for a European damage claim is from a consumer perspective far from optimistic. In order to make the judgment of the ECJ in *Courage* reality, namely to establish liability of undertakings for infringing EC competition rules seems to be a complicated and complex project for the coming years. With regard to consumers the following problems arise in the present Member States.

Consumers and consumer organisations have restricted standing in national laws to bring actions for damages. The most relevant limitation on standing is the requirement of 'interest' of the plaintiff in bringing the action, which exists in nearly all countries, although the content of this requirement varies. The issue of standing is directly related to the question whether passing on defence is allowed and to the quantification of damages. Furthermore, consumers and consumer organizations face significant impediments with regard to financial and legal resources that could facilitate litigation. Access to evidence, high standards of proof, calculation of damages and the costs of litigation form significant barriers for bringing damages claims before national courts.

11 Indirect purchasers' standing and passing on defence

A crucial question with regard to private enforcement is whether indirect purchasers and thus final consumers should be granted legal standing at all to claim damages and whether the passing-on defence should be available. Passing-on defence is when a defendant can claim that an overcharge was passed on and that the plaintiff's damages claim should be reduced accordingly. In the US at federal level the combination of *Hanover Shoe*[37] and *Illinois Brick*[38] has excluded the passing-on defence as well as legal standing for indirect purchasers to claim damages. The logic behind these decisions was that calculating the total overcharge and distributing this between direct purchasers

---

37 Case *Hanover Shoe, Inc. v. United Shoe Machinery Corp.*, 392 U.S. 481 (1968). In 1968 the US Supreme Court ruled in *Hanover Shoe & Co v. United Shoe Machinery Corp* that it was not possible for a defendant to use a passing on defence to a suit by a direct purchaser.

38 Case *Illinois Brick Co. v. Illinois*, 431 U.S. 720 (1977). In 1977 the Supreme Court in *Illinois Brick Co v. Illinois* held that indirect purchasers could not recover damages for violations of antitrust laws under section 4 of the Clayton Act.

establishes a simple and efficient system, which encourages direct purchasers to bring damages actions.[39]

The concerns about passing-on defence are based, on the one hand, on the complexity implied by indirect claims. Anti-competitive behaviours like cartel agreements in the form of price-fixing or excessive pricing by a dominant firm will cause some kind of financial damage to a number of intermediate firms in the production chain as well as to final consumers. The increase in the price of intermediate goods due to over-charging will be, to varying degrees, by direct purchasers absorbing the price increase and suffering reduced profit margins, and/or passed to indirect purchasers, namely other users further downstream in the form of higher prices for the goods and services supplied by the direct purchasers. If standing is given to indirect purchasers, the damages calculation will have to calculate the proportion of an overcharge passed on to indirect purchasers. This is the case irrespective of whether a passing on defence is allowed or not as regards the damages suffered by direct purchasers. This issue extends the damages analysis quite considerably in scope and complexity as compared to the relatively simple question of the extent of any overcharge to direct purchasers. This is because the key determinants of pass on are the nature of costs, demand and competition in the output market served by the direct purchaser, and whether the overcharge affects the position of the direct purchaser in its market relative to its competitors. If indirect purchasers are granted standing and a passing on defence is allowed to defendants, the degree of passing on is crucial with regard to the proportion of the overcharge that is passed on to the direct purchasers' customers. However, calculating the pass on rate and the exact antitrust damages requires a complex and complicated economic analysis. Especially when the group of indirect purchasers is very large such an analysis might amount to an impossible task.[40]

The logic behind *Illinois Brick* is threefold. It is, first, to avoid multiple liability of the defendant and multiple recovery of damages. Second, it is to avoid increasing the complexity of competition cases as a result of apportioning damages along the distribution levels and at the same time driving up the costs of litigation. Third, it has been argued that the direct purchaser is the most efficient enforcer of the competition rules and therefore the greatest economic incentives should be preserved for him to sue and thereby maintain the effectiveness of enforcement. The full right of recovery by direct purchasers allegedly leads to more effective enforcement. Restricting standing to direct purchasers and excluding the possibility of any passing on from direct purchasers' damages claims would promote deterrence by increasing the potential payoffs to direct purchasers who would thereby have greater incentive to bring private enforce-

39 Calculation of the total overcharge forms already a complex and complicated issue. Apportioning this total amount of the overcharge along the supply chain between different claimants at different levels further complicates the issue.

40 Cited above fn. 31 at pp. 14 and 30-31.

ment actions. Moreover it can help to avoid over compensation and overlapping damages claims.[41]

Allowing indirect purchasers to sue raises risk of abuses. There are possible scenarios where indirect purchaser actions could promote frivolous law suits or other inefficient or perverse behavior by plaintiffs.[42] These can be unmeritorious claims by inefficient competitors to fight price competition fuelled by their more efficient competitors. In these scenarios competition rules are invoked in order to demand protection from the defendant's behaviour that allegedly damages the claimants. Firms might decide to 'invest' in competition litigation as a way of competition. Once firms suffer loss of sale as a result of a new or an established competitor on the market, they may react by cutting prices, improving quality or stepping up advertising efforts. They might, however, as a reaction initiate proceedings and bring damages claims in order to subvert the competitive process.[43] The power of competition law suits to subvert competition is very real and can be substantial. Shughart shows that private antitrust cases in the US between 1973 and 1983 were overwhelmingly filed by firms charging their competitors with unlawful conduct and by downstream business entities-dealers, business customers, franchisees, and licensees-charging their suppliers with unlawful conduct. He argues that the significant proportion of private suits that are initiated either by competitors or by firms having an existing or prior business relationship with the defendant and the high settlement rates that characterize these actions reinforce the conclusion that most private antitrust litigation is driven by extortion motives. There is some limited evidence suggesting that more benign compensation and deterrence motives simply do not explain a large number of private suits.[44] This, however, may amount to protection of competitors instead of the protection of competition. For example, in Italy many claims with regard to the abuse of a dominant position were often dressed as unfair competition claims and were brought under general civil law rules to the courts.[45]

---

41 Deterrence objectives may also be achieved through other policy instruments like corporate fines, personal fines, and disqualification of directors. The issue of damage claims should also be considered together with the impact of damages awards on the efficacy of leniency programmes which provide full or partial immunity to government imposed corporate fines and personal sanctions. Cited above fn. 31 at p. 30, 128.

42 W. Breit, K.G. Elzinga, 'Private Antitrust Enforcement: The New Learning' (1985) 28 *Journal of Law and Economics*, p. 405.

43 W.F. Shughart II, 'Private Antitrust Enforcement: Compensation, Deterrence, or Extortion?' (1990)13 *Regulation*, p. 53.

44 'One of the most troubling aspects of private antitrust enforcement is the frequency with which firms bring suits against their competitors. Of course, it is possible that specialized business knowledge puts competitors in the best position to spot unlawful activities. But another possibility is that firms employ the antitrust laws as a weapon to handicap their successful rivals: firms attempt to win in the courts what they are unable to win in the open marketplace.' Ibid, see also McAfee, Mialon, Mialon (2005) P.R.

Another argument against indirect purchaser standing is based on the question whether consumers can indeed be awarded meaningful compensation. It is often put forward that there is little compensation for ultimate consumers that are being awarded as a result of indirect purchaser actions. In the US an overwhelming majority of class actions are settled before trial.[46] These settlements generally lead to the use of coupons or vouchers and a separate payment for the attorney's fees. These so-called coupon settlements mean that class members receive discounts on future purchases from the defendants rather than cash and they involve excessive attorney fees. Cash settlements for indirect purchasers are rare because courts are reluctant to allow consumers to submit claims for cash with the proof of purchase. While the damage suffered by the individual indirect purchaser is often limited in value such class actions often result in multi-million dollar awards. It is, however, the plaintiff's attorneys who stand to receive the most of such awards and the indirect purchasers often does not receive anything or the individual coupon it gets is too small, to bother to redeem it.[47]

These so-called contingency fees may create distorted incentives to settle for coupon compensation that is ultimately of little value, or even no value to the class, provided that the coupons facially appear valuable enough to justify the fees counsel seeks from the court. By promoting excessive litigation that is not only contrary to the interests of the class, but unnecessarily raises the cost of goods and services to consumers generally.[48] Such law suits are also excessive burden for the court system, who have to decide on small claims.

Thus it is argued that indirect purchaser actions enhance costs of proceedings for the plaintiffs and they impose enormous burdens on the court system, moreover such suits fail to achieve any meaningful compensation for those actually injured by price-fixing conspiracies. The benefit to indirect purchasers in terms of their participation in settlements or the value of their individual compensation is far outweighed by the costs of such indirect purchaser litigation. Accordingly, critics of indirect purchaser actions suggest that as indirect purchasers actions cannot result in meaningful compensation such a goal

McAfee, H. Mialon, S.H. Mialon, *Private Antitrust Litigation: Procompetitive or Anticompetitive?* (August 16, 2005). Emory Law and Economics Research Paper No. 05-18 available at SSRN: http://ssrn.com/abstract=784805.

45 P. Giudici, 'Private Antitrust Law Enforcement in Italy' (2004) *The Competition Law Review*, p. 68-69.

46 OECD Roundtable discussion on private remedies: class action/collective action; interface between private and public enforcement, United States of America DAF/COMP/WP3/WD(2006)34, p. 5.

47 E.P. Henneberry, *Private enforcement in EC competition law*; The Green Paper on damages actions, The passing on defense and standing for indirect purchasers, representative organizations and other groups, http://www.era.int/web/en/resources/5_2341_2394_file_en.3235.pdf last visited 7th February 2007 (2006), p. 11.

48 OECD (2006), cited above fn. 46.

should not dictate policy, but rather deterrence and effective judicial administration should take priority.[49]

Therefore, the question that has to be carefully considered is whether these actions and in particular the possible settlements reached in these law suits truly serve consumers' interests and deter unlawful behavior by defendants. There are substantial concerns that such consumer redress does not really provide anything of value. Moreover, excessive attorneys' fees may either reduce consumer redress in meritorious cases or even provide incentives for prosecution of meritless cases that can indirectly harm consumers.[50]

Although, it is true that a system denying indirect purchaser standing keeps things simple, it does, however, seriously endanger the effectiveness of private enforcement. On the one hand, concerns are related to the fact that the pass-on defense can be used to reduce liability and therefore make damages actions less attractive for the plaintiff. On the other, direct purchasers often lack the incentive to bring damages claims either because they were able to pass on the overcharge to the next commercial level, or because of the fear of retaliation and the wish to maintain good business relationship with the wrongdoer or because an upstream cartel may incorporate the direct purchasers tacitly in the cartel agreement.[51] There are instances where direct purchasers consider it to be

49 Henneberry, cited above fn. 47 at. p. 12. Chicagoans take the view that if altering the distribution of wealth is a social goal, tax or other policies are instruments superior to compensatory suits. J.M. Connor, and Y. Bolotova, Cartel Overcharges: Survey and Meta-analysis, (2005) *University of Purdue Working Paper*, p. 4; Connor, J.M., Optimal Deterrence and Private International Cartels June 20, 2005, Available at SSRN: http://ssrn.com/abstract=787927.

50 OECD (2006), cited above fn. 47 at p. 8, Concerns about possible adverse effects of class-actions have been expressed by testimonials before the Antitrust Modernization Commission: 'I am aware of one case in which an individual class member in a state antitrust indirect purchaser class action achieved a meaningful recovery. The class of consumers in 15 states and the District of Columbia whose claims were settled in *Davis v. United States Tobacco Company, supra*, received $48 in coupons towards the purchase of the product, utilizable in $3 increments. This amounted to a small amount per purchase ($3 off a 3 can roll of the product, or a dollar a can) but in the aggregate was sufficiently meaningful that approximately 26% of consumers identified as class members in those states (in excess of 150,000 people) registered to receive the coupons. I believe that this is the result of several factors: (1) the product is regularly consumed, so purchase is not a one time only event; (2) consumers of this product are price sensitive and respond to the defendant's regular promotions in much higher numbers than are typical of other products sold in convenience or grocery stores; and 3) the defendant had agreed to distribute a minimum of 40% of the face value of the coupons to class members and thus undertook to promote the settlement beyond the normal legal notice mechanisms utilized in most class action settlements.'; M.M. Zwisler, *State indirect purchaser litigation and US antitrust enforcement*, testimony before the Antitrust Modernization Commission, June 27, 2005 Washington, D.C., p. 8-9.

51 Rüggeberg, J. M.P. Schinkel, 'Consolidating Antitrust Damages in Europe: A Proposal for Standing in Line with Efficient Private Enforcement', (2006) 29 *World Competition*, pp. 395-420; Heineman, Möllers (2006), cited above fn. 26 at p. 617.

against their interests to sue their suppliers, and often indirect purchasers are substantially injured parties who should retain the right to recover where state law permits.[52]

Denying indirect purchasers right of actions means that direct purchasers can recover the entirety of the overcharge even though they could have passed on part or the total amount of the overcharge. This clearly results in issues of unjust enrichment and leaves downstream consumers without any remedy. In case indirect purchasers are *a priori* excluded from standing private enforcement may fail altogether as a consequence of lack of litigation.

The decision on indirect purchasers' standing is clearly a policy decision. The various options with regard to standing have their pitfalls and raise their own issues in terms of deterrence and consumer redress concerns. The appropriate choice largely depends upon the public policy goals sought to be accomplished. If deterrence and effective judicial administration are the main objectives of private enforcement, then limiting claims to direct purchasers should be regarded as the most feasible option. If, however, the main objective is to enable parties harmed by anti-competitive practices to receive compensation for their injuries sustained, then the argument for allowing an indirect purchaser right of action becomes stronger.[53] The question, therefore, is whether and to what extent should efficiency and ease be sacrificed in order to facilitate corrective justice i.e. recovery for downstream consumers who individually may only obtain small scale compensation.

According to the 2004 study on private enforcement in the EU the combination of the passing-on defence and the difficulties faced by indirect purchasers might seriously restrict private claims.[54] Although the possibility for indirect purchasers to bring claims theoretically exists in the EU Member States, lack of clarity on this point and difficulties of proof (in particular as regards causation and damages) and the existence of passing-on question the practical possibilities for such claims.[55]

In accordance with the consumer welfare oriented competition policy of the EC and taking into account that one of the principal reasons for encouraging private competition enforcement in the EU is redressing the injury to victims, and especially consumers, it would appear that some remedy for indirect

---

[52] L.H.Jr. Montague, Written testimony, Antitrust Modernisation Committee, Regarding State Indirect Purchaser Actions in the U.S. Antitrust Enforcement System, June 27, 2005, p. 3. Recently, in *Crane v. International Paper Co.*, 2005-1 CCH Trade Cas. 74,789 (D.S.C. 2005), the court adopted the 'first non-conspirator in the distribution chain' to allow plaintiffs-indirect purchasers who purchased from distributors who are allegedly co-conspirators but whom the plaintiff class did not name as defendants, to proceed with their claims under the Sherman Act. See also Paper Systems, *Inc. v. Nippon Paper Indus. Co., Ltd.*, 281 F.3d 624, 631-32 (7th Cir. 2002).

[53] Henneberry (2006), cited above fn. 47 at p. 4.

[54] Waelbroeck, Clark, cited above fn. 31 at p. 6.

[55] Ibid. at p. 10.

purchasers is inevitable. This is also in line with the ECJ's judgment in *Courage*, where it has provided standing for 'any individual' who suffered loss by a contract or conduct liable to restrict competition.[56]

Effective private enforcement will require a system for consolidation of the numerous claims for damages and a mechanism that provides consumers meaningful compensation. It is clear that the 'German way' of compensation[57] does not qualify as such and does not lead to corrective justice. The danger of deficient private enforcement leading to under-deterrence as a result of economic and legal impediments to the use of damages actions, or excessive private enforcement is very real when one carefully studies the US example.

12 Access to evidence

Access to information has direct influence on the ability and willingness of private individuals to build their claims on sufficient evidence and meet the burden of proof in damages claims. Access to evidence can, however, often be difficult to obtain for consumers and consumer organizations. Consumers and their organizations often do not have direct access to market data and/or specific commercial information about the supply side. Moreover, their resources are insufficient both for purchasing market information or for conducting the required proper market analysis themselves as compared to the business parties participating in the proceedings.[58] For these reasons, consumers and consumer organizations can significantly profit from gaining access to information which is held by competition agencies. When competition authorities have taken a decision in a certain case access to the non-confidential part of such a decision can assist consumers to provide the necessary substantial evidence before national courts to prove the anti-competitive arrangement they had been victims of. In the EU the principles of the general right to access to documents of the European Parliament, the Council and the Commission is laid down in Regulation 1049/2001.[59] The principles on the right to access to files in competition proceedings is laid down in Regulation 1/2003 and Regulation

56 Case C-453/99 *Courage*, para. 26.

57 Art. 34 a GWB provides that '[W]hoever intentionally commits an infringement within the meaning of 34(1) and thereby gains an economic benefit at the expense of multiple purchasers or suppliers may be required by those entitled to an injunction under 33(2) to surrender the economic benefit to the federal budget, to the extent that the cartel authority does not order the skimming off of the economic benefit by the imposition of a fine, by forfeiture or pursuant to 34(1).'

58 Comments of the European Consumers' Organisation – Bureau Européen des Unions de Consommateurs (BEUC), Public Consultation Access to File Notice comments received, p. 14-15.

59 Persons making an application for access to documents under this Regulation do not have to give reasons for their request and any document which has been released following an application enters into the public domain. Regulation (EC) 1049/2001, O.J. 2001 L 145/43.

773/2004. The relevance of this issue has been demonstrated in another recent case before the CFI which concerned the above mentioned Lombard-club' cartel: *Verein für Konsumenteninformation v Commission*.[60]

The *Verein für Konsumenteninformation* (VKI) is an Austrian consumer organization which has the right to bring proceedings before the Austrian civil courts in order to assert certain financial claims of consumers, which the latter have previously assigned to it. By the time of the dispute before the Court the VKI had brought several sets of proceedings against one of the banks participating in the 'Lombard-club' cartel, BAWAG before the Austrian courts. In those proceedings, the VKI claimed that as the result of an incorrect adjustment of the interest rates applicable to variable-interest loans granted by BAWAG the latter charged its customers too much interest over a number of years. In that context, the VKI applied to the European Commission for access to the administrative file relating to the 'Lombard Club' decision. When the Commission rejected that request in its entirety, the VKI brought an action for annulment of that rejection before the CFI.[61]

The VKI stated, *inter alia* that, in order to secure damages for the consumers on whose behalf it was acting, it had to be able to put forward specific claims regarding both the illegality of BAWAG's conduct under competition law and the effects of that conduct. To that end, consultation of the Lombard club file would have been a significant, or even indispensable, help to it. The CFI ruled that the Commission was bound, in principle, to carry out a concrete, individual examination of each of the documents referred to in the request in order to determine whether any exceptions applied or whether partial access was possible.[62]

This judgment has two main implications. On the one hand, the Court's ruling considerably strengthened the procedural rights of third parties in competition cases. The VKI did not have a right of access to the file under the competition rules which only envisage such a right for interested parties, but do not recognize a special right for third persons. Access to the file is a fundamental procedural guarantee protecting the rights of defence in competition proceedings, in particular their right to be heard. The right of access to documents concerning competition cases was, at the material time, governed only by Regulation 17/62. Even though the new procedural measures have extended the right to access to the file,[63] access to the file is still restricted to the undertakings to which the Commission addressed its statement of objections. In accordance with Article 27 (1) (3) Regulation 1/2003 these undertakings are referred to as the 'parties *vis-à-vis* the 'complainants' and 'other natural or legal persons' whose right to be heard depends on the Commission's discretion when they can show sufficient interest'.[64] In accordance with Article 7 (1) Regulation 773/2004

60 Case T-2/03 *Verein für Konsumenteninformation v Commission* [2005] ECR II-13.

61 Ibid. at paras. 6-9.

62 Ibid. at para. 92.

63 Art. 27(2) Regulation 1/2003, cited above fn. 16, Regulation (EC) 773/2004, O.J. 2005 L 133/55.

64 Art. 27(3) Regulation 1/2003 and Art. 13 Regulation 773/2004.

complainants can only request access to the file when their complaint has been rejected by the Commission. No further procedural right has been granted to them or to other natural and legal persons.

The Commission has also adopted a Notice on the rules for access to the Commission file in cases pursuant to Articles 81 and 82 of the EC Treaty, Articles 53, 54 and 57 of the EEA Agreement and Council Regulation (EC) No 139/2004.[65] This is a revised version of the 1997 Notice and it clarifies that access to file is granted only to addressees of a statement of objections.[66] However, the Notice recognises a separate right, granting limited access to specific documents on the file to complainants in competition cases and other involved parties in merger cases. These rights are dealt with separately as their scope, nature and timing are different from the right of access to file given to addressees of a statement of objections.[67] The participation of complainants in competition proceedings is restricted to receiving a non-confidential copy of the statement of objections and affording the opportunity of expressing their views at the oral hearing of the parties or submit written comments.[68] Third parties are, therefore, not entitled to access to the file.

Regulation 1049/2001 does, however, grant the right of access to any third person without having to give reasons for their request.[69] The broad scope of Regulation 1049/2001 is due to the fact that it seeks closer participation of the citizen in the decision-making process and greater legitimacy of the administration,[70] whereas the competition rules on access to the file were designed as procedural safeguards intended to protect the rights of the defence to be heard and to apply the principle of equality of arms.[71] The annual statistics of the Commission show that an increasing number of law firms request access to files on the basis of Regulation 1049/2001 in competition investigations.[72]

The dilemma this judgment poses is one between two policy choices: facilitating the conditions of private enforcement or safeguarding the legal guarantees of effective public enforcement by means of public investigatory powers

---

65 Notice on the rules for access to the Commission file in cases pursuant to Arts. 81 and 82 of the EC Treaty, Arts. 53, 54 and 57 of the EEA Agreement and Regulation (EC) 139/2004, O.J. 2005 C 325, p. 7-15.

66 Point 3 Notice on access to file.

67 Points 29-34 Notice on access to file.

68 Art. 6 Regulation 773/2004, cited above fn. 63.

69 Art. 2(1) Regulation 1049/2001 provides that '[A]ny citizen of the Union, and any natural or legal person residing or having its registered office in a Member State, has a right of access to documents of the institutions, subject to the principles, conditions and limits defined in this Regulation.'

70 Recital 2 Regulation 1049/2001, cited above fn. 59.

71 S. Bartelt, Case T-2/03, Verein für Konsumenteninformation v. Commission (2006) 43 *Common Market Law Review*, p. 197-198.

72 Report from the Commission on the application in 2004 of Regulation (EC) No 1049/2001 of the European Parliament and of the Council regarding public access to European Parliament, Council and Commission documents, COM(2005) 348 final.

and leniency applications. This judgment confronts the Commission with two questions. Should the Commission limit the increased disclosure of documents from a cartel file, which imposes serious threat to confidentiality and to the competition investigation, in particular threatening the effectiveness of leniency policy? Or should the Commission facilitate private enforcement by providing third parties a detailed assessment of the documents in the investigatory files of the Commission? The answer is not easy, especially considering the fact that both leniency applications and private enforcement are means to achieve the same goal, namely more effective enforcement of competition rules and deterring anti-competitive behaviour.

13 Burden of proof and damages calculation

According to Article 2 of Regulation 1/2003 the burden of proof rests on the claimant. This means that the plaintiff has to prove the infringement of the competition rules, the causal link between the infringement and the damage suffered and that he has to quantify the damages. The proof of all these three elements imposes highly complex issues on both claimants and the national courts hearing the cases. While all claimants will have difficulties providing courts with substantial evidence on these issues it must be made clear that the difficulties consumer claimants will face are even more burdensome.

First, in order to prove the anti-competitive behaviour of undertakings consumers need access to relevant market information. The inherent information asymmetry between the supply and the demand side as well as the further obstacles of obtaining this information has been explained above. Moreover, the current body of European competition law demands a high standard of economic evidence. A standard, which has been developed by the European courts and which in the first place demands solid economic evidence from the Commission.[73] The Commission has accordingly established a more economic based analytical framework, which significantly differs from its own past practice and policy. The Commission's more economics based approach has been communicated on the one hand with regard to Article 81 through its Notice on the application of Article 81 (3) and, on the other, with regard to Article 82 through its recent Discussion Paper. [74] The new, more economics based

[73] The Court of First Instance has made it clear in judgments like *Airtours* (Case T-342/99 *Airtours v. Commission* [2002] ECR II-2585), *Schneider* (Case T-310/01 *Schneider Electric v. Commission* [2002] ECR II-4071), *Tetra Laval* (Case T-5/02 *Tetra Laval BV v. Commission* [2002] ECR II-4381) and *GE/Honeywell* (Case No. COMP/M.2220 *General Electric/Honeywell* OJ L 048/1 18/02/2004 *Commission decision of* July 3 2001) that it demands well-founded and extensive economic analysis from the Commission.

[74] The Commission's future approach to the criteria under Art. 81 (3) EC is now made clear in the Guidelines: efficiency gains will gain more weight in the future assessment under Art. 81 (3) EC. Art. 81 (3) EC is first of all to take account of efficiencies of objective economic nature.

approach of the Commission requires the assessment of complex legal and economic issues.[75] It seems obvious that the same standard of proof will apply to private individuals bringing damages claims and thus consumers will be required to provide similar economic evidence before national courts. Relying on previous decisions of the competition authorities can be essential in these, so-called follow-on, cases.

Second, consumers at the end of the distribution line will always face legal difficulties proving the causal link between the anti-competitive behaviour and the harm they have suffered. In many jurisdictions general rules of tort law requires the proof of the fact that the damages are the direct and immediate consequence of the tort. The lack of proximate causation can itself prevent recovery of damages.

Third, calculation of damages and especially the rate of passing on downstream the distribution line requires the application of complex economic models. Anti-competitive behaviors like cartel agreements in the form of price-fixing or excessive pricing by a dominant firm will cause some kind of financial damage to a number of intermediate firms in the production chain as well as to final consumers. As has been mentioned above when standing is given to indirect purchasers, the damages calculation will have to calculate the proportion of an overcharge passed on to indirect purchasers. As has been mentioned above the degree of passing on is crucial with regard to the proportion of the overcharge that is passed on to the direct purchasers' customers. Calculating the pass on rate and the exact antitrust damages requires a complex and complicated analysis for private claimants and for the courts hearing the case. Especially when the group of indirect purchasers is very large such an analysis might amount to an impossible task.[76]

14 Costs

Private actors are much more influenced by costs and benefits than public bodies enforcing the law. Policy decisions on encouraging private enforcement of the law has to take account of the fact that private parties have to bear the costs of accessing information in order to discover the infringement, litigation costs, consisting of the lawyer's fees and perhaps expert witnesses.

---

75 The difficulties of enforcing the consumer welfare standard inherent in Arts. 81 and 82 EC concerns two aspects. On the one hand, the consumer welfare standard will permit a certain trade practice when there is no net reduction in consumer surplus irrespective of the increase or decrease in total surplus. It discriminates between different efficiencies depending on whether consumers or producers will benefit from them. On the other, the inherent requirement that consumers have to be provided a fair share of the overall economic welfare, the so-called passing-on requirement is difficult to prove.

76 Waelbroeck, Clark (2004), cited above fn 31 at pp. 14, 30-31 (Part II: Economics report: Analysis of economic models for the calculation of damages).

Duggan discusses the role of costs in litigation and the benefits of civil justice system from a law and economics perspective. Adjudication has social benefits in terms of lowering the social costs of disputes by facilitating well-organized dispute resolution instead of costly disorder and in terms of limiting the number of disputes by guiding future behaviour through the judge made law. It operates as a deterrent through encouraging private individuals to take cost-effective preventive measures and by avoiding liability in future cases. The main objective is to achieve an optimal amount of litigation, i.e. an 'equilibrium in the market for consumer justice'.[77] There are factors on both the supply and demand side that discourage litigation. Direct legal costs, such as court fees and lawyers' fees have a fixed and a variable component. High fixed costs inherent in civil litigation discriminate in favour of large claims and makes small claims uneconomical.[78] Indirect costs, such as information, opportunity, emotional costs favour repeat players who can achieve economies of scale and who can spread costs over a large number of claims.[79] These insights show that conventional civil justice system is biased against consumer litigation, which often involves small value claims and one-shotters. Solutions for consumers could be litigation methods that can either spread or avoid litigation and other associated costs.

All jurisdictions of the EU Member States provide for some kind of rules on allocation of costs in civil proceedings. The costs of litigation are often borne by one of the parties, in most jurisdictions by the losing party. While the recovery costs are often to some degree limited and do not cover the whole amount of fees for lawyers or/and experts and other witnesses, the threshold for individual and sometimes even for groups of consumers is too high. The European Commission has acknowledged that the application of the 'loser pays principle' will be problematic in cases where small amounts of damages are being claimed. In those cases the actual cost of the action might be disproportionate, even with regard to recoverability under cost rules.[80] Clearly, the costs of bringing damages claims need to be seriously addressed if private enforcement is to be encouraged. Consumers and their organizations might even need special rules that alleviate their costs and provide optimal circumstances to bring such claims.

The above mentioned barriers consumers face with regard to exercising their rights as 'private attorney generals' of EC competition law in the future can be summarized and their implications for future policy decisions can be evaluated

77 Duggan, A.J. Consumer access to justice in common law countries: a survey of the issues from a law and economics perspective in: C.E.F. Rickett, T.G.W. Telfer (eds.), *International perspectives of consumers' access to justice* (Cambridge, 2003), pp. 46-47, 65-66.

78 Ibid at p. 48-49.

79 Ibid. at p. 49-50.

80 Commission Staff Working paper Annex to the Green Paper Damages actions for breach of the EC antitrust rules COM(2005) 672 final, p. 60-61.

on the basis of a recent Italian cartel case that has been referred through the preliminary ruling to the ECJ.

15 Motor car insurance saga: the limitations of actions at EC level

This case demonstrates that if the objective is to provide compensation for final consumers and to encourage them taking action to enforce competition rules then consumers will choose only the redress avenue that provides them optimal conditions to have their claims adjudicated in a swift, flexible and effective way. This case shows that if claims are small and there is no possibility to consolidate and aggregate the separate claims then consumers' lawyers prefer small claims judges where procedures are less formal and less demanding in terms of evidence and burden of proof.

In July 2000, the Italian national competition authority declared that three insurance companies had implemented an unlawful agreement for the purpose of exchanging information on the insurance sector. The Italian NCA (AGCM) revealed that the agreement facilitated an average 20% increase in premiums for compulsory civil liability insurance relating to accidents caused by motor vehicles, vessels and mopeds not justified by market conditions.[81] Motor insurance is compulsory in Italy and therefore every car has to be insured by the owner or by the usual driver against accident and third party risk. Accordingly, the number of individuals who have been victims of the overcharge is massive. In the absence of standing for consumers under Article 33 of the Italian competition law No 287/90[82] and in the absence of collective actions under Italian law, consumers brought individual damages claims before the Italian small claims judge, the *Giudice di pace*, in order to obtain orders against the insurance companies for restitution of the increase in the premiums paid by reason of the arrangement declared unlawful. Even though the Italian *Corte di Cassazione* in its judgment of 4 February 2005 declared that consumers can also bring damages claims under Article 33(2) of the Italian competition law, consumers did not bring actions before the *Corte d'appello* who has exclusive territorial jurisdiction in damages claims based on the competition rules. Consumers decided to turn to the small claims court because the proceedings before the *Corte*

[81] Autorità garante per la concorrenza e del mercato Decision No 8546 (I377) of 28 July 2000 (Bolletino 30/2000 of 14 August 2000).

[82] Art. 33(2) of the Italian Competition Act (Law No 287 of 10 October 1990 on the rules for the protection of competition and markets (Legge 10 ottobre 1990 No 287, Norme per la tutela della concorrenza e del mercato, GURI No 240 of 13 October 1990, p. 3) states that actions for annulment and damages and applications for interim measures in relation to infringements of the provisions referred to in Titles I to IV of that law, including Art. 2, are to be brought before the Corte d'appello having territorial jurisdiction.

d'appello take much longer and the costs are much higher in comparison to the proceedings before the *Giudice di pace*, which could compromise the outcome of their damages claims. As the small claims judges did not have jurisdiction to rule on the damages claims on the basis of the Italian competition rules, they awarded restitution for consumers on the basis of civil liability rules, in particular on the basis of unjust enrichment.[83]

Manfredi and other injured individuals then brought proceedings before the Giudice di pace di Bitonto. This court took the view that as insurance companies of other Member States carrying on their activities in Italy also took part in the agreement ruled unlawful by the AGCM, the alleged agreement infringed not only Article 2 of Law No 287/90 but also Article 81 EC (2). The Italian court considered that any third party, including the consumer and end user of a service, may consider itself entitled to rely on the invalidity of an agreement prohibited under Article 81 EC and claim compensation in damages where there is a causal relationship between the harm suffered and the prohibited arrangement. It argued that if that was the case, then a provision such as that in Article 33 of Law No 287/90 could be regarded as contrary to Community law. The national court reasoned that the timescales were much longer and the costs much higher in proceedings before the *Corte d'appello* compared to those in proceedings before the *Giudice di pace*, which could compromise the effectiveness of Article 81 EC.

The insurance companies in the main proceedings pleaded, *inter alia*, that the *Giudice di pace di Bitonto* did not have jurisdiction under Article 33 of Law No 287/90 and that the right to restitution and/or compensation in damages was out of time.[84]

The Italian court stayed proceedings and among others referred two questions to the ECJ for preliminary ruling that are relevant from the consumer perspective.[85] On the one hand, the Italian court asked whether Article 81 EC should be interpreted as meaning that it precludes the application of a national provision similar to that in Article 33 of Law No 287/90 under which a claim for damages for infringement of Community and national provisions for anti-competitive arrangements must also be made by third parties before a court other than that which usually has jurisdiction for claims of similar value, thus involving a considerable increase in costs and time. On the other, it asked whether Article 81 EC is to be interpreted as meaning that it entitles third parties who have a relevant legal interest to rely on the invalidity of an agreement or practice prohibited by that Community provision and claim damages for

83 Giudici explains that the *Corte d'appello* is located only in large cities and it is perceived by lawyers as very demanding court in terms of quality of the legal paperwork. At the same time the *Giudice di Pace* is local and undemanding also because it can apply equity instead of formalized legal rules. Giudici (2004), cited above fn. 45 at p. 73-74.

84 Joined cases C-295/04 to C-298/04 *Manfredi* [2006] ECR I-6691, paras. 23-25.

85 Joined cases C-295/04 to C-298/04 *Manfredi* [2006] ECR I-6691.

the harm suffered where there is a causal relationship between the agreement or concerted practice and the harm.

The ECJ was clear on both points. It explicitly stated that '[A]rticle 81 EC must be interpreted as meaning that any individual can rely on the invalidity of an agreement or practice prohibited under that article and, where there is a causal relationship between the latter and the harm suffered, claim compensation for that harm'.[86] Thus the ECJ has reaffirmed that final consumers must be able to bring damages claims before national courts for losses caused by infringements of EC competition law.

Furthermore, the ECJ has repeated again in the present case as it has always consistently held that '[I]n the absence of Community rules governing the matter, it is for the domestic legal system of each Member State to designate the courts and tribunals having jurisdiction and to lay down the detailed procedural rules governing actions for safeguarding rights which individuals derive directly from Community law, provided that such rules are not less favourable than those governing similar domestic actions (principle of equivalence) and that they do not render practically impossible or excessively difficult the exercise of rights conferred by Community law (principle of effectiveness).'[87] While a legal basis does exist in European law for the application of EC competition rules in civil disputes before national courts, there are no Community rules and the European courts have no jurisdiction in the matter. The private law consequences of competition law infringements fall within the competence of the Member States in accordance with the so-called national procedural autonomy.[88] It is, therefore, for the Member States to provide for remedies to effectuate damages actions and it is for the national courts to hear cases.[89]

In accordance with Article 3 (1) of Regulation 1/2003 where the national courts apply national competition law to agreements, decisions or concerted practices within the meaning of Article 81 EC, which may affect trade between Member States within the meaning of that provision, they should also apply Article 81 EC to such practices. As AG Geelhoed explained in the present case, this means that in principle a claimant would be able to choose depending on whether he had based his claim solely on an infringement of European competition law or based it partly thereon. In the first case the *Giudice de Pace* would have jurisdiction in the second the *Corte d'Appello* has jurisdiction, given its exclusive competence to deliver judgments on claims for damages based on an infringement of Italian competition law.[90]

---

86 Joined Cases C-295/04 to C-298/04 *Manfredi* [2006] ECR I-6691, para. 63.

87 Joined Cases C-295/04 to C-298/04 *Manfredi* [2006] ECR I-6691, para. 62.

88 Joined Cases C-295/04 to C-298/04 *Manfredi* [2006] ECR I-6691, para. 62, Case 33/76 *Rewe-Zentralfinanz eG and Rewe-Zentral AG v Landwirtschaftskammer für das Saarland (Rewe I)*, [1976] ECR 1989, para. 5, Case C-261/95 *Palmisani* [1997] ECR I-4025, para. 27, Case C-453/99 *Courage and Crehan*, para. 29.

89 Green Paper Damages actions for breach of the EC anti-trust rules, COM (2005) 672 final, p. 4.

90 Opinion of Advocate General L.A. Geelhoed delivered on 26 January 2006 in Joined Cases C-295/04 to C-298/04 *Manfredi* [2006] ECR I-6691, para. 48.

The principles of effectiveness and the principle of equivalence apply merely to the enforcement of individual rights based on Community law. The possible procedural obstacles of damages actions that consumers face in national law can, on the basis of national procedural autonomy, be dealt with by neither the Community courts nor other Community institutions. Disproportionate duration and costs of such proceedings can be capable of frustrating the exercise of consumers' rights conferred by the Italian legal system, but it is not capable of frustrating rights conferred to them by the Community legal system. [91] And as such the Community has no competence to rule on this issue.

The facts and the outcome of *Manfredi* demonstrate the inherent obstacles consumers face when they want to make use of the substantive rights conferred on them by the Community legal order.[92] Compensating the loss consumers suffered as a consequence of an anti-competitive behaviour has been advocated as 'fundamental to the idea of private damages actions'[93] in EC competition law.

Even though Commissioner Neelie Kroes and her DG Competition has declared on numerous occasions that '[T]he EC Treaty gives the victims of anti-competitive behaviour a basic right to reparation for the damage caused'[94] the same Treaty has provided neither Community rules nor jurisdiction for the European institutions to rule in this matter.

Such policy declarations will remain empty words without credible actions. However, credible actions begin with setting realistic goals and with acknowledging the actual legal, economic and practical problems that private individuals, in particular consumers will face when they want to effectuate their substantive Community rights before their respective national courts. Without seriously investigating the legal and economic infrastructure consumers need to bring compensatory claims, the policy plans of the European Commission will remain a mere illusion.

The above discussion has demonstrated that today consumers and consumer organizations lack the financial resources and the economic expertise to bring successful damages claims. As Gavil points out private parties need the procedural and evidentiary infrastructure to collect, present and assess economic evidence. The absence of such infrastructure might altogether undermine their capacity to make effective use of private rights actions, which have been made

91 Ibid. at para. 51.

92 The European Court of Justice held in *Courage*, that the full effectiveness of Art. 81 would be at risk if it were not open for individuals to claim damages for losses caused by infringements of EC competition law. Case C-453/99 *Courage and Crehan*, paras. 26 and 27.

93 'It is fundamental to the idea of private damages actions that the victim of a violation of the law is entitled to compensation for the loss suffered as a result of the violation in question.' Point 4 Commission Staff Working paper, Annex to the Green Paper on damages, SEC (2005) 1732, p. 6.

94 The Green Paper on antitrust damages actions: empowering European citizens to enforce their rights Neelie Kroes, speaking at the European Parliament Workshop on damages actions for breach of the EC antitrust rules, Brussels, 6 June 2006.

possible by legislation.[95] Suggestions on how consumers could be empowered to make effective use of their procedural rights under competition law will be reviewed below.

16 How to empower consumers to make effective use of their procedural rights?

Since the European Commission has launched its new policy aiming at outsourcing the enforcement of competition law to private individuals, consumers have been in the frontline of competition policy discussions. They have been appointed a relevant role in bringing competition law closer to the citizens by disseminating and raising the awareness of competition law principles and thereby contributing to improved deterrence of anti-competitive conducts and to overall increased effectiveness of the Commission's enforcement of competition law. The relevant policy question now is how to encourage consumers to bring compensatory claims before national courts despite the above mentioned lack of legal and economic incentives and without endangering the effectiveness of competition law enforcement. In other words, how should the law or other regulatory measures empower consumers to make effective use of their substantive rights and at the same time safeguard the efficiency of the private enforcement of competition law?

It seems commonly agreed that the success of private enforcement of competition law in Europe depends on the improvement of both the incentives of private actors and the institutional capacity of the respective jurisdictions. In order to encourage private individuals to go to court and play the role of 'private attorney generals' a system of optimal conditions has to be created.[96]

Private actors' and in particular consumers' readiness to bring damages actions to courts is hindered by the limited access to courts in the form of various limitations on standing, low degree of awareness of competition rules, the

---

95 A. Gavil, 'The Challenges of Economic Proof in a Decentralized and Privatized European Competition Policy System: Lessons from the American Experience,' (2006) *JCEL* (forthcoming).

96 The alleged factors of the success of private damages claims in the US such as treble damages, class actions, discovery rules and contingency fees touch upon fundamental principles of national private law in Europe. Therefore, they have limited chances to be introduced in the same way in the European jurisdictions. The term 'private attorney general' refers to the use of private litigation as a means of bringing potential antitrust law infringements into courts. In the U.S. public enforcement has long been assumed to be inadequate to achieve effective enforcement, and therefore private litigation has been used as a means of public enforcement. By giving private litigants incentives to bring civil suits, it is thought, government can more efficiently and effectively achieve compliance with the antitrust laws. Private litigants play a public role by assisting public authorities in their enforcement role. Gerber, D.J. (2006) forthcoming 'Private enforcement of competition law: a comparative perspective' in: Heineman, Möllers (2006) forthcoming, cited above fn. 26 at p. 416-417.

lack of legal certainty including the lack of confidence in the expertise of judiciary and the significant time, costs and complexity litigation means.[97] The legal position of consumers and consumer organizations is often even more restricted in the new Member States than in the old Member States. Access to justice of consumers and consumer organizations within and outside of the court system is often problematic or despite existing legal rules practical difficulties hinder them to make effective use of those substantive rights. In these Member States even collective consumer actions are rare either because of the lack of legal basis or other practical financial problems.[98]

While nearly all Member States provide for some kind of collective or representative actions, the diversity of these actions is substantial and terminology differs through the 25 Member States. However, US style class actions do not exist in Europe.[99] Although litigation by representative associations seems to rise, these are often limited to injunctions or cease and desist orders to the exclusion of damages actions.[100]

The perceived financial risk and lack of incentives of private individuals to bring damages actions on the basis of competition law calls for actions that target more the practical side of the problems than pile up another layer of legislative rules. The gap between the adoption of ambitious legal rules and effectively enforcing the law may have a negative impact on both private individuals' and national authorities (courts) capacity to deal with private law suits. This gap has to be addressed by making use of a multiple toolbox consisting of legislative measures, education by investing in competition advocacy, academic research and practical solutions.

Consumers are often claimed to be the ultimate beneficiaries of competition law. However, their position to get compensation for the damages they have suffered as a result of cartel agreement or an abuse of a dominant position is limited or not possible at all in most of the Member States.[101] Facilitating private damages claims will include legal measures such as widening the standing, the introduction of some type of collective actions either in the form of private group actions, claims by consumer associations or by public authorities. The Commission's Green Paper on damages has also acknowledged that collective actions can protect consumer interests and they can serve to consolidate a large number of smaller claims into one action, thereby saving time and money.

However, more is needed. Besides providing standing for consumer organizations, litigation and other associated costs need to be reduced, the burden of proof has to be alleviated and relaxed rules of evidence and procedure should be

97 Waelbroeck, Clark (2004), cited above fn. 31 at pp. 9-13 (Part I: Comparative Report).

98 Ibid. at p. 2 and the National reports of Czech Republic (p. 20), Lithuania (p. 17), Latvia (p. 17), Estonia (p. 21-22), Slovenia (p. 21-22), Hungary (p. 16).

99 Although Sweden comes extremely close and Spain has a similar albeit more limited action.

100 Waelbroeck, Clark (2004), cited above fn. 31 at p. 2.

101 Heineman, Möllers (2006) forthcoming, cited above fn. 26 at. p. 618.

introduced. The need for strengthening the position of consumer organizations in order to bring collective actions as well as alleviating their burdens in terms of access to evidence, burden of proof and reduced court fees have been equally stressed. Providing ways to obtain meaningful compensation will be a critical factor in the overall system.

Moreover, mechanisms that make effective use of certain elements of public enforcement such as the expertise and the assistance of competition authorities and other market regulatory agencies have to be encouraged. Most of the NCAs have by now built up sufficient legal and economic expertise with regard to competition law issues and this should be channelled into the avenues of private enforcement. Establishing specialized courts hearing both national and European competition cases or involving experts in the courts proceedings have also been suggested.[102]

The expertise of the NCAs can assist national courts in adjudicating damages claims in competition cases. In Hungary, for example, on the basis of Article 88/B of the Competition Act, a court shall immediately notify the Competition Office if the application of the competition law rules on cartels or abuse of dominant position arises in a civil action before the court. The Competition Office may submit observations or set forth its standpoint orally before the closing of the hearings. Upon a request of the court, the Competition Office shall inform the court about its legal standpoint concerning the application of the competition law rules in the given case. Thus, the Competition Office acts as an 'amicus curiae' to the courts. Furthermore, if the Competition Office decides to initiate proceedings in a matter that is pending before the court, then the court shall stay its own proceeding until the Competition Office issues its final and legally binding decision, and the court is also bound by the final and legally binding decision of the Office concerning the finding of breach of the competition law rules or the lack thereof. A similar solution exists in Finland[103] and has been proposed in Estonia[104] as well.

Rüggeberg and Schinkel propose an alternative procedure, which consolidates all individual claims into one centralized and complete assessment of total damages corresponding to one and the same infringement. They suggest to place the responsibility for the overall assessment with a central authority, most probably the NCA or the European Commission, that oversees the passed-on damages related to the infringement, and has the economic and industry expertise, investigation powers and means to quantify them in the required detail. The authority acts as an advisor to the court on the assessment of total damages and to whom they accrue.[105]

[102] Waelbroeck, Clark (2004), cited above fn. 31 at pp. 121-122 (Part I: Comparative Report).

[103] Ibid at p. 2 (National Report, Finland).

[104] Ibid at p. 20 (National Report, Estonia).

[105] Later consequential damages can refer to this advice. The procedure combines decentralized damages litigation before national courts with a centralized and coherent calculation of total damages. The latter

Heinemann and Möllers propose a registration system in which consumers have to establish the degree to which they have been affected. In order to limit administrative expenses flat-rate amounts should be possible.[106]

The Member States have come up with several suggestions as well to solve the above mentioned problems. Latvia and Lithuania emphasized that the European Commission could issue certain instructions or guidelines on the different methods of calculating damages and explaining the application of various economic models.[107] Lithuania even suggested the introduction of statutory damages.[108] In order to ease the proof of causation Latvia suggested to facilitate the indirect purchaser's action by creating an express rule stating that the choice of a middleman to pass on increased costs either wholly or partially would not be sufficient to break the chain of causation.[109] In order to increase the general awareness of competition issues both the judiciary and businesses should be further educated. Furthermore, the Member States emphasized the need for concentrating these kinds of cases in a single court acting as a specialized court or an exclusively competent court.[110]

Private actors are not yet familiar and recognize themselves in the role of a responsible and sovereign market actors. It takes time to educate the old generation and to bring up a new generation of consumers and business undertakings, especially in the new Member States. However, paying more attention to the role of institutions in the new enforcement system of EC and national competition law can prove to be the solution. In both the old and new Member States the NCAs are the motors behind effective enforcement and competition advocacy. They can assist the national courts who often face competence problems in competition cases.[111] The role of lawyers will be also significant to make private enforcement workable. Hopefully they will assist their clients and not 'hijack' them.

In the following sections the enforcement of consumer interests through consumer rules will be reviewed and discussed from a competition law perspective.

---

decreases the litigation cost faced by parties discovering competition law infringements willing to bring a private damage action. It achieves efficiency gains by preventing fragmented, duplicative litigation, while respecting the Community remedy principle and interconnecting with the European legal system. Rüggeberg, Schinkel (2006), cited above fn. 51.

106 Heineman, Möllers (2006) forthcoming, cited above fn. 26 at. p. 620.

107 Waelbroeck, Clark (2004), cited above fn. 31 at p. 17 (National Report, Lithuania and National Report, Latvia).

108 Ibid.

109 Ibid.

110 Waelbroeck, Clark (2004), cited above fn. 31 at p. 10 (Part I: Comparative Report).

111 One significant trade-off of the NCAs amicus curiae role could be that the independence of courts come into danger through cooperation with NCAs.

17 Enforcement of collective consumer interests on the basis of consumer law

In the last decade consumer policy objectives have been increasingly refocusing on redress schemes and enforcement issues all around the world. The challenge for finding effective and low cost ways for consumers to resolve their disputes and to provide access to remedies that are not disproportionate to the economic value at stake have become one of the key objectives of consumer policies at national, European and international levels.[112]

In the EU a number of legislative measures and other initiatives have been taken to stimulate the discussion and to achieve this policy objective. Even though access to justice and consumer redress have been part of the Community's policies since 1975 they have only been reinforced in soft law documents. A specific legal basis for consumer redress is absent in the EC Treaty.[113] While previously Directives in the consumer protection field have left enforcement of the law entirely to the Member States, Directive 98/27 EC on injunctions and Regulation 2006/2004 on consumer protection cooperation have squarely put the issue on the top of the consumer protection agenda. The discussion on the enforcement of consumer rules since then has been very similar if not identical to the discussion on effective enforcement methods in competition law circles. The objectives of the enforcement of competition law and consumer law partly coincide as they both aim to achieve deterrence and efficiency. Both sets of rules are aimed at effectively influencing and imposing a meaningful impact on corporate policy and behaviour. While the underlying legal rules and the subject matters differ there seem to be numerous insights that merit broader consideration and cross-fertilization in both fields.

The particular characteristics of consumer problems and the objectives of consumer redress need to guide this study. The goal is, on the one hand, to establish effective means of collective consumer redress providing an efficient supplement to individual redress schemes such as small claims procedures and ADR. On the other, the deterrent effect of currently available remedies and sanc-

[112] This increased awareness of enforcement issues are witnessed by initiatives like OECD Guidelines for Consumer protection in electronic commerce, OECD Cross-border fraud Guidelines, UNCTAD UN guidelines for Consumer protection. Further initiatives include the setting up of the International Consumer Protection en Enforcement Network, which is a worldwide network of national authorities with the aim of strengthening and improving the enforcement of consumer protection legislation (except product safety and the prudential regulation of financial institutions). The Network of European Consumer Centres is there to help with such questions and any other problems you may have concerning your activities as a consumer in Europe.

[113] Art. 153 EC says that '[I]n order to promote the interests of consumers and to ensure a high level of consumer protection, the Community shall contribute to protecting the health, safety and economic interests of consumers, as well as to promoting their right to information, education and to organize themselves in order to safeguard their interests.'

tions has to be reviewed. The question whether the present set of remedies and sanctions that mostly comprise injunctive relief and administrative fines should be extended to recovery of damages and how to make private enforcement a valuable complement to public enforcement colludes again strikingly with the policy issues in competition law. The issue of providing consumers with meaningful compensation for damages suffered as a consequence of 'anti-consumer' or anti-competitive practices can provide useful insights in both areas worth of cross-fertilisation. In the following these areas of cross-references and insights worth of cross-fertilisation will be discussed.

The enforcement of consumer rules

Adhering to the principle that substantive rights are of little value without effective enforcement of these rights and easy access to justice, it has to be emphasized that substantive and procedural issues are interdependent. The behaviour of consumers can be the source of frictions in markets. Different market failures trigger different remedies and call for different redress schemes. Therefore, a discussion on enforcement methods that serve consumer interests in the most effective and efficient way cannot disregard the nature of the interests that have to be protected and the nature of the harm suffered by consumers. Consumer concerns are complex, diverse and diffuse both over consumer groups and over time. The adverse effects of consumer offences might realize later in time. They are moreover unpublicized and therefore difficult to detect and address. Prospective enforcement methods have to take account of this diversity and complexity of consumer concerns.

The rapid technological changes, globalisation and deregulation of formerly regulated monopolies have expanded the range of consumer products and services, made product- and service-specific regulation increasingly complex and complicated and magnified the informational challenges consumers face today. The complexity and the wide range of trade practices consumers meet on present markets have a direct influence on the one hand, on what consumer interests should be protected and on the other, which kind of enforcement tools can achieve such protection and assist consumers in the best way. The present complexity and variety of trade practices determine the kind of resources of investigation and the detection methods needed.

Furthermore, consumer concerns are not always of economic nature. This a relevant difference with competition law, which is aimed at improving economic efficiency and as such it is first of all to benefit consumers in terms of price and output and it is less capable of taking account of broader consumer interests, like health, safety or information problems. Although competition enforcement might incidentally address consumers' non-economic interests, it is neither fit nor effective in doing so. Accordingly, competition rules are suited to target consumers' economic welfare and to remedy economic losses that they have suffered as a result of anti-competitive trade practices.

A large amount of consumer problems are related to information inefficiencies like imperfect information, information asymmetries and even cognitive constraints such as bounded rationality. Many consumer concerns have economic repercussions related to price, output and quality of products and services and variety and choice between those. Consumer problems are not only directed at economic, but also at social aspects of the market. The protection of consumers is thus not limited to preventing enterprises from asking excessively high prices and to oppose the one-sided communication structure on the market. Consumers also attach great importance to the quality of living standards. These non-economic interests include health and safety concerns and in a broader sense also environmental protection, culture or even sports.

The fact that consumer concerns are diffuse and diverse is not conclusive to argue that consumer interests cannot be represented and protected. Nevertheless, the discussion of enforcement methods have to take account of this diversity and complexity of consumer concerns. Moreover, it needs to take into account that the assumption that consumers (can) behave in a rational way and (can) make rational choices and purchases often proves to be an illusion. The extent to which consumers deviate from the model of rational decision-making calls for discussions on the bounded rationality or even irrationality of consumers' decisions and for a more refined approach. The competence of consumers to process available information and make rational decisions is proved to be subject to cognitive constraints.[114] Such an approach needs to be based on the fact that rational decisions require sufficient motivation, capacity and opportunity to take place.[115] This requires regulators and enforcers to change their focus points to how they want to assist consumers and ultimately achieve more competitive and socially optimal and economically efficient markets.

The assessment and the design of the various procedural models have to take account of the underlying substantive issues in order to provide consumers such enforcement tools that are capable of addressing the market failures, repair the damage and prevent future violations of consumer rights. Accordingly, enforcement methods should be designed and selected by studying the various ingredients that determine their actual operation. These ingredients include the nature of consumer concerns (health, safety issues or economic loss as result of for example information problems), practical matters such as economic incentives, financial resources but also time and ease of access to justice and last but definitely not least the remedies sought (declaratory, injunctive or monetary

[114] H.A. Simon, 'A Behavioral Model of Rational Choice' in: *Models of man: social and rational: mathematical essays on rational human behaviour in a social setting* (New York: Wiley 1957); T.S. Ulen, 'Information in the market economy – Cognitive errors and legal correctives' in: S. Grundman, W. Kerber, S. Weatherhill, (eds.), *Party autonomy and the role of information in the Internal Market*, de Gruyter, Berlin, 2001, pp. 98-129.

[115] Th.B.C. Poiesz, 'The free market illusion: psychological limitations of consumer choice' in: *Market regulation: lessons from other disciplines*, Ministry of Economic Affairs, (The Hague 2004), pp. 17-36.

remedies) and deterrent sanctions (criminal law or civil law). These elements will be further discussed below by making cross-references to their implications for business and competition law.

Cross-fertilisation: useful lessons from (and for) competition law

Despite the fact that the discussion on the enforcement of both competition law and consumer law is related to similar issues there have been little cross-references and even less attempts to channel the useful lessons into the parallel discussions. In the following a number of questions will be raised that are suggested to be carefully thought through before policy decisions are made about proposing one or another consumer redress scheme. These questions can be grouped around three subjects that all indicate a certain policy choice. Below these choices and their implications for both competition and the different consumer redress schemes will be dealt with.

Public v. private enforcement

The effectiveness of the institutional framework has a direct impact on the efficiency of the redress system. When it comes to the choice whether to entrust enforcement to public bodies or private individuals or private organizations, the question is not so much an 'either-or' but rather what is the most effective allocation of enforcement between public law and private law techniques and how to achieve an optimal combination between these two techniques so that they can effectively complement each other. A further question and perhaps one which is more relevant in consumer law enforcement is which substantive issues should be outsourced to private consumers and which can be better left to public agencies. In consumer law enforcement this demarcation line also depends on which market philosophy a certain legal system adopts. When consumer law and policy is based on the principle of consumer sovereignty there will be strong incentive to encourage consumers to make use of their possibilities on the market and to provide instruments that make the market more transparent and consumer decisions more rational. Intervention by public regulatory tools will be limited to the most necessary as consumers are believed to be the best judge of their welfare and thus capable of being self-responsible by making rational economic decisions. A more paternalistic approach will have stronger preference for enforcement by public bodies thereby leaving a smaller segment of enforcement to the consumers.

Thus on the one hand, the selection between the institutional options depends, on the one hand, on the underlying particular interest that policy makers or the legislature wants to protect and on the other, on the institutional capacity of the different players. Whether public authorities or private organizations should enforce consumers' interests or private individual consumers should do so needs careful consideration on the basis of factors such as costs, delay, access and the quality and quantity of dispute resolutions. Public authorities will be more efficient in cases where they can realize economies of scale, specialization in investigating and prosecuting claims and impose penalties and other deterrent measures that private individuals could not in civil proceedings.[116]

Outsourcing the enforcement of consumer rights to private individuals or their representative organizations can be an effective policy option, when they have better access to information and when such an enforcement is less disruptive for market transactions. Private claims can be also a valuable option where the financial resources or the legal constraints prevent public authorities from acting.

When deciding on who should enforce the rules in both legal fields the starting point should be to ask who has the economic resources, the legal tools and the incentives to do so. When private individuals have the capacity, the motivation as well as been provided with optimal conditions to enforce their rights then private enforcement should be given preference. However, the ways in which public and private enforcement can complement each other and how practically useful elements can be channelled from one to the other should be also considered. The way to achieve such an efficient combination could be through, on the one hand, setting clear lines of demarcation regarding where public agencies and where private enforcement is better placed to act and then create what Trebilcock calls a socially appropriate incentive structure where individuals are given the possibility to make their choice about avenues of redress.[117] These issues are equally applicable in competition law as has been explained above with regard to the private enforcement of competition rules.

Civil law innovation v. market regulation

There is also a broader institutional dimension of the discussion whether private or public actors should be entrusted with enforcement powers. This dimension refers to the level where the dispute is decided on, namely by civil courts, by other independent third parties such as arbitrators, mediators or regulatory agencies.

When private individuals or private organizations enforce the law by filing law suits and civil courts adjudicate on the matter the enforcement is both more costly and time consuming and complicated from legal, economic and practical points of view as has been explained above with regard to competition law enforcement. Therefore, there seem to be good arguments in consumer law enforcement for regulation of the market by public authorities by setting market regulatory standards and pecuniary fines for violations of the standards.[118]

[116] M.J. Trebilcock, 'Rethinking consumer protection policy' in: Rickett, C.E.F., Telfer, T.G.W. (eds.), *International perspectives of consumers' access to justice* (Cambridge 2003), pp. 83-84.

[117] Ibid. at p. 81.

[118] H-B. Schaefer, 'The Bundling of Similar Interests in Litigation. The Incentives for Class Action and Legal Actions taken by Associations' (2000) *European Journal of Law and Economics*, p. 202.

Public regulation of the market seems to be a more efficient solution not only because of the various limitations on consumers' capacity and motivation to take action but also because of the limited competence and in certain jurisdictions the limited readiness of civil courts to rule on consumer standards and to influence business behaviour.[119] Moreover, courts are deciding disputes on a case by case basis, which is not capable of building long-term policy lines. Individual cases cannot address systematic consumer problems that would have a meaningful impact on corporate policy and behaviour and that would be capable of addressing collective interests.[120] Regulatory agencies have the expertise and the specialisation rather than civil courts to deal better and in a more cost-efficient way with market regulatory issues. Furthermore, they are in a better position to impose behavioural standards and sanctions as well.

The selection of the appropriate public authority is a further question. Here the role of competition authorities in enforcing consumer interests can be thought over. Combining competition law and consumer protection matters under one administrative institution has practical benefits and produces useful synergies through taking a broader look at the whole market. It helps to achieve complementarities and to avoid potential conflicts between the enforcement of competition law and of consumer protection. The combination of functions allows the consideration of whether competition or consumer protection remedies are most appropriate and permits consumer protection decisions to be informed by considerations of economic efficiency.

Bringing a 'consumer welfare' perspective to competition law enforcement can also increase public awareness and approval of the agency's activities, with potential derivative benefits for competition enforcement.[121] Moreover, there are cases where both competition law and consumer law violations are present that can give rise to a mix of competition and consumer issues and which can be more efficiently viewed and solved together. Considerations in one policy area can provide useful guidelines in the other policy area and mutually draw the attention of enforcers in one area to the concerns of the other area. Handling both supply and demand side problems under one agency could provide relevant insights, which help to avoid drafting rules or making policy decisions that would trigger or aggravate problems on the consumer or producer side of the market. It may also help to answer questions like what are the specific reasons to tackle a certain market failure on the supplier or on the consumer side? Whether competition agencies could assist consumers in other ways, for example, by enforcing fair trading rules requires further consideration. The influence

---

[119] C. Scott, J. Black, *Cranston's Consumers and the Law* (Cambridge 2000), p. 513-514.

[120] G. Howells, R. James, 'Litigation in the Consumer Interest', (2002) *ILSA Journal of International & Comparative Law*, p. 30.

[121] Consumer outreach by ICN Members, A report on outreach undertaken and lessons learned, April 2005 p. 41.

of such a combined institutional setting or more integrated policy-making on the consumer welfare standard could be further examined.

Examples of such combined agencies can be found in the US, Australia, the UK, Italy and Hungary just to mention a few.[122] Characteristic of these agencies is the great emphasis they place on truthful and useful consumer information as the key to making effective choices possible for consumers and in turn to making markets work effectively.

Individual v. collective action

When we accept that most of the consumer problems are individual problems, then the logical conclusion would be that these problems should be solved through taking individual actions. This argument is also supported by the fact that a large part of consumer law is private law and as such was intended to assist consumers to make use of their protected rights. In this line of argument consumers themselves are responsible for initiating actions, to solve their dispute with business and to seek redress. The assumption that consumers know their rights and are sufficiently motivated to enforce them implies that private enforcement of consumer rights is a direct consequence of the economic self interest that in the case of business wrongdoing forces them to take action. Private individual enforcement is, therefore, to be preferred because it overcomes government failures of enforcement such as lack of resources and capture. In public choice theory and political science, capture is said to occur when bureaucrats or politicians, who are supposed to be acting in the public interest, end up acting systematically to favor particular vested interests. Individuals also have the best knowledge of the harm suffered and they have the incentive and motivation to take action.[123]

When the consumer offence is specific to an individual and does not affect a larger group of consumers there should be simple and cost-efficient ways to act. These avenues should be chosen besides taking into consideration the ease of consumers also the ease and efficiency benchmark of business. While the main objective is obviously dispute resolution for the consumer when several options are available the least market disruptive solution should be selected. This will also encourage businesses to participate in the redress procedure and comply with its outcome.

The options for individual redress schemes allowing individuals to resolve disputes and obtain redress at a cost and burden proportionate to the amount of their claim range from informal attempts to resolve complaints directly with the company, to alternative dispute resolution services and formal legal action in small claims courts. Out-of-court procedures and especially ADR seem to be

[122] The Hungarian Office of Economic Competition also has jurisdiction in cases of misleading and comparative advertising. The Italian Competition authority has a similar jurisdiction. Besides cartel law, it has jurisdiction in deceptive advertising as well.

[123] Scott, Black (2000), cited above fn. 119 at p. 513.

best suited for individual consumer disputes. The advantages of such schemes include informality, efficiency of solving disputes in a speedy way, low costs, confidentiality, simplicity and flexibility. These factors are also relevant for business. Swift, low cost and informal solutions are also meaningful for business as they create better opportunity for settlement and can in turn increase business compliance with the agreed solutions and thus improve satisfaction with the outcome or manner in which the dispute is resolved. Certainty and trust in these schemes is equally important for the supply and demand side.

The disadvantages of these alternative schemes are equally well-known: the willingness of business to participate, the non-enforceable legal nature of decisions of some ADR bodies, lack of independence and competence of the ADR bodies. There are generally accepted principles that address the reduction of these disadvantages such as accessibility, independence, fairness, accountability, effectiveness and efficiency.

However, individual consumer action has numerous limitations and is not an optimal solution in all cases. When individual consumers have suffered similar harm and when the economic loss suffered by each consumer is small and widespread, individual consumers often do not have the incentives or the capacity to act individually. In these cases some kind of collective action can be more efficient. From a competition and business point of view effective models for collective actions also enjoy a preference. However, collective actions can also create incentives to bring meritless claims simply to pressurise defendants to settle and to avoid the nuisance of defending themselves. Moreover, collective actions do not always serve the goals they have been created for. They can facilitate opportunistic attacks on innocent parties. Consumers might be 'hijacked' by their lawyers, who claim excessive class action attorney fee awards. Such contingency fees represent a significant source of consumer harm, as they diminish the total compensation available to injured consumers. To the extent that such fees do not accurately reflect the amount of work performed by the attorney, or the value of the settlement to the class, they may also create distorted incentives, thereby promoting excessive litigation that is not only contrary to the interests of the class, but unnecessarily raises the cost of goods and services to consumers generally. Especially settlements involving coupon or other non-pecuniary compensation raise conflict-of-interest concerns. The interests of private class attorneys and defendants align to the detriment of the class members, injured plaintiffs may be offered insufficient redress while defendants obtain broad releases from liability and class counsel receive generous fees.[124] The potential pitfalls of these private damages actions have to be avoided. The lessons earned in the private enforcement of both competition and consumer rules should be shared and discussed in order to avoid the risks of abuses.

---

[124] OECD (2006), cited above fn. 46 at pp. 2 and. 5.

Remedies and sanctions

Perhaps the greatest overlap and most useful field of cross-fertilisation between competition law and consumer law enforcement takes place in the discussion on remedies and sanctions. The objectives of sanctions are deterrence and prevention in both fields. The target of both sets of rules is to modify corporate behaviour and policy and to impose such an impact on business that will prevent future violations of the law. Effective deterrence requires that undertakings that might otherwise engage in illegal activities perceive a reasonable probability of being detected, as well as a sufficiently severe punishment when indeed they are.[125] The question is whether the threat of the potential punishment is sufficiently large to assure compliance with the legal rules and behaviour within the boundaries set by the law. In both competition law and consumer law enforcement the effectiveness of administrative fines proves to be limited. Corporate fines are not capable of efficiently deterring either cartels, other anti-competitive practices or anti-consumer behaviour. In the following the remedies and sanctions that are presently available in consumer law will be discussed in the light of the discussion of effective enforcement in competition law.

Sanctions

The present set of administrative sanctions in the form of corporate fines has limited impact on corporate behaviour in both areas. While in competition law there are recent economic studies that show that fines based on a percentage of sales concerned are substantially less than the estimated benefits related to the average infringement,[126] the effectiveness of fines has not been extensively examined in consumer law. It can, however, be reasonably argued that the low level of fines for consumer law violations are often seen as a fee to stay on the market. In both areas a relevant drawback of these sanctions is that they affect the corporation and not the private individuals, which can be both higher and lower management, who decide on the undertakings' business strategy including possible anti-competitive and anti-consumer acts. Detection of violation of competition and consumer rules is another significant concern.[127] Consumer offences are often complex, diffused over time and unpublicised, which makes detection highly complicated or sometimes even impossible before a certain period of time has elapsed.

---

[125] D.I. Baker, 'The use of criminal law remedies to deter and punish cartels and bid-rigging' (2001) 69 *George Washington Law Review*, p. 697.

[126] Connor and Bolotova (2005), cited above fn. 49; Connor (2005), cited above fn. 49. W.P.J. Wils, 'Optimal Antitrust Fines: Theory and Practice' (2005) 1 *Journal of Competition Law & Economics*.

[127] P.G. Bryant, E.W. Eckart, 'Price fixing: The probability of getting caught' *The* (1991) *Review of Economics and Statistics*, p. 531-536; The OECD estimates the chance of detection at one in six, so substantial dark numbers are likely to subsist. OECD, *Report on the nature and impact of hard core cartels and sanctions against cartels under national laws*, April 2002, DAFFE/COMP(2002)7, p. 3.

The publicity for violations of competition law is increasing and certain consumer law violations receive broader media attention. Still, in both cases the level of public awareness of the seriousness of antitrust and consumer law violations, incurring a negative reputation with regards to compliance with the rules does not seem to worry many companies in Europe. While the political climate seems to be changing for tougher or alternative punishments of competition law violations, for violations of consumer law criminal sanctions have existed for a long time. Criminal law sanctions in the case of for example product quality and safety prove to be powerful enforcement tools. In certain cases civil law redress is unavailable as the damage has not yet materialized. Problems, however, seem to exist with regard to detection and prosecution.[128]

It is clear that sanctions need to affect the economic disincentives of business attached to a certain course of action. Breaches of competition and consumer law are the result of deliberate business decisions aiming at clearly set and straightforward managerial objectives. They are executed by mature and risk neutral companies with a straightforward profit motive, which in itself is the responsibility of professional management, as well as in-house counsel advising on compliance with the law.[129]

There is an extensive body of corporate governance literature, based on principal-agent problems relating to asymmetric information and imperfect monitoring, which points out that managerial incentives are often difficult to reconcile with corporate profit maximization objectives. Managers may strive at objectives other than firm profits including personal monetary gain, status, expensive business trips, as well as discretionary powers over decision-making for which the company incurs the unnecessary costs. Corporate penalties may, therefore, not constitute the appropriate sanction, because they are the individuals within the corporation who take the decisions and, hence, actually commit the corporate crimes. A fine imposed on the corporate entity may not hurt those actually responsible for the breach of law, in particular not when shareholder control over management is weak. In order to prevent company liability acting as a shield behind which managers can hide and collude to their personal advantage, a direct intervention from the authorities on individuals responsible, in the form of individual fines, disqualification orders or even jail sentences may provide for more effective deterrence.[130] Imposing criminal sanctions has important economic, social and political implications. Besides introducing new procedural rules, it will need enhanced and strong investigative powers, courts that take an active role as well as high standards of proof as the offence will then have to be proven beyond reasonable doubts. It also requires the readiness and willingness of courts to impose strict criminal liability also when the punish-

[128] Cranston (1985), cited above fn. 10 at p. 143.

[129] K.J. Cseres, M.P. Schinkel, F.O.W. Vogelaar (eds.), *Criminalization of Competition Law Enforcement, Economic and Legal Implications for the EU Member States* (Cheltenham 2006), pp. 1-29.

[130] Ibid.

ment is imprisonment. The application of criminal sanctions requires more complex, more careful and most probably more time-consuming procedures.

Sanctions need to bite into business profits in order to be effective. Businesses know that few consumers take action, even less take legal action and even less succeed in their actions. Moreover consumer offences are often hidden from the public and therefore the reputation of business is not affected. When fines are too low business will consider whether the economic gains still outweigh the fine and other associated costs. The deterrent effect of fines is further weakened because business can shift the burden in form of increased prices to the public. The fine will be regarded as licence fee to infringe the law.[131]

Cartwright defends the use of criminal sanctions in consumer protection as an effective tool to discipline business behaviour. He argues that instead of decriminalization, criminal sanctions should retain their central role in the protection of consumers. He rather calls for a reassessment of the ways in which regulatory crime operates. He further points out that while health and safety measures are to protect consumers' physical safety they can raise potential barriers of trade. He suggests reassessing the role of criminal sanctions against this background.[132] Similar conclusions have been made by Parry, who has argued that in the area of product quality the interplay between civil law redress and criminal law sanctions when both physical and economic harm has been caused prove to be valuable tools.[133] Both of these authors, however, base their arguments on studying UK law. Similar studies would be needed in other jurisdictions as well. Especially the interplay between civil and criminal liability in consumer law could be useful in future policy and legislative decisions in competition law.

Beyond criminal sanctions such as jail sentences for high-executives, the role of media is very important in both consumer and competition cases. In fact criminal prosecutions carry a powerful deterrent effect through the publicity they receive. The power of adverse publicity for example by setting up black lists has earned some experience in consumer law enforcement.

Other means to achieve effective enforcement can be freezing business assets or requiring the creation of compliance programmes. In some jurisdictions courts can issue provisional remedies before a case is decided in order to maintain the *status quo* pending the outcome of the case. One important type of provisional remedy is a temporary order that 'freezes' a defendant's assets to ensure that there will be funds available at the conclusion of the case to satisfy the judgment. An asset freeze places a temporary hold on the assets of the defendant, pending the outcome of the case. This protective tool, where permit-

131 Cranston (1985), cited above fn. 10 at pp. 141-142.

132 Cartwright, P. *Consumer protection and the criminal law: theory, law and policy in the UK* (Cambridge 2001).

133 D.L. Parry, 'Product Quality and the Criminal Law' (2005) *Journal of Consumer Policy*, p. 454.

ted, greatly increases the likelihood of collecting on any money judgment that is ultimately issued for return to consumers.[134]

Compliance programmes have to form an integral part of good corporate governance for these mechanisms to become effective and self-evident. For competition and consumer rules to play a more prominent role in day-to-day business, it could also include explicit compliance obligations and mechanisms in the audit requirements of companies, so that compliance with the competition and consumer rules becomes an integral part of their corporate governance obligations and policies.[135]

The legal, economic and social aspects of the experience with criminal sanctions in consumer protection can be useful for the present discussion on criminalization of competition law violations. Whether anti-competitive practices or which anti-competitive practices could be regulated by criminal law might be answered on the basis of this experience. The experience earned in consumer law enforcement could be used when the possibilities to impose sanctions on individual directors, managers or employees of the undertakings that are responsible for the anticompetitive acts are being considered.

Remedies

Cohen argues that the major remedies for consumer protection refer to prevention, restitution, and punishment. Preventive measures must be designed so that sellers' rights are not unfairly restricted to protect consumers' rights. Punishment applies in cases involving only the most abusive practices. Restitution offers the promise of developing remedies that are equitable to both buyers and sellers.[136]

In most European jurisdictions the present arsenal of remedies for consumer offences is limited to declaratory remedies and injunctions. Monetary remedies in the form of damages claims can provide consumers with compensation for damages suffered as a consequence of 'anti-consumer' practices. When a consumer offence causes economic losses some kind of action for claiming damages seems justified as well as efficient to remedy harmed consumers. The difficulties of such damages actions in the context of competition law have been explained above. Some of those barriers of litigation equally apply in the consumer law context.

---

[134] OECD, Workshop on Consumer Dispute Resolution and Redress in the Global Marketplace: Background Report, 2005, p. 36.

[135] At present, there is an increasing number of companies that establish competition rules oriented compliance programmes including commitments to dismiss employees whenever these act in breach of competition rules. B.J. Rodger, 'Competition Law Compliance Programmes: A Study of Motivations and Practice' (2005) *World Competition*, p. 363; F.O.W. Vogelaar, 'Mededingingsclean gedrag als onderdeel van een goede Corporate Governance' (2005) *Markt & Mededinging*, pp. 113–15.

[136] D. Cohen, 'Remedies for Consumer Protection: Prevention, Restitution, or Punishment' (1975) *Journal of Marketing*, pp. 24-31.

While issues such as passing on and standing for consumers seem of little relevance in the case of consumer offences, still access to evidence, detection and investigation, the costs of identifying injured parties and estimating damages pose serious limitations on individuals' readiness to bring such claims. Introducing damages claims in the consumer law context faces the same hurdle as in competition law: compensating individuals stands in contrast with the lack of legal and economic incentives of consumers. A solution seems to lie in creating some kind of collective actions that can be a cost-efficient solution when consumer offences have caused widespread but small economic harm to individual consumers and the individual motivation to take action is low.

There seem to be two other concerns related to damages calculation and cross-border enforcement. With regard to damages the question of actual damages calculation rises in relation to consumer offences such as health and safety issues and when the damage has not yet materialized, for example when dangerous products are detected but no one has suffered physical or economic harm. Moreover, what is the actual damage in these cases or when there is 'moral damage' to consumers? Damages claims are even further complicated when the group of consumers who suffered harm includes consumers outside of the territory of one Member State.

18 Conclusions: the comparative advantage of collective consumer actions

Private parties are driven by private gains and private interests. As has been explained above when individual consumers face costs and burden disproportionate to the amount of their complaint they will decline to seek redress and resolve disputes. Especially in cases where damage is widespread and individual losses are low rational apathy prevails among the injured individuals who will not sue. Private actors are much more influenced by costs and benefits than public bodies enforcing the law. Policy decisions on encouraging private enforcement of the law has to take account of the fact that private parties have to bear the costs of accessing information in order to discover the infringement, litigation costs, consisting of the lawyer's fees and perhaps expert witnesses.

Another concern is that private interests do not always coincide with public interests. Therefore private parties might lack the incentives to litigate, which in turn results in less enforcement or they may exceed the level of litigation which is socially desirable and optimal. In other words, private enforcement carries considerable risk of both under-deterrence and over-deterrence. Private enforcement does not always and not necessarily meet the socially desirable level of litigation.

Collective actions can provide solutions to both the individual incentive problem and the public policy concern. Collective actions can consolidate widely dispersed small-scale claims. They form avenues of litigation that are less disruptive for the market than individual litigation. They are cost-spreading solutions that can overcome reluctance of consumers to bring complaints. Collective actions can solve the incentive problem of many individual consumers in cases where the harm caused by a violation of the law is vast but the harm caused to individuals is so fragmented that they refrain from litigating. Consolidating these claims is therefore essential for consumers who have suffered harm. Collective actions can reduce litigation costs, enlarge litigation possibilities and provide optimal representation of consumers in court proceedings. In a 2004 Eurobarometer survey in the 15 old Member States 67% of the European Union citizens indicated that they would be more willing to defend their rights before a court if they could join with other consumers who were complaining about the same thing.[137]

Bundling these fragmented individual claims can also considerably enhance law enforcement. It is argued that collective actions have a higher probability of preventing future harm to consumers and thus have a stronger deterrent effect than individual claims. Moreover, it carries efficiency benefits both for business and the judicial system by providing a less disruptive and fragmented way of litigation and increasing the merits of the claims brought before the courts. This saves costs, resources and time for business and for the courts as well.

Nevertheless, the adverse effects of collective actions are also well-known and have been explained above. Collective actions can create incentives for lawyers' misconduct to bring frivolous suits that result in unfavourable or too early settlements for consumers but those which guarantee excessive attorney fee awards.[138] These adverse effects call for an approach that develops mechanisms that on the one hand, aggregates and consolidates claims and provides an efficient manner for bringing these claims to courts and to adjudicate these claims. On the other, an approach that can avoid excessive litigation and provide consumer meaningful compensation is needed. Such a system will need to be based on 'strict management'[139] and on an optimal coordination between private and public enforcement.

Such a strict management could make use of the recent reforms taken in the US in order to ameliorate its class action system and which clearly attempts to impact on indirect purchaser actions. The Class Action Fairness Act (CAFA)[140] enacted in 2005 takes considerable measures to make indirect purchaser actions less burdensome and more manageable. While CAFA does not prohibit the use of coupons in settlements, it does restrict the fees paid to class attorneys who obtain coupon settlements for the class. CAFA requires that federal and state officials are notified of proposed settlements and the law also limits attorney's fees awarded in coupon settlements. As attorneys fees in coupon settlements are typically calculated on the large aggregate face value of the coupons, but

[137] Eurobaromater, *European Union citizens and access to justice*, October 2004, p. 36.

[138] Schaefer (2000), cited above fn. at p. 183-184.

[139] Henneberry (2006), cited above fn. 47 at p. 13.

[140] 28 U.S.C., s. 1332(d), 1453, and 1711-1715.

most coupons are never redeemed, CAFA restricts the fee award to the value of coupons redeemed if coupons are used as the basis for awarding fees to class counsel. Moreover, the court may require that a proposed settlement agreement include the distribution of a portion of the value of unclaimed coupons to one or more charitable or governmental organizations, as agreed to by the parties.[141] These provisions are intended to discourage non-pecuniary coupon settlements that provide little value to class members, overcompensate the legal counsel, provide unclear notice and have burdensome claim procedures. While the CAFA does not address the complexity of determining and allocating damages, it is expected to streamline the settlement process by consolidating multiple proceedings before one federal court.[142]

Optimal coordination between private and public enforcement could include deciding on issues like who would be a rational tort-feasor. While the adverse effects of class actions, such as contingency fees and unfavourable settlements might disappear when a consumer organization or other association brings damages claims, other limitations become clear. Consumer organizations enjoy the advantage that they can stay close to the marketplace and have easy access to information from individual consumers and they are less subject to capture and principal agent problems. However, they often lack the resources and powers of detection and investigation as well as the means to bring claims to civil courts.

Therefore, while public intervention should be limited and decided on the basis of a cost-efficiency, their expertise, investigative powers and sanctions might be indispensable and necessary. In the EC Regulation 2006/2004 on consumer protection cooperation has already created a framework for the Member States' competent public authorities. The Regulation sets up an EU-wide network of national enforcement authorities and enables them to take co-ordinated action for the enforcement of the laws that protect consumers' interests and to ensure compliance with those laws. Within this framework the role and cooperation between the various public authorities such as competition authorities and public consumer protection agencies should be further explored. Whether there are synergies from handling both supply and demand side problems under one and single agency or multiple and separate agencies are more effective needs further consideration as well.

Last, but not least the following comment. Nearly all Member States provide for some collective or representative actions of some type. Class actions that would correspond exactly to the US definition of the term do not exist in Europe.[143] However, the diversity of collective actions is substantial and terminology differs as well. Before new legislation is proposed these existing redress schemes should be reviewed and their effectiveness needs to be carefully

[141] Such distributions (typically referred to as cy pres awards) are used when it is impossible to distribute all of the settlement fund directly to the class. It is believed that this is a second-best solution of the use of settlement funds that cannot be distributed directly to class members.

[142] Henneberry (2006), cited above fn. 47 at p. 13; OECD (2006), cited above fn. 46 at pp. 7-8.

[143] Although Sweden comes extremely close and Spain has a similar albeit more limited action.

studied. Without being familiar with the reasons why these redress schemes are underused and unused, no new initiative will lead to more success.

Closing word: two proposals

These conclusions lead to two main suggestions. First, the choice for a particular consumer redress scheme has to be decided by considering the various elements of the consumer offence and the consumer complaint. The choices and combinations depend on a number of factors that considered together provide the best arrangement. Without providing a complete list of the possible factors, the following questions seem relevant for such an analysis.

- what is the nature of the consumer concern?
- who is best placed to bring an action?
- who has the necessary resources, incentives and legal tools to act?
- which adjudication avenue in terms of cost, time and ease corresponds to the consumer concern at stake?
- what are the remedies sought by consumers and which sanctions are the most effective in order to deter future violations of the law?

For example, collective actions brought by consumer organizations or public agencies seem to be suitable for widespread small scale economic losses. Health and safety issues should be enforced by public agencies applying criminal sanctions, but when economic loss has been suffered civil damages claims should remain possible. Individual enforcement should take place through simplified or small claims procedures and ADR. Criminal sanctions seem to have a powerful role in safety and health issues.

Second, the gap between the law in the books and its actual enforcement has to be addressed. It is not enough to provide the legal tools. The economic and social setting of the application of the rules have to be studied before new rules are adopted. While this might be valid as a general guideline in the enforcement of law, the economic and social context of consumer rules and the behaviour of consumers have a more direct impact on the actual success of the legislative models. Without studying the practical problems and the psychological circumstances of consumer decisions it seems difficult to draft legislative or other tools that can increase consumer activity and improve redress options. Such a study actually needs to take into account the economic resources, appropriate incentives of both supply and demand side.

Facilitating consumer redress needs to be based on the improvement of the institutional capacity of consumers and their organizations. This in turn requires investments in consumer advocacy, 'consumer policy R&D',[144] academic

[144] Muris, former Commissioner of the FTC in the US, argued that a competition agency needs to make substantial investments in what might be called competition policy research and development in order to make intelligent contributions to competition policy. Competition policy R&D stands for continuous improvement of the competition agency's knowledge base in order to establish a firm base for competition advocacy through establishing intellectual leadership. W.E. Kovacic, 'Competition policy and

infrastructure, education in law and economics, professional associations and consumer groups who can contribute to disseminate consumer but also competition principles. Furthermore, a sufficient judicial system, sufficient expertise in terms of sufficient understanding of both competition and consumer issues, market processes and the awareness of competition and consumer rules as well as a receptive political environment are all indispensable for successful legislative and policy models.[145] Moreover, for laws to be effectively enforced, it is important to understand what strategies individuals and undertakings choose to operate under the law. To that end, the impact of laws and regulations on private actors' behaviour should be studied and evaluated when new policy decisions are made.

cartels: the design of remedies' in: K.J. Cseres, M.P. Schinkel, F.O.W. Vogelaar (eds.), *Criminalization of Competition Law Enforcement, Economic and Legal Implications for the EU Member States* (Cheltenham 2006), pp. 41-59; For more details see T. J. Muris, *Looking Forward: The Federal Trade Commission and the Future Development of U.S. Competition Policy* (New York 2002) (remarks for the Milton Handler Annual Antitrust Review), available at http://www.ftc.gov/speeches/muris/handler.htm#N_103_ (last visited in July 2006).

145 W.E. Kovacic, 'Getting Started: Creating New Competition Policy Institutions in Transition Economics' (1997) 23 *Brooklyn Journal of International Law*, pp. 403-453; W.E. Kovacic, 'Institutional Foundations for Economic Legal Reform in Transition Economies: The Case of Competition Policy and Antitrust Enforcement' (2001) 77 *Chicago-Kent Law Review*, p. 265.

CHAPTER 8

Should consumer protection law be publicly enforced?

An economic perspective on EC Regulation 2006/2004 and its implementation in the consumer protection laws of the Member States

Roger van den Bergh

1 Introduction

Regulation 2006/2004 on consumer protection cooperation[1] lays down the conditions under which national authorities responsible for the enforcement of consumer protection laws must cooperate with each other in order to ensure compliance with those laws. Cooperation between public authorities is deemed necessary for the smooth functioning of the internal market and the protection of consumers' economic interests. A lack of effective enforcement in cross-border cases is said to enable sellers and suppliers to evade enforcement attempts by relocating within the Community (consideration 2). Public authorities of Member States where the infringement originated or took place, or where the responsible trader is established, or where evidence pertaining to the infringement can be found will have to cooperate with public authorities of Member States where the 'collective interests' of consumers are harmed. In this way, distortions of competition to the detriment of law-abiding sellers will be avoided. According to the second consideration of the Regulation, the lack of effective enforcement in cases of intra-Community infringements of consumer protection laws also undermines the confidence of consumers to engage in cross-border shopping and hence their confidence in the internal market.

It may be doubted whether the market integration objectives of Regulation 2006/2004 are founded on solid economic grounds and will be reached. There is no convincing empirical evidence supporting the fear that traders will relocate within the European Community to profit from a more lenient system of enforcement of consumer protection laws.[2] The costs of complying with rules of consumer law are only a minor component of the costs of doing business and other factors, such as taxes, wages and the quality of infrastructure, are likely to have a much greater impact on location decisions. It must also be doubted whether consumers will more often engage in cross-border transactions as a result of an increased enforcement of consumer protection laws. The barriers faced by consumers are not only differences in enforcement of their rights but also factors like language, culture, distance, and travelling costs. In this paper, the doubts concerning the market integration argument as a major justification for harmonisation of the substantive rules of consumer law are not further discussed.[3] Instead, the analysis focuses on the desirability of public enforcement of consumer protection laws. Traditionally, there have been major differences in the enforcement of consumer protection laws across the European

---

1 Regulation (EC) 2006/2004, O.J. 2004 L 364/47, pp. 1-11.

2 If this were the case, it would not necessarily imply a need for harmonization at the EC level. It would suffice to change traditional conflict of law rules to enable action against the tortfeasor in the country where the wrongful practices originate, rather than at the place where the injury occurs. See H.W. Micklitz, 'Cross-Border Consumer Conflicts – A French-German Experience' (1993) *Journal of Consumer Policy* 411-434.

3 See R. Van den Bergh, 'The Uneasy Case for Harmonising Consumer Law', in: K. Heine and W. Kerber (eds.), *Zentralität und Dezentralität von Regulierung in Europa* (Stuttgart 2007, forthcoming).

Community. Some Member States have relied mainly on private enforcement[4], whereas others have empowered public agencies to enforce consumer law, either under their own authority[5] or by way of application to courts competent to grant the necessary decision.[6] Since Regulation 2006/2004 requires that each Member State designates the competent public authorities, the effect will be that such authorities will need to be established in Member States where they did not exist before. For example, in the Netherlands the prevailing model of enforcement relied primarily on self-regulatory arrangements and claims by individual consumers to enforce their private rights in civil law courts. To comply with the Directive, meanwhile a proposal of law to create a Consumer Authority has been submitted to the Dutch Parliament.[7]

In the legal literature, consumer law is often presented as a set of rules which aim at protecting 'weak' consumers from manipulation and abuses by intellectually and economically superior traders.[8] The Law and Economics literature starts from the insight that consumer interests are hurt if markets do not function properly. Market failures may be caused by restrictions of competition, information asymmetries and negative externalities. To some extent, the market itself is able to cure these failures by means of the reputation mechanism, but in many cases (for example, when there are no repeat purchases) regulatory intervention will be needed. Whereas competition law may cope with the monopoly problem, consumer protection laws (in particular information remedies and liability rules) may cure the other instances of market failure.[9]

---

4 This has been the case in the Netherlands, where the enforcement system has heavily relied on protection of individual rights by means of self-regulatory arrangements. See Ministry of Economic Affairs, *Strategic Action Programme: Policy Paper on Consumer Protection* (Den Haag 2004). From 2007 on, a newly established Consumer Authority will enforce a large part of the consumer protection rules, but the bill stresses that this must be seen as a complementary possibility where the collective interests of consumers are harmed and self-regulatory arrangements or civil law suits fail (Tweede Kamer, 2005-2006, document 30 411, nr. 3, p. 28).

5 For example, the British Office of Fair Trading controls the functioning of the market mechanism by withholding credit licenses to business (see the contribution by Howells in this volume).

6 In the Nordic countries, the Ombudsmen bring cases before specialized market courts (see the contribution by Viitanen in this volume).

7 See the paper by Ammerlaan in this volume.

8 Th. Bourgoignie, *Éléments pour une théorie du droit de la consommation* (Brussel 1988); S. Weatherill, *EU Consumer Law and Policy* (Northampton MA 2005).

9 Information remedies have received a lot of attention in the neo-classical Law and Economics literature. The traditional view that consumer protection laws curing problems of asymmetric information will improve the efficiency of consumer goods markets has been criticised in the Behavioural Law and Economics literature (see e.g. Th. Ulen, 'The Growing Pains of Behavioral Law and Economics' (1998) *Vanderbilt Law Review* 1747-1763). This literature emphasises that improving information flows is not a sufficient remedy if consumers behave irrationally. It also stresses the risk of an information overload; too much information may be worse than no information at all. These different views have a clear impact on the desirable content of substantive rules of consumer law.

In addition, consumer law may provide remedies to mitigate the consequences of irrational behaviour. Currently there is a great variety of consumer protection laws in the EC Member States, ranging from liability rules to information remedies, cooling-off periods and direct regulation of quality. The European harmonisation efforts concern only a part of this large body of consumer protection laws. The 'consumer acquis' covered by Regulation 2006/2004 consists of 15 Directives and one Regulation. The relevant rules of EC consumer law relate to: misleading and comparative advertising (including specific rules for television advertising and medicines), unfair terms in consumer contracts, guarantees, consumer credit, package travel, time-sharing, sales negotiated away from business premises and distance contracts, electronic commerce, indication of prices, unfair business-to-consumer practices, and compensation in the event of denied boarding and of cancellation or long delay of flights.[10]

From a legal perspective, Regulation 2006/2004 may be criticised because it seriously disrupts national legal orders by requiring public enforcement mechanisms for rules that traditionally belong to the field of private law. Remarkably, the Regulation does not harmonise the form of the sanctions and the stage of intervention but restricts itself to impose public enforcement for the rules of the 'consumer acquis'. Violation of these rules is sanctioned in different ways: criminal or administrative fines, cessation of prohibited practices (injunctions) or payment of damages. By leaving the form of the sanctions intact, the Regulation creates islands of publicly enforced Community law in the ocean of privately enforced national consumer protection laws. This seems to endanger the internal consistency of the legal system. As stressed in the Dutch bill, the consequence will be a hybrid and complex 'dual' system.[11] Another concern is that the implementation of the Directive may cause 'reverse discrimination'. The Regulation only imposes a duty of cooperation between public authorities of the Member States in enforcing the rules of EC consumer law, as they are transposed in the national legal orders, in cross-border transactions. This may have the consequence that rights of consumers who do not engage in cross-border shopping are less well protected than the rights of those who buy in another Member State. 'Reverse discrimination' will occur if infringements of national consumer law, which do not generate intra-Community effects, are sanctioned by private remedies only and the respective rules cannot be enforced by public authorities. To avoid this outcome, the Dutch proposal stipulates that national infringements will also be enforced by the newly established Consumer Authority.

This paper will not further elaborate on the legal criticisms but relates to the efficiency of public enforcement in the field of consumer law. The central research question will be whether enforcement by public authorities in the areas of consumer law covered by Regulation 2006/2004 can be supported

10 See the references in the Annex to Regulation (EC)2006/2004, O.J. 2004 L 364/11.

11 Tweede Kamer, 2005-2006, 30 441, nr. 3, p. 6.

by economic arguments. At the outset it should be made clear that an optimal allocation of enforcement powers to either private parties and/or public agents is only one component of an efficient system of enforcement. Equally important from an efficiency perspective are the choice of the sanction(s) and the timing of the intervention (before or after a harm has occurred). The structure of this paper is as follows. After this introduction, the economic criteria for allocating enforcement powers will be introduced. The second section of the paper examines the comparative advantages of either private or public enforcement in the field of consumer protection laws. Thereafter, the third section of the paper focuses on systems of public enforcement in a number of EC Member States and discusses their strengths and weaknesses from an economic perspective. Within the confines of this paper, a full discussion of the enforcement of the wide variety of consumer protection laws of all Member States is not possible. For this reason, the analysis uses examples which are best suited to illustrate the relevance of the economic insights. Finally, the fourth section summarises the most important conclusions.

2 Economic criteria for allocating enforcement powers to public authorities

To answer the question under which circumstances public enforcement of consumer protection laws is preferable to private enforcement of those laws, use will be made of the criteria provided by the economic analysis of law enforcement.[12] Two determinants allow to make an informed choice between public or private enforcement, – or opt for a combination of both. The first criterion relates to the availability of information concerning law infringements and the identity and location of the wrongdoer. The second criterion refers to the need to achieve an efficient level of law enforcement, excluding both under-enforcement and over-enforcement. Private enforcement will be economically optimal if: i) private parties possess information on violations of consumer protection laws and ii) the private interests of law enforcement coincide with the socially optimal enforcement level. Conversely, public enforcement is preferable to private enforcement if: i) public agents enjoy an information advantage over private parties in discovering law infringements, and/or ii) the social motives to bring law suits are not identical with the private benefits of law enforcement.

At the outset, it should be pointed out that both criteria in favour of either private or public enforcement may not be simultaneously satisfied. Private parties possessing information about infringements may not have incentives

[12] C.G. Veljanovski, 'The Economics of Regulatory Enforcement', in: K. Hawkins and J. Thomas (eds), *Enforcing Regulation* (Boston 1984), pp. 171-188; S. Shavell, 'The Optimal Structure of Law Enforcement' (1993) *Journal of Law and Economics* 255-287; A.M. Polinsky and S. Shavell, 'The Economic Theory of Public Enforcement of Law' (2000) *Journal of Economic Literature* 45-77.

to initiate proceedings if the costs of enforcement exceed the benefits (for example, in cases of trifle damage). This 'rational apathy' problem will lead to under-enforcement. Private parties may also expand their enforcement activities beyond the socially optimal level for opportunistic reasons, thus causing over-enforcement. Even if public enforcement succeeds in avoiding the latter problem, enforcement agencies may remain unaware of law infringements, thus causing again the reverse problem of under-enforcement. For these reasons, in cases where there is a risk of suboptimal enforcement, it may be preferable to opt for a combination of private and public enforcement, so that they can mitigate each other's disadvantages. Both economic criteria for allocating enforcement powers will be further explained below. Thereafter, it will be investigated to what extent the conditions in favour of public enforcement are satisfied for the rules contained in the European 'consumer acquis'.

2.1 Information advantages of public authorities

In designing an economically optimal system of enforcement, the first determinant is the availability of information. If private parties can easily discover law infringements, other things being equal, then it is not socially desirable to have the state spend its resources on enforcement activities. By contrast, if it is very difficult and/or costly to identify law infringers and the location of the infringements, then public enforcement may be more adequate.

Two examples may illustrate the relevance of the information argument. The prohibition of horizontal (price) cartels in competition law (Article 81 EC Treaty and its counterparts in national laws) is best enforced by a public agency (Competition Authority) since consumers often possess no information about such infringements. Competition authorities are better at discovering and proving infringements of the cartel prohibition since they have wider investigative powers than private parties.[13] In cases of hard core cartels (such as price-fixing) private parties may not even realise that they are harmed. They may also face difficulties in proving the size of the damage and the causal link between the infringement and the harm. Without the investigative powers of competition authorities, very serious infringements will remain undiscovered and unpunished.[14] Conversely, tort law is best enforced by private parties. In a typical tort case, private parties initially possess information unknown to the state about the identity or location of liable parties. The victim will usually have incentives to supply this information to the courts in order to be able to collect tort damages. Society would spend its resources needlessly if it was relying on the state to report harms leading to civil liability.

13 This may be different in cases of vertical restraints or abuse of a dominant position, but the parties that could claim – typically traders – may still refrain from bringing claims out of fear of retaliation.

14 For further discussion, see: W.J. Wils, 'Is Criminalization of EU Competition Law the Answer?' (2005) *World Competition* 117-159.

2.2 The social benefits of enforcement deviate from the private benefits

Generally, legal rules do not only protect the private interests of harmed individual parties but also the interests of society at large. If private interests and social interests do not coincide, private parties will have no incentive to bear enforcement costs even if this would be in the public interest.

As indicated by Shavell, the possibility of financial reward coupled with the desire to avoid future harm and the retributive motive (the desire to see people who have acted wrongly suffer sanctions) may create a set of incentives sufficient to induce people to report the information they possess about wrongdoers.[15] However, the size of these private benefits will vary across different fields of law and not always generate optimal law enforcement efforts.

Again examples are appropriate to illustrate how benefits for society at large may differ from the private benefits, and why this state of affairs may justify public enforcement of law. Competition law will again be contrasted with tort law. In the case of price-fixing, which constitutes a major infringement of EC competition law, there are two detrimental effects: (i) consumers have to pay more for the product, since the price cartel charges a super-competitive price (price effect), and (ii) consumers will purchase less of the product, even though it would be utility maximising for them to buy additional goods (allocation effect). The price effect is a mere distribution from the consumers to the cartel members, but the allocation effect causes a 'dead-weight loss' which is not captured by the price cartel.[16] From an economic perspective, both types of losses should be compensated to force the firms involved to internalise the negative welfare effects of their behaviour. However, private enforcement will at most partially sanction the price effect and will leave the allocation effect intact. The reason is that private parties will initiate proceedings only if the private benefits of doing so are higher than the private costs. The private costs consist of the information costs that must be borne to discover the infringements, the costs of the court procedure and the costs to prove the size of the damage and the causal link between the infringement and the harm. The private benefits consist of the monetary sanction imposed on the law offender (assuming that there is no 'judgement proof' problem[17]), as far as this will improve the financial situation and/or the competitive market position of the private claimant. This private cost-benefit calculus has no systematic relation with the social costs and benefits. The social costs also comprise the harm suffered by victims who do

15 Shavell (1993), cited above fn. 12.

16 R. van den Bergh and P. Camesasca, *European Competition Law and Economics: A Comparative Perspective*, 2d ed. (London 2006), pp. 23-29.

17 A law infringer is 'judgement proof' if the loss he or she caused is larger than his or her assets, so that liability will not lead to a full internalisation of the harm. See S. Shavell, 'The Judgment Proof Problem' (1986) *International Review of Law and Economics* 45-58.

not sue and other losses that cannot easily be attributed to individual victims.[18] Since potential plaintiffs are driven only by the private gains and expenses of their claims, they will have insufficient incentives to invest in detecting and litigating meritorious cases. In addition, a system of private enforcement also creates a 'free riding' problem. Every victim of an antitrust infringement has an interest to leave the enforcement efforts to other victims, so that profits can be obtained without having to spend own resources. The 'free riding' problem will reduce the number of private actions below the level of enforcement that would be socially optimal. For these reasons, public enforcement of competition law by competition authorities is needed and sufficiently high fines should be imposed to deter infringements.[19]

As was the case with the first economic argument in favour of public enforcement, tort law offers again a different picture. In many cases, the private benefits from successfully suing a tortfeasor will be identical with the social benefits. If a house burns down in a fire caused by negligent behaviour of a tortfeasor, the value of this house is lost for society as a whole. The private loss equals the social loss. By contrast, if a company charges super-competitive prices, the benefits of private parties who claim compensation do not include the losses suffered by potential consumers who refrained from buying the products. Contrary to price-fixing cases, private losses and social losses will generally be equal in cases of tortuous liability. An exception is claim for compensation of pure economic losses. If electricity supply is cut off for a number of hours due to negligent behaviour of a contractor charged with repair works, bars and restaurants in the affected area will have to close and will loose business. Since consumers will go to different places to have a drink or enjoy a dinner, the value of this business is not lost but simply moves to competing traders. In the latter example, private losses and social losses are not equal. This economic reasoning may explain the reluctance of some tort systems to compensate pure economic losses.[20] In most jurisdictions, liability is acknowledged only in cases of intentional instigation of pure economic loss without justification.[21]

2. 3 Economic reasons for public enforcement of consumer protection laws

2.3.1 Consumers have no information about law infringements

The insights from the previous sections will now be applied to the field of consumer law. At first sight, the information argument seems

[18] Dead weight loss, costs of rent-seeking, losses of dynamic efficiency.

[19] To cope with the 'judgement proof' problem, US antitrust law provides for the possibility of imprisonment. Competition laws of some Member States also include imprisonment of directors of companies which have violated the prohibition of horizontal price cartels. See Wils (2005), cited above fn. 14.

[20] H.-B. Schaefer and C. Ott, *The Economic Analysis of Civil Law* (Cheltenham 2004), pp. 253-259.

to plead against public enforcement of consumer protection laws. Why would the state spend resources on finding out which contracts concluded between traders and consumers negatively affect the economic interests of the latter? This information is available to the individual consumers who are harmed and it seems more efficient that they come forward and initiate legal proceedings. Relying on public authorities to report harm would amount to an inefficient spending of scarce financial resources. However, this reasoning is subject to two important qualifications. First, it may be difficult for individual consumers to recognise poor quality in markets characterised by serious information asymmetries. Examples include unsound investment advice by a financial consultant or non-transparent price calculations. Second, consumers will often remain unaware of infringements before harm has occurred. Public enforcement will be preferable if it is costly to identify the infringement and/or the law infringer. A consumer who was deceived by a false statement in a commercial advertisement knows the identity of the trader who engages in such misleading advertising. The same holds for a consumer who comes across a liability disclaimer in contract terms, which exculpates a seller for intentional faults in fulfilling his contractual duties. However, before the harm has occurred, consumers may face great difficulties in discovering infringements. It may be very costly to check whether statements in advertisements are true or false. Also standard form contracts are usually signed without a prior reading of the contract terms, since the opportunity costs of time exceed the expected benefits from discovering harsh clauses.[22] Compared to private parties, public agencies enjoying investigative powers have a comparative advantage in discovering false statements in advertising and the use of unfair contract terms by traders. As long as private parties are not deceived by advertisements or not confronted with a liability disclaimer, they will remain unaware of the risk of misleading advertising or the risks of unfair contract terms.

The comparative advantage of public authorities in discovering infringements of consumer protection laws is clearest in the case of safety and quality regulation. From an economic perspective, it can be easily understood why enforcement of regulation of safety and health is primarily public. Private parties are not aware of the full size of the risks. If a restaurant kitchen is unclean but a consumer does not get ill when he goes to the restaurant, how will he or she know the status of the kitchen? The state will need to spend resources on public enforcement, in order to guarantee that law infringers are identified and sanctioned. Another example is the requirement of a licence to practise a certain trade or profession, which aims at excluding incompetent service

21 See W.H. van Boom, H. Koziol and C.A. Witting, 'Outlook', in: W. van Boom, H. Koziol and C.A. Witting (eds) *Pure Economic Loss* (Wien/New York 2004), pp. 191-205, no. 31.

22 G. de Geest, 'The Signing-Without-Reading Problem: An Analysis of the Directive on Unfair Contract Terms', in : H.-B. Schaefer and H.-J. Lwowski, *Konsequenzen wirtschaftsrechtlicher Normen* (Wiesbaden 2002), pp. 213-235.

providers from the market. Individual consumers may be unaware of the licence requirements and will face great difficulties in controlling compliance with the (often very technical) applicable regulations.

The absence of harm is a strong factor explaining why it can not be expected that people know who needs to be sanctioned for violating regulations. In some cases consumers may have this information and may wish to prevent harm to themselves or to the community. But in general consumers will become aware of the existence of infringements and the identity of the wrongdoer only after harm has occurred. The above examples relating to misleading advertising and the use of unfair contract terms have shown that also large parts of the European 'consumer acquis' covered by Regulation 2006/2004 may be in need of public enforcement. The economic reason is that private consumers remain unaware of violations of those consumer protection laws as long as no harm has occurred. To achieve efficient outcomes, society will need to spend resources to discover violations of consumer protection laws. The discussion of the first economic argument for allocating enforcement powers thus leads to the conclusion that a combination of private and public enforcement, through which the latter system mitigates the problems of the former system, is economically optimal.

2.3.2 The private benefits of individual consumers differ from the social benefits

Besides incomplete information on the side of individual consumers, the case for public enforcement of violations of legal rules may be based on differences between the private and the social benefits of sanctioning infringements. Rules of consumer law protect the private interests of individual consumers but are also indispensable for the proper functioning of markets. As a consequence, both private values and public values are served by consumer laws. A useful analogy may be drawn with rules of competition law. Individuals may invoke these rules to protect their subjective rights: for example, by claiming compensation in cases of violation of the cartel prohibition. However, the social interests in prohibiting infringements of competition law exceed the private benefits; they include avoidance of the losses caused by allocative inefficiency (dead-weight loss), dynamic inefficiency and rent-seeking.[23] Also in the field of consumer law, the losses to individuals are smaller than the social losses. Individual consumers benefit from prohibitions in as far as these protect their individual rights. The harm to society is larger than the loss suffered by individual consumers who initiate legal proceedings. The social loss consists of the overall quality deterioration in markets plagued by information asymmetries. As is the case with the 'deadweight-loss', the social loss exceeds the private loss. Individual consumers are unlikely to benefit personally from the marginal

[23] Van den Bergh and Camesasca (2006), cited above fn. 16 at pp. 23-29.

benefit in deterrence created by suing a trader who violates consumer protection laws, even though this deterrent effect represents the major social reason for identifying law infringers. These insights will be further elaborated on below. First, the social benefits of consumer protection laws will be described. Second, it will be explained why the incentives of individual consumers may be inadequate to initiate an optimal number of enforcement actions. Particularly, the risk of enforcement efforts below the socially optimal level (under-enforcement) merits attention, but also the risk of opportunistic claims (over-enforcement) cannot be excluded.

a) The social benefits of consumer protection laws

The case for public intervention in markets for consumer goods can be based on the important insights of Nobel Prize Laureate George Akerlof.[24] This famous economist convincingly argued that asymmetric information leads to quality deterioration and may ultimately even destroy particular markets for consumer goods. In his seminal article 'The Market for Lemons', Akerlof has shown that quality uncertainty may cause a process of adverse selection through which good quality products are driven out of the market by bad quality products. Akerlof has considered formally a market where information is imperfect. The seriousness of the information problems depends on both the nature of the goods and the personal qualifications of the buyers (professional buyers or consumers). It is useful to distinguish between search goods, experience goods and credence goods. The quality of search goods may be inspected prior to their purchase; examples include fresh fruit, which can be tasted before buying, and the colour of textiles. In other cases the buyer will only learn about quality after purchase. Experience goods include, among others, houses, cars and stereo equipment. When experience goods are bought regularly, quality uncertainty may be reduced through the 'repeat purchase mechanism'. The use of the goods may provide the necessary information about quality enabling the consumer to decide whether he will make a repeat purchase or not. For some products and services, consumers will not be able to assess quality even after purchase. In such cases quality uncertainty is replaced by 'trust'. Credence goods, such as complex medical services, are bought whenever buyers are sufficiently confident about the professional qualifications of the supplier. If consumers are not fully informed, two problems arise. First, in the short run inefficient contracts may be concluded. Consumers may also buy goods if the purchase price is lower than the utility they derive from those goods; transfers of goods will not be Pareto optimal. Second, in the long run bad quality may drive out good quality, as described by Akerlof.

If consumers cannot distinguish beforehand between good quality and bad quality, the price will be based on average quality. Sellers of good quality face a

---

24 G. Akerlof, 'The Market for Lemons: Qualitative Uncertainty and the Market Mechanism', (1970) *Quarterly Journal of Economics* 488-500.

situation in which the price consumers are willing to pay is below the real value of the product. At this market price, those sellers may decide not to sell the product and withdraw from the market. If sellers of good quality withdraw from the market, average quality drops and, hence, the price goes down. More sellers of good quality will decide to leave the market and, in the end, only the lowest quality will be offered for sale. This process of adverse selection leading to a general lowering of quality is the consequence of a market failure: uninformed buyers are confronted with informed sellers (asymmetric information). Akerlof has used the example of the second-hand car market to illustrate his argument. Similar risks occur in other markets for consumers goods that are not regularly bought (restaurant services at tourist places, stereo equipment) or the quality of which is difficult to assess (standard terms in contracts, professional services). To some extent, the market itself may cure these problems. Reputation may play a disciplinary role in case of repeat purchases; also trade marks and (true) advertising may signal quality.[25] However, consumer protection laws will be necessary to guarantee the quality of both experience goods, which are not regularly bought, and credence goods, the quality of which cannot be assessed by its buyers.

b) The risks of under- and over-enforcement

Individual consumers will have insufficient incentives to report infringements of consumer protection laws, if their private benefits are lower than the social losses resulting from an overall quality deterioration in consumer markets. As mentioned above, the possibility of financial reward coupled with the desire to avoid future harm and the retributive motive create a set of incentives sufficient to induce people to report the information they possess about wrongdoers. These conditions do not seem sufficiently satisfied in the case of infringements of consumer protection laws. The extent to which the economic criteria in favour of private enforcement are satisfied may differ across different areas of consumer law. This is illustrated by the following examples.

An individual consumer who is hurt by an unfair clause in a consumer credit contract will find out the harm when the first payment is due and avoiding substantial future harm by going to court will not benefit other consumers. In the latter case, public enforcement does not seem efficient since the state would need to spend huge resources in analysing thousands of consumer credit contracts without generating social benefits that diverge from the private interests. Conversely, several causes may explain why individual consumers will not spend efforts on enforcement. The prospect of financial reward will not generate sufficient incentives to initiate proceedings in the following three cases: First, it will be non-existent if the law infringer is insolvent. Second, it will be uncertain if the law infringement cannot be assessed with certainty, such as in the case of violation of open-ended norms. Third, it will be too small if the loss consists of trifle damage; the costs of the law suit may even then

[25] P. Nelson, Advertising as Information (1974) *Journal of Political Economy* 729-754.

exceed the expected compensation.[26] The desire to avoid future harm may not provide incentives in cases where the harm is already suffered (such as misleading advertising), because of the free riding effects generated by private enforcement. Why would a consumer who has been deceived bring a claim to stop misleading advertising after he has discovered deception? He will not buy the product or service again and avoiding future harm will result in benefit to other consumers who did not bear the financial burden of the enforcement action ('free riding' problem). Finally, the retributive motive does not seem sufficient to neutralise the above problems and provide sufficient incentives for private actions in cases of violation of consumer protection laws.

It may be noted that private parties may also have a greater motive to sue than is socially desirable. Competition law offers an example: a large reward (treble damages) may create scope for abuses and lead to the prohibition of practices that are not welfare reducing (such as pro-competitive price reductions that are banned as 'predatory pricing').[27] Also in the field of unfair trade practices law, similar problems may occur: individual traders may initiate abusive proceedings that aim at protecting competitors from competition. However, the scope for abuses by individual consumers in enforcing consumer protection laws seems negligible. The picture may be different in the case of collective actions ('American style' class actions, actions by consumer associations which are not truly representative of consumers' interests) but these problems are outside the scope of this paper.[28]

3 Public enforcement of consumer protection laws in EC Member States: an economic assessment

The arguments in the previous section of this paper provide useful insights for the policy debate on public enforcement of consumer protection laws. Economic analysis of law may help in clarifying the following four issues: first, why public enforcement is needed; second, how to set an agenda of priorities for public enforcement agencies; third, the choice of sanctions and timing of the intervention, and fourth, the role of private enforcement. Each of these subjects will be discussed in turn. The insights from the Law and Economics literature will be illustrated by a discussion on different ways to enforce consumer protection laws in a number of EC Member States.

---

26 See also: W.H. van Boom, *Efficacious Enforcement in Contract and Tort* (Den Haag 2006), pp. 17-18.

27 See for an elaboration: R.P. McAfe and N.V. Vakkur, The Strategic Abuse of the Antitrust Laws (2005) *Journal of Strategic Management Education* 37-54.

28 See for a discussion of these issues: H.-B. Schaefer, 'The Bundling of Similar Interests on Litigation. The Incentives for Class Actions and Legal Actions taken by Associations' (2000) *European Journal of Law and Economics* 183-213.

3.1 The need for public enforcement: deterrence

The economic analysis of law enforcement makes clear that public enforcement is needed to complement private enforcement. Whereas private actions are indispensable to protect consumers' individual rights, they may fall a long way short of providing sufficient incentives to deter infringements of consumer protection laws. There are two major reasons why private enforcement will be deficient as a deterrence mechanism: i) lack of information about infringements on the side of private parties, and ii) the risk of under-enforcement. Consequently, if the policy goal is to decrease the number of infringements of consumer law, public enforcement will be indispensable. Policy documents of public agencies, which are active in the area of consumer protection laws, confirm that deterrence of infringements is a major goal.[29] To achieve this goal, public enforcement agencies will need to have sufficient resources to detect violations of consumer protection laws and initiate proceedings against traders who commit infringements if the collective interests of consumers are harmed. Looking at the different approaches towards enforcement of consumer protection laws discussed in other contributions of this book, the following two questions arise. Is it preferable to establish a separate and specialised Consumer Authority or can (parts of) the enforcement tasks be entrusted to generalist public agencies? And: How must the criterion of 'collective interests' be interpreted to make sure that the goal of deterrence is reached? These questions will be discussed below.

In the EC Member States, there are different approaches with regard to the allocation and division of competences across different enforcement agencies. In the Nordic countries, the Consumer Ombudsmen have the sole task to enforce consumer protection laws; this competence is not shared with other supervisory public agencies, such as the competition authorities.[30] In the United Kingdom, the Office of Fair Trading is responsible for the enforcement of both competition law and consumer protection laws (including unfair terms in contracts, misleading advertising and rules on fair trade practices).[31] In the Netherlands, the choice has been made not to expand the powers of the Dutch Competition Authority (NMa) and to create a new Consumer Authority. How should these different approaches be evaluated? At the outset it must be made clear that both competition law and consumer law are concerned with a good functioning of markets and that, from a perspective of efficiency, it is logical that they are (also) publicly enforced. The question whether a separate Consumer Authority must be established can be answered only by way of a cost-benefit analysis of specialisation.

29 See, for example the statement by the Dutch Consumer Authority: Consumentenautoriteit, *Consultatie-document* (Den Haag 2006), p. 3.

30 See the contribution by Viitanen in this volume.

31 See the contribution by Howells in this volume.

Creating specialised enforcement agencies has two advantages. First, consumer protection laws have become so complex and specialised that it no longer seems possible to have them fully covered and enforced by a generalist public authority. Second, reserving resources for the supervision of marketing practices and standard contract terms avoids the risk that other activities, such as the enforcement of competition law, dominates the agenda of the competent public authority.[32] However, creating specialised authorities for enforcing consumer protection laws also entails disadvantages. First, the goals of consumer protection and the objectives of competition law are not always perfectly consistent with each other. For example, improving information flows may benefit consumers but may make it at the same time easier for firms to reach collusive agreements.[33] If competition law and consumer protection law are enforced by the same public authority, it may be easier to avoid inconsistent decisions. Second, multiplication of enforcement agencies entails additional administrative costs, which may exceed the benefits resulting from a greater degree of specialisation. Apart from administrative costs, there is also the risk that decisions of regulatory agencies are influenced by private interests of the industry groups they are supposed to control (regulatory capture).[34] Both in the UK[35] and in the Netherlands[36] there is a strong proliferation of enforcement agencies, which creates the impression that sometimes every newly emerging problem gives rise to the creation of a new public authority. Obviously, having a specialised regulator and enforcement agency for each sector of industry may generate costs, resulting form lack of coordination and increased risk of regulatory capture, which outweigh the benefits of specialisation.

As a general rule public enforcement authorities initiate proceedings only when the 'collective interests' of consumers are harmed. The concept of collective interests is rather vague. Even though consumer authorities will not intervene in disputes between an individual consumer and an individual trader, the scope of potential intervention still remains unclear. Economic analysis may be helpful in interpreting the vague notion of collective interests. Such an economic interpretation will make sure that public enforcement can step in where private enforcement fails. As mentioned above, public enforcement is a remedy to the information problem and the risk of under-enforcement. This has two important implications.

First, initiatives of public enforcement agencies should not be dependent on prior complaints of individual consumers. To cure the information deficiencies on the side of consumers, public authorities must take a pro-active approach.

32 See the contribution by Viitanen in this volume.

33 See J. Tunney, 'The Neglected Tension between Disclosure of Information in Consumer and Competition Law Contexts' (2002) *Journal of Consumer Policy* 329-343.

34 A. Ogus, *Regulation. Legal Form and Economic Theory* (Oxford 1994), pp. 57-58.

35 See the contribution by Howells in this volume, footnotes 19 to 26.

36 See the overview in Consumentenautoriteit (2006), cited above fn. 29 at p. 23.

Consequently, they must have investigative powers and dispose of sufficient resources to detect and punish violations of consumer protection laws. According to Ogus, Faure and Philipsen, a reactive approach may suffice in countries where there is a culture of consumer activism and consumer associations take the initiative in publicising problems and seeking out defaulting traders.[37] However, consumer associations do not enjoy investigative powers and may not be appropriately funded. As a consequence, a reactive approach will fall short of curing the information asymmetry with regard to the existence of consumer protection law infringements.

Second, the aim to protect consumers' collective interests should allow aligning the decision to initiate proceedings with the social motive for enforcement of consumer protection laws and thus cope with the problem of under-deterrence. Illegal activities may cause similar damages to a large group of consumers. Therefore, the harm suffered by a single consumer may significantly diverge from the total harm and the damage caused to the functioning of the market mechanism (adverse selection). In such cases the private cost-benefit calculus of an individual consumer dramatically deviates from the social cost-benefit calculus. Examples include misleading advertising, exculpation clauses in standardised contract terms and violation of health and safety regulations. Public enforcement will be needed to minimise economic and physical harm caused by unfair marketing practices, unfair standard contract terms, or unsafe or poor-quality products. Again, a culture of consumer activism may not be sufficient to guarantee enforcement activities in all cases where this would be socially desirable. Consumer associations might also misuse their enforcement powers for opportunistic reasons, by suing a trader where this may attract a lot of public attention and add to the consumer association's profile without generating net social benefits. In sum, well-funded public authorities are needed to enforce consumer protection laws. An economic interpretation of the notion of collective interests requires a pro-active approach enabling these authorities to discover infringements at an early stage and prevent adverse selection in consumer markets.

3.2 An agenda of priorities for public enforcement agencies

Resources of public authorities are generally constrained and cannot be expanded without limits. For this reason, it is important that public enforcement agencies make an efficient use of their scarce resources. Setting an agenda of priorities is a way to achieve this goal. The Dutch Consumer Authority has proposed to use the following criteria in order to make a selection of priorities: i) the size of the harm caused to consumers, ii) the impact on consumers' confidence and iii) the impact on the functioning of the market. Upon

[37] A. Ogus, M. Faure and N. Philipsen, *The Effectiveness of Penalties for Breaches of Consumer Protection Legislation* (Maastricht 2006), unpublished manuscript, p. 75.

the basis of these selection criteria the Authority has suggested to concentrate its activities during the first year of its functioning (2007) on the following problems: unfair terms in consumer contracts, electronic commerce, lotteries, package travel and guarantees.[38]

The criteria suggested by the Dutch Consumer Authority are not very clear and do also partly overlap. Markets will not function properly if there is no consumer confidence, and this confidence will disappear if consumers are harmed. Economic analysis suggests rephrasing these criteria in the following way. Markets for consumer goods do not function properly in case of information asymmetries which cause adverse selection. In such cases, consumer confidence will be undermined and serious harm to consumers will occur. The case for public enforcement will be stronger the more serious are the information asymmetries and the risk of under-deterrence. Consequently, public enforcement agencies should prioritise intervention in markets with the following characteristics: i) there is a serious risk of adverse selection, ii) individual consumers face difficulties in discovering law infringements, and iii) the size of the total harm substantially exceeds the damage suffered by individual consumers. The above criteria may enable public enforcement agencies to set their agenda of priorities, in order to make optimal use of their scarce resources. These criteria also raise some doubts about the choices made by the Dutch Consumer Authority for the year 2007. Two prioritised areas may serve as an illustration of how economic analysis may contribute to the optimal use of scarce enforcement resources. On the one hand, standard terms in contracts deserve close scrutiny from public enforcement agencies. On the other hand, the sector of holiday trips seems less in need of supervision by a public authority, since the market mechanism itself may be able to cope with potential market failures.

The proposal to scrutinise standard contract terms is a wise choice provided attention is directed mainly to markets where there is a serious risk of adverse selection, in particular markets for expensive experience or credence goods which are not regularly bought. Examples include sophisticated electronic equipment and cars. Consumers will not discover harsh contract clauses (such as liability disclaimers in cases of intentional fault and clauses allowing unilateral modifications of the object of the contract) since they use to sign standard form contracts without having read them before. This 'signing without reading' is a result of rational behaviour[39], since the (opportunity) costs of checking the quality of the contract terms exceed the expected benefits (the loss in case harsh clauses are effectively invoked, discounted by the probability that such harm materialises). As a result of the persisting unawareness of the presence of unfair standard terms in contracts, a 'market for lemons' can easily develop. Therefore, consumer authorities should check standardised contracts in markets where 'signing without reading' may result in an overall quality deterioration of the

[38] Consumentenautoriteit (2006), cited above fn. 29 at pp. 13-14.

[39] De Geest (2002), cited above fn. 22.

contract terms. Their intervention should make sure that unfair contract terms are not included.

It may be doubted whether the sector of holiday trips deserves priority from a perspective of an efficient enforcement policy. On the one hand, consumers focus their attention on choosing a holiday destination which best fits their preferences and do not wish to spend time on reading the contract terms. Consequently, the use of harsh clauses in violation of consumer protection laws may remain hidden until harm occurs. As far as the use of standardised contracts is concerned, our arguments above fully apply: public enforcement is needed to cure the information deficiencies. On the other hand, the risk of under-enforcement may be lower in the holiday sector than in other markets for consumer goods. The 'rational apathy' problem seems less serious since consumers are more likely to complain if the holiday trip they have been intensively longing for did not meet their expectations. In addition, error costs of public enforcement may be high if authorities focus on practices which attract great public attention but are rather innocuous. For example, the concerns of the Dutch Consumer Authority also relate to price advertisements, such as 'Special offer: 8 days on Ibiza – from 300 euro', which are considered to be not transparent. It is thought that consumers are deceived if only few holiday trips are available at the advertised low price. In our view, a general indication of a price level which explicitly mentions the lowest possible price is not necessarily deceptive. The final full price often depends on options for which the consumer has the possibility of choice. Price transparency requires that consumers have the possibility to easily calculate the final full price before deciding to book the holiday trip. A duty imposed on the travel agents to indicate in their advertising the prices of all available options seems to be an unduly burden, if interested consumers can receive additional information upon request. Another important consideration is that a prohibition to advertise the lowest possible price (even if there is only a limited number of holiday trips available at that price) may produce counterproductive effects. Such a prohibition would deny consumers valuable information. Moreover, travel agents may be forced to offer discount prices less frequently, and this will have a dampening effect on price competition.[40] In both cases, overall consumer welfare will be reduced. As this example illustrates, efficient law enforcement also requires a minimisation of error costs.[41]

3.3 Sanctions and timing of the intervention

The Law and Economics literature on law enforcement indicates several determinants which may have an impact on the level of deterrence: the role of public and private enforcement actions, the choice of the sanctions

40 P.H. Rubin, 'Information Regulation (Including Regulation of Advertising)' in: B. Bouckaert and G. De Geest (eds) *Encyclopedia of Law and Economics* (Cheltenham 2000), pp. 273-274.

41 See below; section 3.3.1.

and the timing of the intervention. European law has influenced the institutional design of the first two determinants: Regulation 2006/2004 has forced Member States to set up a system of public enforcement and Directive 98/27[42] has promoted the use of injunctions as a sanction. Up until now, the timing of the intervention has remained the exclusive domain of national consumer protection laws. The previous sections of this paper have shown the need for public enforcement and have indicated how economic criteria may be helpful in setting an agenda of priorities for public enforcement agencies. Hereinafter, the focus will be on the choice of the sanctions and the timing of the intervention.

3.3.1 Choice of sanctions

In EC Member States, there are a number of infringement proceedings which can be initiated in case of violation of consumer protection laws, ranging from administrative action to civil proceedings and criminal prosecution. The sanctions which can be imposed include: informal and formal warnings, injunctions strengthened with conditional fines[43], withdrawal of (credit) licenses, administrative fines and criminal sanctions (fines, imprisonment). The economic analysis of law enforcement offers criteria to decide which sanctions are economically optimal for the enforcement of consumer protection laws. Two central lessons from Law and Economics should always be kept in mind when judging the efficiency of sanctions. First, the costs which traders will face as a result of infringements must be higher than the benefits (utility) they derive from engaging in unlawful activities.[44] Although the precise value of the utility will rarely be known, compliance will be achieved by policy measures which influence the magnitude of the costs and the likelihood that traders will have to face these costs. The level of deterrence will therefore depend on the following variables: the formal sanction (cease and desist order, fine), adverse publicity, costs of lawyers, and the amount and quality of the monitoring by public agencies. Second, an optimal enforcement system minimises the sum of the social costs resulting from infringements and the costs of enforcement. The latter cost category includes not only administrative costs but also error costs. The expenses of the public sector (cost of enforcement agencies, prosecutors and courts) fall ultimately on taxpayers; besides these expenses further costs (management costs, costs of lawyers) are borne by traders, who may pass on parts of these costs to the consumers. Error costs occur when practices that harm consumer welfare are allowed (type I errors) or innocuous practices are falsely prohibited (type II errors). Both insights are helpful in assessing current enforcement mechanisms in a number of EC Member States.

---

42 Directive 98/27/EC, O.J. 1998 L166/51, pp. 51-54.

43 Conditional fines have to be paid when the trader does not comply with a court order.

44 The basic model was developed by Becker. See G. Becker, 'Crime and Punishment: An Economic Approach' (1968) *Journal of Political Economy* 169-217.

The overview of enforcement systems in this book and in other publications[45] shows that the use of criminal sanctions is relatively rare. In the United Kingdom, where the criminal justice system can be used to impose financial penalties, a much more powerful instrument for enforcing consumer protection laws is the (threat of) refusal or withdrawal of a credit licence, which almost every trading business needs to obtain for being active in markets for consumer goods. In other countries where criminal prosecution is possible (such as Belgium), large parts of consumer law have meanwhile been 'de-criminalized', mainly because public prosecutors and judges in the general courts mainly took a dismissive attitude towards infringements of consumer protection laws. In jurisdictions where there is a significant degree of investigation by administrative agencies and they themselves have the power to impose sanctions, financial penalties are generally modest.[46] The recent trend is moving farther away from repressive actions. Recent statements of public enforcement agencies express the desire to put more emphasis on informal warnings and giving advice; preventing infringements by informing traders and negotiating with them are preferred to penalties.[47] This 'soft' approach is followed in the hope that it will generate voluntary compliance.

Even though public enforcement agencies consider it to be their main task to deter infringements of consumer protection laws, it may be doubted whether the 'soft' approach can reach the goal of optimal deterrence. Economic analysis stresses that traders comply with the law only when the costs that they will incur by acting unlawfully exceed the benefits they will receive from committing the unlawful act. Besides management costs, informal warnings and advice do not impose any further burden upon traders. It seems unlikely that the prevention goal will be reached solely by non-repressive actions. In the United Kingdom, the OFT found that the success of voluntary codes drafted by trade associations depended on the availability of a strong sanction, a plausible threat of statutory regulation and a clear wish by the good players in the industry to distinguish themselves.[48] This confirms that the successes of voluntary compliance depend on the functioning of the reputation mechanism; repressive actions by public enforcement agencies remain necessary to achieve optimal deterrence in markets which do not function reasonably well. In particular, unscrupulous traders who do not worry about bad reputation will need to be deterred by financial penalties. In such cases, penalties will need to be of a substantial magnitude in order to make sure that the costs of law infringements exceed the utility of 'rogue traders'. Thereto, the expected sanction (magnitude of the fine discounted by the probability that it will be imposed) must exceed the amount of the premium for opportunistic behaviour that can be earned.

---

45 Ogus et al. (2006), cited above fn. 37.

46 For an overview, see Ogus et al (2006), pp. 78-81.

47 See, for example: Consumentenautoriteit (2006), p. 6-7.

48 See the contribution by Howells in this volume.

At this point, it should be recalled that the ultimate goal of consumer protection laws is to avoid adverse selection and maximize consumer welfare. This goal can be achieved only if it does not pay for firms to engage in acts which lower consumer welfare; remedies should therefore provide the correct amount of deterrence. Ideally, the sanction to be imposed in case of violation of consumer protection law should equal the harm caused by adverse selection in consumer markets multiplied by a factor which is inversely related to the probability of detection and punishment of the violation. Are criminal sanctions the right instrument to achieve optimal deterrence? Criminal fines carry a stigma effect (a clear sign that society morally disapproves a certain behaviour) and may therefore be a more effective deterrent than civil law sanctions (injunctions, damages) and administrative fines. Still, even when criminal sanctions can be imposed, the level of deterrence may easily remain too low since not all infringements will be detected and brought to court. In this context, it should be noted that criminal enforcement of consumer law does not have a high priority for public prosecutors, whose resources are, in any event, limited. Viewed *ex ante* traders will perceive the probability of a criminal penalty to be low. As a consequence of the low probability of being caught, the expected costs of law infringement are likely to be lower than the expected benefits. To remedy this problem, criminal courts could impose relatively large penalties but they may be reluctant to do so for what they consider to be minor offences. In addition, the possibility of imprisonment may cure the 'judgement proof' problem: if companies are insolvent, the possibility to send corporate directors to jail will effectively deter the latter to violate rules of consumer protection.[49] However, a major disadvantage of criminal sanctions (in particular imprisonment) is that they carry the risk of high error costs, in particular type II errors. For these reasons, one should look for alternative sanctions which are a powerful deterrent but at the same time minimise the error costs.

Ogus, Faure and Philipsen (2006) have suggested a system of administrative financial penalties, which avoids the language associated with the criminal process. Fixed penalties should be used for minor offences but in other cases agencies imposing fines should enjoy discretion to determine the amount. In their view, criminal prosecutions should be reserved for repeat offenders who cannot be deterred by other instruments and for repugnant moral conduct, which must be sanctioned irrespective of deterrence considerations. The proposal of these authors merits some comments. If deterrence is the goal of public enforcement, consumer authorities must have power themselves to impose substantial financial penalties. In choosing the amount of the penalty, they should enjoy discretion to apply a multiplier in inverse proportion to the probability of detection and punishment of the infringement of consumer protection laws. Here, a useful parallel can be drawn with the discussion

[49] Compare the related discussion on the desirability of criminal sanctions (fines, imprisonment) in the field of competition law. See Wils (2005), cited above fn. 14.

on optimal fines for violations of competition law. Both competition law and consumer protection laws protect at the same time individual rights and public values. In case of infringement of rules of competition law, the harm caused to society equals the dead-weight loss. In case of violation of rules of consumer protection, the social loss consists of the overall quality deterioration in consumer markets caused by adverse selection. As it is the case with infringements of the cartel prohibition, the detection rate of several infringements of consumer law may be low. Under EC competition law, the administrative fines that can be imposed by competition authorities amount to 10 percent of the world-wide turnover. Since infringements of consumer law cause a social loss (adverse selection on markets of consumer goods) which is comparable to the deadweight loss caused by monopoly, enforcement mechanisms of competition law may also be suitable for consumer law. An interesting example is the Swedish 'market disruption fee', which a trader may be ordered to pay in serious cases of intentional or careless violation of the substantive rules of the Swedish Market Act. The market disruption fee can amount to 10 per cent of the trader's annual turnover.[50] Even though this fee can be easily justified as an administrative penalty for the loss due to adverse selection, it may still be to low to effectively deter and cope with 'judgement proof' problems. To improve deterrence of violations of competition law, a number of EC Member States has introduced criminal sanctions for hard-core violations of the cartel prohibition, including imprisonment of directors; the latter sanction may be an appropriate remedy for the judgement-proof problem. In Sweden the possibility to use criminal sanctions was abolished when the market disruption fee was introduced. This choice may be justified by the risk of error costs. Compared to the field of competition law, it may be more difficult to define hard core infringements of consumer law where the risk of error costs is sufficiently low.

From a viewpoint of efficiency, under-deterrence (when sanctions are too low) is not the only problem. Over-deterrence results in a situation in which penalties are too high is equally worrisome from a consumer welfare perspective. For some prohibitions of consumer protection laws, criminal penalties may cause over-deterrence and injunctions (cease and desist orders) may be the preferable sanction. The current prohibition of misleading advertising, which equally bans false and true but deceptive statements, offers an example. It is difficult to determine whether an advertisement is deceptive and many advertisements may be innocently written and later misinterpreted by consumers.[51] Penalties more severe than a cease and desist order could easily cause firms to reduce the information provided in advertisements, in order to limit the number of claims. If firms resort to image advertising or puffery, which is allowed in most legal systems, the informative contents of advertisements will decrease. To avoid such a counterproductive result sanctions should not be too severe. A cease

50 See the contribution by Viitanen in this volume.

51 Weatherill (2005), cited above fn. 8.

and desist order may be the appropriate choice; an injunction is required where continuing the law infringement will lead to a decrease in consumer welfare.

3.3.2 Timing of the intervention

The next determinant in designing an enforcement regime for consumer protection laws relates to the timing of the enforcement actions. Intervention may take place before an undesirable act is committed (*ex ante* control) or after harm has occurred (*ex post* monitoring). Under the former regime, firms may inform the public authorities on practices they are contemplating, so that the authorities may screen contracts or marketing techniques before they are used or practiced. Under the latter regime, public authorities try to achieve deterrence by imposing sanctions if rules of consumer law are violated. In the Nordic countries, use is made of advance opinions, marketing guidelines and negotiations with trade organisations.[52] In the Netherlands giving guidance to businesses is equally contemplated and presented under the motto 'prevention is better than cure'.[53] This raises the question how timing of the intervention influences the outcomes of the system of enforcement.

Again a useful parallel with competition law may be drawn. In European competition law, a shift from an *ex ante* to an *ex post* control has occurred.[54] Until May 2004, undertakings could notify their agreements to the European Commission, asking for a formal decision implying that the agreement did not constitute a restriction of competition (negative clearance) or that it did, but could profit from an exemption. The European Commission was the only agency empowered to grant individual exemptions. This notification system has been abolished and replaced by a directly applicable legal exception regime. Under the new enforcement system, the European Commission as well as all competent national competition authorities and judges will fully evaluate the agreements, including the conditions to grant an exemption. Economic analysis has shown that firms may react differently to these divergent regimes and that this will have an impact on the level of law compliance.[55] These insights are also useful for judging the desirability of *ex ante* monitoring in the field of consumer law.

Generally, *ex ante* enforcement will be preferable if firms have limited knowledge about whether the action they are contemplating will violate the rules of consumer law or not. Under such circumstances, *ex post* enforcement will impose risk bearing costs on firms, which may prevent that beneficial practices are adopted. The decrease of information costs for enforcement authorities due to communications of potential infringements is a further argument in favour

52 See the contribution by Viitanen in this volume.

53 See the contribution by Ammerlaan and Janssen in this volume.

54 For a comment from an economic perspective, see V. Hahn, ' Antitrust Enforcement: Abuse Control or Notification?' (2000) *European Journal of Law and Economics* 69- 91.

55 For an overview, see Van den Bergh and Camesasca (2006), cited above fn. 16 at pp. 337-345.

of an *ex ante* monitoring regime. On the contrary, if firms are well informed, *ex post* enforcement may be superior provided that enforcement authorities have sufficient resources and that the quality of their assessments is sufficiently high. In the field of competition law, *ex ante* monitoring has been replaced by *ex post* enforcement. Only if the second scenario is closer to reality than the first, may one welcome the change of enforcement regime; in the opposite case, welfare losses may occur. In the field of consumer law, *ex ante* monitoring (if available) co-exists with *ex post* enforcement. This may allow improvement of the knowledge of market participants by giving advance opinions on the legality of certain sales practices. It also promotes the negotiation of contract terms in consumer markets, where the reputation mechanism is a powerful disciplining force. At the same time, *ex post* enforcement can be focused on clear-cut violations of consumer protection laws in markets for expensive experience goods (particularly those not regularly bought) and credence goods, where the harm caused tends to be the largest.

3.4 The role of private enforcement

It follows from the above that there are powerful economic arguments in favour of public enforcement of large parts of consumer law. However, this does not imply that there is no scope left for private enforcement. The story cannot end here, since also public enforcement exhibits a number of weaknesses. Public agencies have limited resources and cannot take action against every infringement of consumer law which is socially undesirable. Legal actions by private parties will draw additional means into the enforcement system and may contribute to reaching an efficient enforcement level. Another danger is that public enforcement agencies may be 'captured' by interest groups[56], which may lead to under-enforcement of consumer protection laws in certain sectors of the industry. The risk of regulatory capture will be greater with specialised authorities than with generalist public agencies. Given these weaknesses, private enforcement should play a complementary role. It must also be added that the strength of the arguments favouring public enforcement varies according to the type of infringement. From an economic perspective, the crucial question is whether the consumer protection laws covered by EC harmonisation are best enforced by public authorities. Some parts of the 'consumer acquis' lend themselves best for public enforcement (for example, unfair standard terms in contracts, misleading advertising), whereas the case for public enforcement is (much) weaker in other areas of EC consumer law (for example, package travel and consumer credit).

By allowing private enforcement next to public enforcement, there will also be competition between different enforcement systems. Such competition may be as important as competition on ordinary goods markets. The co-existence of

[56] Ogus (1994), cited above fn. 34 at p. 69-71.

public and private enforcement will allow learning processes and also limit the scope for regulatory capture.[57] Competition between private and public enforcement may be intensified by creating scope for self-regulation. The Law and Economics literature has stressed that self-regulation may have a number of advantages compared to public regulation: i) self-regulatory agencies have better information about the markets to be controlled; ii) there may be a high degree of self-compliance if the rules are set by the industry itself rather than by a distant public authority; iii) self-regulation may be more flexible and more innovative; and iv) the costs of self-regulation are borne by the industries themselves.[58] But also self-regulation is not without disadvantages: i) the rules may lack democratic legitimacy and ii) self-regulation may be abused for anti-competitive purposes. Consequently, also self-regulation must take place within an institutional framework which allows to profit from its advantages while at the same time limiting its disadvantages. On the one hand, a competition authority should retain the right to intervene to combat distortions of competition. On the other hand, the major benefit could be the development of innovative solutions, which remain needed if enforcement efforts are unsatisfactory.

4 Conclusions

The main conclusion from this paper is that there is a clear need for public enforcement of consumer protection laws. Private enforcement may play a useful complementary role but it cannot replace public enforcement. Since Regulation 2006/2004 forces national legislators to establish public enforcement agencies in EC Member States, the Regulation may be welcomed from an economic perspective. However, this does not imply that enforcement of consumer protection laws will be optimal in all EC Member States. An optimal allocation of enforcement powers to either private parties and/or public agents is only one component of an efficient system of enforcement. Optimal enforcement can be achieved only through a fine-tuning of four relevant parameters: i) an optimal mix of public and private enforcement, ii) the choice of an optimal sanction (injunction, administrative fine, criminal fine), iii) an optimal timing of the intervention (*ex ante* monitoring and/or *ex post* enforcement) and iv) allocation of enforcement powers to the optimal government level, either centralised or decentralised. Injunctions may pose problems of under-deterrence and in the absence of harmonisation it is left to the Member States to find the best ways to solve problems of under-deterrence. Also the efficiency of other parameters of enforcement will crucially depend on choices made by national legislators.

---

57 See R. Van den Bergh, 'Towards an Institutional Legal framework for Regulatory Competition' (2000) *Kyklos* 435-466.

58 See J. Miller, 'The FTC and Voluntary Standards: Maximizing the Net Benefits of Self-Regulation' (1985) *Cato Journal* 897-903.

A major effect of Regulation 2006/2004 is that public enforcement of important parts of consumer law, such as the prohibitions of misleading advertising and unfair terms in consumer contracts, will have to be organised in Member States where it did not exist before (at least as far as intra-Community infringements are concerned). Economic analysis of law enforcement teaches that public enforcement is to be preferred to private enforcement if i) private parties possess insufficient information about the infringements, and/or ii) the social net benefits from enforcement exceed the private net benefits of successful claims. Private parties may not be able to assess the infringement with certainty or discover the infringement only after harm has occurred. Rules of consumer law protect the private interests of individual consumers but are also indispensable for the proper functioning of markets. Losses to individuals may be smaller than the social losses, which result from an overall quality deterioration in markets plagued by information asymmetries (adverse selection). These insights are particularly useful for economically justifying public enforcement in different areas of consumer protection law.

In spite of the positive evaluation above, Regulation 2006/2004 may also entail problems. The extent to which the economic criteria in favour of public enforcement are satisfied differs across different areas of consumer law. For example, compared to private parties, who lack the investigation powers necessary to find infringements, public authorities are better able to find out whether particular firms respect prohibitions of unfair standard terms in contracts. Public enforcement is also called for in cases of misleading advertising, which does not only hurt an individual consumer who bought a worthless product but also impairs the proper functioning of the market (adverse selection) to the detriment of all sellers and buyers. However, private enforcement may be preferable in other cases, such as infringements of rules on consumer credit and package travel. In the latter cases, consumers do not face information problems concerning the identity of the wrongdoer and there will no serious 'rational apathy' problem since the private benefit of suing (not only the financial reward but also the desire to see traders who caused harm punished) tends to be substantial. Regulation 2006/2004 might thus cause inefficiencies to the extent that public enforcement is favoured in areas of consumer law where private parties possess better information than public authorities and there is no serious risk of under-deterrence.

CHAPTER 9

Collectivism: Evaluating the effectiveness of public and private models for regulating consumer protection

Christopher Hodges*

The thesis that sparked this conference is that Europe has evolved in its approach towards consumer interests, and that a reappraisal may be fruitful. Whereas the preoccupation during the 1970s and 1980s was with the acquisition of consumer rights and their definition in legislation, the primary focus now is on improving the ability of consumers to realise their rights. Realisation of rights has traditionally involved the separate streams of public law and private law, hence there has been concentration on, firstly, regulatory mechanisms and enforcement and, secondly, civil justice systems.

The paper attempts to identify at least some of the major forces that have been in operation in bringing about the current situation, so as to provide illumination for a re-examination of current trends and developments, and an evaluation of whether policies should be changed. Embarking on such an overview inevitably runs the risks of selectivity and of generalisation but, with that caveat and apology, it is worth doing if the exercise proves fruitful. The analysis presented adopts a deliberately questioning approach, in order to stimulate debate by challenging some hitherto orthodox views.

It will be argued that a new assessment is necessary of what role consumers should play in the enhancement of European policies on economic development and market regulation. Certain options, such as the involvement of consumer organisations in exercising regulatory enforcement functions, or the trend towards regulation through litigation, should be re-evaluated, and lessons learned. Alternative solutions should be adopted towards the challenge of how to provide adequate solutions for collective redress. Systems should be constructed that will deliver appropriate data on which future policy can be soundly based. The focus will be on EU measures, and some illustrations from the UK, with apologies to other member States.

1 Policy considerations

The starting point for this enquiry is the finding that EU policy on consumer affairs has changed. European countries have introduced extensive substantive consumer rights since at least the 1970s. However, scope for further progress may be limited, partly because the substance of what has been achieved in the past 50 years may leave limited opportunities for further ground-breaking legislation.[1] Instead, current preoccupations have shifted to the realisation of rights and redress mechanisms.

The trends and reforms identified above take place in the context of a particular political and policy environment. What are the prevailing policies and how

---

* Centre for Socio-Legal Studies, University of Oxford.

1 This is not to undervalue possible progress in relation to services.

are they likely to affect future developments?[2] It will be argued that the authorities have stated seven main policies that are relevant for present purposes. However, it will be seen that there are some inconsistencies between them and over how they are being implemented. Further, the impact of change occurring simultaneously in so many areas raises questions over whether the stability of the internal market and the Community can be maintained, as well as whether the primary goals are achievable or should be modified.

The primary policy of the Barroso Commission is to *enhance European competitiveness, growth and jobs*. The authorities also make an express link between competitive markets and innovation.[3] The Commission's 'revised Lisbon agenda' has not delivered these objectives, and there is some urgency to make economic progress, not least when faced with the cost of assisting the ten States who acceded to the EU in 2004 to undertake significant modernisation of their economies. All European harmonising legislation must have the goal of reducing the costs on business and of business transactions, by producing unified and therefore simplified rules.

Secondly, the authorities wish to improve European competitiveness by *encouraging competition* in markets. The principal methodology is to do this by maintaining both strong rules and their enforcement.[4] However, the Commission asserts that these mechanisms are currently insufficient,[5] although it has produced little evidence to substantiate such an assertion,[6] and has proposed to encourage private damages claims. The EU Competition Commissioner Neelie Kroes has said: 'I am personally convinced that there is a lot of potential in advancing private enforcement of the European competition rules. [...] it could really contribute to our number one priority in Europe: creating a more competitive environment for business and industry, and thus growth and economic and

2 It is not intended to record here a history of consumerism over the past 50 years, but to note particularly important forces and trends so as to illuminate the present situation and where we are heading or ought to go next.

3 See Communication from the Commission: Fostering structural change: an industrial policy for an enlarged Europe, COM(2005) 274, 20.4.2004; Commission consultation paper "Innovate for a Competitive Europe" A new Action plan for innovation, 2.4.2004; Implementing the Community Lisbon programme: More Research and Innovation – Investing for growth and Employment: A Common Approach, COM(2005) 488, SEC(2005) 1253.

4 Hence the modernisation of Community competition law. In relation to substantive rules, see Council Regulation (EC) 139/2004, O.J. 2004 L 24. In relation to enforcement see Council Regulation 1/2003 O.J. 2003 L 1/1; D. J. Gerber, 'The "Modernisation" of European Community Competition Law: Achieving Consistency in Enforcement: Part 1' E.C.L.R. 2006, 27(1), 10-18.

5 Green Paper: Damages actions for breach of the EC antitrust rules, COM(2005) 672, 19.12.2005; Commission Staff Working Paper: Annex to the Green Paper 'Damages actions for breach of the EC antitrust rules', SEC(2005) 1732, 19.12.2005.

6 C. Hodges, 'Competition enforcement, regulation and civil justice: what is the case?' (2006) *CMLR* 43, 1381-1407.

social welfare for our citizens. [...] the threat of having to pay damages for the harm caused by an infringement of the competition rules has a strong additional deterrent effect.'[7]

Thirdly, although EU policy is to increase pressure on business to ensure a dynamic, competitive and innovative market, the authorities at the same time aim to *reduce regulatory burdens* on business, so as to cut costs and thereby improve profitability and encourage innovation.[8] A principal manifestation of this approach is to undertake impact assessments of proposals for Community legislation,[9] although this is a notoriously difficult task, and may even be practically useless. It is interesting that there seems to be no programme of retrospectively analysing the actual costs of compliance with new regulatory measures.

Fourthly, a link is made between *consumer power* and economic improvement, notably through enhancement of competition.[10] This is only possible given the establishment of a corpus of consumer protection legislation, and appropriate organisations, such as a Directorate-General on Consumer Protection. A former Consumer Commissioner identified a major 'objective of our strategy [as] the proper involvement of consumer organisations in EU policies. [...] The integration of consumer interests in other EU policies is of vital importance to our aims, and in particular to empower consumers in the internal market.'[11] Similarly, a former Director General of the UK Office of Fair Trading expressed the point: 'Competition is increasingly being recognised as a core consumer issue. [...] competition policy and consumer interest should, and indeed, must be seen as inextricably linked and interdependent.'[12] This approach can justify strands of legislation on consumer protection, but is now extended to strengthening consumers as an economic force within the market.

The Commission has stated in 2005 'there is still a lack of a credible EU consumer movement'. Accordingly, its Health and Consumer Protection Strategy for 2007-2013 has a priority to increase consumers' capacity to promote their own interests. The budget for the combined EU health and consumer protection agenda is EUR 1,203 million. A European Consumer Institute will be created to assist the implementation of this policy, and assist with building the capacity of consumer organisations (training, knowledge, networking and pooling of efforts). Specific consumer protection objectives to be pursued are:

---

7 Speech by N. Kroes, Competition Commissioner, Harvard Club, New York, 22 September 2005.

8 See Commission press release 'Less red tape = more growth: Commission package for better regulation' 16 March 2005.

9 Commission Impact Assessment Guidelines, 15 June 2005, SEC(2005) 791.

10 See J. Stuyck, 'EC competition law after modernisation: More than ever in the interests of consumers' (2005) *Journal of Consumer Policy*, 28: 1-30.

11 "EU Consumer Policy: Making it work!", speech by Commissioner D. Byrne, Dutch presidency Conference on EU Consumer Policy, Amsterdam, 21 October 2004.

12 J. Vickers, 'Healthy Competition and its Consumer Wins' (2002) 12 *CPR* 142.

- a better understanding of consumer markets;
- better consumer protection regulation;
- better enforcement, monitoring and redress;
- and better informed and educated and responsible consumers.

Fifthly, there is the enhancement of *access to justice*. At one level, this issue arises from human rights considerations, against a background of widely differing standards in the efficiency, costs and speed of court systems across Member States.[13] However, the Community's economic health arises from a realisation that it is somewhat pointless to enact extensive substantive legal rules to further the internal market unless traders, consumers and regulators were enabled to enforce infringements and claim compensation through speedy and cheap procedures.[14]

The Commission has for some years been encouraging Member States to improve their access to justice and increase their expenditure on legal aid.[15] A considerable programme of activity on harmonisation of redress mechanisms and civil justice systems is underway, albeit at an early stage.[16] Of particular relevance for present purposes is the trend towards introduction into national legal systems of rules for the collective resolution of multiple individual disputes, colloquially known as 'class actions'.[17]

Items four and five above can be seen at work in two further aspects that are relevant here. The first of these, the sixth feature, is a trend towards *regulation through litigation*. The direct involvement of consumers in enforcing legislation to their benefit may partly be motivated in the desire of governments to save money by reducing direct expenditure on regulatory agencies at a time when voters wish to avoid increases in direct taxation. At the same time, there is a political dimension, in that the Community wishes to increase the involve-

---

13 *Cost-effective measures taken by States to increase the Efficiency of Justice: Report prepared by the European Committee on Legal Co-operation (CDCJ) in consultation with the European Committee on Crime Problems (CDPC)*, 23rd Conference of European Ministers of Justice, 8-9 June 2000; Green Paper: Access of consumers to justice and the settlement of consumer disputes in the single market, COM(93) 576, 16.11.1993, p. 57.

14 A seminal realisation of this point occurred with the Sutherland Report: P. Sutherland et al., *The Internal market after 1992: Meeting the Challenge* (Commission, 1992).

15 Memorandum from the Commission: *Consumer redress*, Commission of the European Communities, COM(84) 692, 12.12.1984; see also *Supplementary Communication from the Commission on Consumer Redress*, COM(87) 210, 7.5.1987; Council Resolution of 25 June 1987 on consumer redress, OJ No C 176/2, 4.7.87; Green Paper: Access of consumers to Justice and the settlement of consumer disputes in the single market, COM(93) 576, 16.11.1993; Directive 2002/8/EC O.J. 2003 L.26/41; Council Decision of 9 November 2004, 2004/844/EC on the standard form for legal aid applications and their transmission.

16 See C. Hodges, 'Europeanization of Civil Justice: Trends and Issues' (2007) 26 *CJQ* 97-123.

17 Laws exist in England, Germany, Spain, Sweden, Netherlands and are likely to be introduced in Finland, Norway, Denmark, Italy and France.

ment of consumers not only in the market (as economically powerful operators, as discussed above) but also in order to encourage increased political support for the Community, its institutions and even its basic concept and goals. This political issue has become more urgent since the rejection in 2005 of the draft European Constitution by voters in France and the Netherlands. There appears to be a desire to communicate the relevance of the Community to voters. The point can be seen in the Commission's justification for proposals to encourage private damages claims as an integral part of competition regulatory policy: 'Easier enforcement of legal rights and increased ability to recover economic losses are essential to bringing European citizens and their associations closer to European laws and policies.'[18]

Many of the above policy items, notably the enforcement of competition and empowerment of consumers, can be seen in the final, seventh, policy item, which is the spread of *collective actions* by consumer organisations or groups of individuals. The ability for consumer organisations to take action to protect the collective rights of consumers, usually being limited to seeking injunctive relief, has of course existed in civil law Member States, often for many years.[19] The involvement of consumer organisations can also now be seen at Community level as enforcement mechanisms in various consumer protection measures, namely the Directives for misleading advertising,[20] unfair contract terms,[21] cross-border injunctions for breach of specified consumer protection Directives,[22] the Regulation on consumer protection cooperation,[23] and the recent Directive on unfair business-to-consumer commercial practices ('UCP').[24] A further manifestation may be in the competition field.[25]

In summary, a sequence of fundamental policies exists in which economic considerations are paramount. Enhancement of the economic health of Member States, and of the Community, is currently a matter of considerable concern. This essential goal gives rise to subsidiary goals, which may be viewed as implementation methodologies by which the primary goal is to be achieved. However, each goal can be pursued independently. Issues of EU integration, innovation

18 Commission Staff Working Paper: Annex to the Green Paper 'Damages actions for breach of the EC antitrust rules', SEC(2005) 1732, 19.12.2005, para 194.

19 See C. Hodges, 'Europeanization of Civil Justice: Trends and Issues' (2007) 26 *CJQ* 97-123.

20 Directive 84/450/EEC, O.J. 1984 L 250/17, Art. 4.1. Most Member States have accorded consumer associations the right to bring actions under this provision: Green paper: Access of consumers to Justice and the settlement of consumer disputes in the single market, COM(93) 576, 16.11.1993, p 10.

21 Directive 93/13/EEC, O.J. 1993 L.095, Art. 7.

22 Directive 98/27/EC, O.J. 1998 L 166/51, Arts. 1-3.

23 Regulation 2006/2004, O.J. 2004 L 364/1, Arts. 4.2 and 8.3.

24 Directive 2005/29/EC, O.J. 2005 L 149/22, Art. 4.

25 Green Paper: Damages actions for breach of the EC antitrust rules, COM(2005) 672, 19.12.2005; Commission Staff Working Paper: Annex to the Green Paper 'Damages actions for breach of the EC antitrust rules', SEC(2005) 1732, 19.12.2005.

and access to justice may not be controversial in themselves. But the further one goes down the above list of policies, the more questions of quantification arise: how far should each individual goal be pursued without adversely affecting other policies and values, such as economic, social and environmental goals? For example, to what extent might empowerment of consumers, or reduction of burdens on business, or regulation through litigation, give rise to adverse effects? Indeed, it is not difficult to analyse potential conflicts between some or all of the individual goals, and in this case there is a need for the subsidiary goals to be kept in balance. It may follow that the over-enthusiastic pursuit of one or more subsidiary goals may produce undesirable consequences. If this is so, questions arise over what attempts have been made to assess the individual and collective effects of the individual measures and proposed reforms that are taken in pursuit of each goal, as well as general trends. These issues will be examined further in the following section.

However, two surprising things may be noted at this point. Firstly, there appears to be little discussion or debate such questions appear to receive, whether amongst policy makers or in the public arena. Evidence of attempts by the authorities to analyse and balance these subsidiary factors is strikingly lacking. Secondly, there seems to be little empirical data on costs and effects, and no criteria, even in the broadest terms, against which value judgements could be made. In the absence of general debate or general criteria, how is one to judge whether a sensible balance has been achieved?

2 Evaluations

It would be difficult not to support the primary goal of enhancing the health of the economy, with resultant potential benefits for employment, innovation and competitiveness. But *how much* increased competition is required; how much regulatory red tape needs to be removed; how much increased access to justice is needed? Further, *what methods* should be used in implementing the policies?

2.1 Oppositions

There seem currently to be two sets of contrasting approaches. The first contrast is between whether the correct methodology for exerting pressure is through regulation, for which the traditional approach involves public agencies, or through private litigation. The latter echoes US theory under which citizens or lawyers act individually as private attorneys general. The second contrast is an historical opposition between consumers and industry, and the question that arises is whether this is of continuing relevance for the future. Both sets of contrasts obviously also raise the issue pluralism: although a possible solution may be to prefer one or the other policy as dominant or even exclusive (ie to prefer public law to private law litigation as the enforcement mechanism), might there be some mixture of the two mechanisms, or would that be fudging the issue?

The advantages of state-run or centralised regulation over more diffuse or privatised mechanisms are well known.[26] The main issues are consistency, expertise, efficiency, resource, accountability, and independence. As noted above, however, in the current economic climate governments are resistant to providing funding for regulatory agencies. A clear example of this at Community level is the Commission's frustration with the limitation on both the resources of both itself and many national regulators in the competition field, which has directly prompted the proposal to involve private actors on the US model of 'private attorneys general'.[27] A national example of refusal to fund public regulation is the UK's decision not to implement the findings of its own report on the rationalisation of local consumer protection agencies and creation of a single national coordinating authority with which national industries could deal more cheaply.[28]

2.2 Consumers and business

The relationship between consumer and business interests is trite, but rarely stated. Business ultimately exists only if consumers purchase its goods and services. Healthy business provides employment, pensions and shareholder income. Successful business depends on quality, efficiency, and sometimes innovation. Consumers ultimately pay for the costs invested in practices necessary to ensure quality, safety and fairness that legal businesses need

26 The academic literature is consistent: see A.I. Ogus, *Regulation: Legal Form and Economic Theory* (Oxford 1994); R. Baldwin, *Rules and Government* (Oxford 1995); C. Hood, H Rothstein and R. Baldwin, *The Government of Risk: Understanding Risk regulation regimes* (Oxford 2001).

27 Green Paper referred to above.

28 The Hampton Review identified that there were 63 national regulators and 468 local authorities in the UK, employing 61,000 people, carrying out over 3 million inspections each year, and costing around £4 billion. The Review recommended that the regime should be simplified by consolidation of 31 of the 63 national regulators into seven bodies, and creation of a single centralised Consumer & Trading Standards Agency, and enforcement be made subject to a risk assessment approach: P. Hampton, *Reducing administrative burdens: effective inspection and enforcement* (H M Treasury, 2005) and Better Regulation Executive, *A Bill for Better Regulation: Consultation Document* (Cabinet Office, 2005). The Department of Trade and Industry accepted the recommendation and consulted on implementation: *Reducing the Administrative Burdens – the Consumer and Trading Standards Agency: Consultation* (Department of Trade and Industry, 5 July 2005). However, the Treasury decided that, although the reform would save costs for business, it was too expensive for public finances, and a much more restricted centralised office would be created, with limited functions, whilst other functions would be transferred to the Office of Fair Trading: Chancellor of the Exchequer, *Pre-Budget Report* (Treasury, 2005); *Moving towards the Local Better Regulation Office: The way ahead* (Department of Trade and Industry, 2006).

to deliver. Accordingly, over-regulation is not in consumers' interests. To what extent does current consumer policy assist business? A recent study found that EU consumer law does very little, if anything, for innovation.[29]

It is also trite that unchecked corporate power will lead to abuse. There can ultimately be no objection by industry to balanced regulation: the only requirements are for certainty as to what rules are to be observed and that the result should properly balance all competing interests. It is clear that the consumer rights movement has influenced the construction of extensive consumer protection legislation during the past 50 years. However, previous models may not be optimal for future conditions.

It is striking that the Kok Report included a conclusion that 'the impact of regulation on competition and ultimately on consumers should be systematically reviewed so as to ensure that it does not unnecessarily impede economic activity'.[30] In other words, given the finding of that Report that the performance of the European economy has been 'disappointing', the prevailing policy should be that regulation and consumer protection should both be kept subsidiary to, and proportionate with, striving for the economic priority, and cannot be absolute or exclusive goals.

What form should collective consumer power take given the changed focus towards redress? Whilst organised consumer pressure can be effective in lobbying for new legislative rights, this may not be so with regulation and enforcement of rights. For example, consumer bodies may be of limited effectiveness in lobbying for improvements in civil justice systems, because of the technical nature of the subject matter. If that is correct, should consumers desert the field, enlist technical assistance, or seek to work through new structures? Might the way forward even be to combine with industry in order to achieve reform that is balanced and effective?

At a more detailed level, what role should consumers take in redress mechanisms? What substantive benefit does this promise? Do consumers even seek greater involvement in the enforcement of regulation? Or has the involvement only come from the Commission or governments as a result of furthering their own reasons of saving money and presenting consumer involvement to their political advantage? Theoretical arguments in favour of the involvement of private enforcers may include failure by a public regulator to take effective action, usually because of lack of resources, or misapplication of the rules, or capture by the regulates. However, none of these theories has been put forward by the Community in explaining the justification for the involvement of private individuals or consumer organisations noted above. The result is a strong suspicion that the motivation for the involvement of consumers is based on political

29 C. Twigg-Flesner, 'Innovation and EU Consumer Law' (2005) *Journal of Consumer Policy*, 28: 409-432.

30 Facing the Challenge: The Lisbon strategy for growth and employment, Report from the High Level Group chaired by Wim Kok, November 2004, p. 25, available at http://ec.europa.eu/growthandjobs/pdf/2004-1866-EN-complet.pdf.

and ideological considerations, rather than pursuit of the primary economic goal. If these considerations are well founded, what should future policy be?

The involvement of consumer organisations in enforcing regulation does not score highly if measured against standard criteria for regulatory legitimacy.[31] Assuming that there is legislative mandate, the criteria of expertise and accountability for the exercise of coercive investigative powers and sanctions, are presumably unfavourable: would consumer organisations possess sufficient technical or legal expertise, and be effectively accountable to a sufficiently wide-ranging body of the population? The study on implementation of Directive 98/27 on injunctions for the protection of consumers' interests concluded that consumer organisations could only claim to be integrated into the enforcement of consumer law if they are professionalized, but that this situation does not currently exist.[32] It would be unclear whether the criteria of due process or efficiency would be favourable. Individual organisations may or may not act fairly and even-handedly, or in an efficient manner or take economically efficient actions. Expansion of the number of regulators raises obvious problems of inconsistency between decisions of different regulators, as well as between individual regulators and courts.

For precisely these reasons, some governments have sought to impose constraints on consumer organisations when empowering them to exercise regulatory powers. The latest proposals from the UK are striking in this regard. Recent government policy is 'a strategy to empower consumers and support business success'.[33] However, the number of consumer organisations that are permitted to exercise certain regulatory functions, is significantly limited. Thus, only one consumer organisation, the Consumers' Association, is empowered to take action against infringements under the Unfair Terms in Consumer Contracts legislation, on the basis of satisfying criteria published by the government.[34] Secondly, both the empowered consumer body and the various other sectoral public regulatory authorities which are empowered to act under the legislation, have to notify the primary public body (the Office of Fair Trading [OFT]) before any action is taken and of the outcome of any proceedings.[35] The aims of these mechanisms are to retain control with the primary regulator, thereby assisting consistency in enforcement policy, and to prevent frivolous and disproportionate enforcement activity.

Similarly, several significant controls were introduced in UK competition law from 2002. First, a designated consumer body may make a 'super-complaint' to the regulator, the OFT, that any feature, or combination of features, of a market

---

31 R. Baldwin, *Rules and Government* (Oxford 1995).

32 M.U. Docekal, P. Kolba, H-W. Micklitz and P. Rott, *The Implementation of Directive 98/27/EC in the Member States* (Bamberg/Vienna 2005).

33 *Extending Competitive Markets: Empowered Consumers, Successful Business* (Department of Trade and Industry, 2004).

34 The Unfair Terms in Consumer Contracts regulations 1999, SI 1999 No 2083, Schedule 1, Part Two.

35 The Unfair Terms in Consumer Contracts regulations 1999, SI 1999 No 2083, regs. 10 – 14.

in the UK for goods or services is or appears to be significantly harming the interests of consumers.[36] It is the OFT, rather than the consumer body, which is empowered to take action, but the OFT must publish a response explaining its position. The power to designate a consumer body for these purposes rests with the Secretary of State, who may do so only if it appears to him to represent the interests of consumers of any description, and only subject to any other criteria which he has published.[37]

Secondly, any person who has suffered loss as a result of an infringement may institute a claim for damages before the Competition Appeal Tribunal.[38] Multiple individual claims that all relate to the same infringement may also be brought in a representative capacity by a 'specified body', provided each individual has consented to the claim being brought. A typical example of such a claim is said to be where consumers have bought goods for personal use where the price has been inflated by a price-fixing agreement. Any body may apply to the Secretary of State to be 'specified', on the basis of published criteria. However, no damages claim may be brought until it has been established (by either the OFT or the European Commission) that an infringement of competition law has occurred. Thus, there is a two-stage process, which separates the functions of infringement enforcement from the consequential issue of compensation. Further, responsibility for enforcement remains with an independent regulator, not with a consumer organisation.

Thus, the result is that the UK is wary of affording consumer organisations unfettered regulatory power, and prefers to continue to rely on the primacy of the public bodies, especially the OFT. The vigilance of consumer organisations is harnessed in market surveillance, which may overcome deficiencies in the resources of the regulator in surveillance, and pressure is exerted on the regulators to take enforcement action where it is proportionate to do so, but regulatory authority of the public body is not ceded to any private organisation. In short, consumers are involved in the system as a watchdog, and may bark but not bite: biting is reserved to the public authority. The advantages of this model for constructing self-regulatory mechanisms will be seen in the discussion below.[39]

---

36 Section 11, Enterprise Act 2002.

37 Section 11, Enterprise Act 2002.

38 Section 47B, Competition Act 1998.

39 As at 2000, the right of initiative under the unfair terms in consumer contracts Directive similarly rested in other member States not with consumer organisations, but with pubic bodies responsible for upholding the public interest: Report from the Commission on the Implementation of Directive 93/13/EEC of 5 April 1993 on Unfair Terms in Consumer Contracts, COM(2000) 248, 27.4.2000. The bodies are the Director General of Consumer Affairs in Ireland, consumer ombudsmen in the Nordic states, the Verbraucherschutzvereine in Germany, and the relevant ministries in Spain and Portugal. France and Belgium were reported as having created collegiate bodies whose main mission is to recommend the elimination of unfair terms, and the courts are reported to refer to the recommendations of such bodies. The Commission noted that the UK's system, in which the OFT is the principal regulator, was notably more effective than other States.

At EU level, the test for consumer organisations to qualify to exercise autonomous cross-border enforcement powers is where the body has a 'legitimate expectation'.[40] Two questions may arise here. Does the legitimate expectation test afford sufficient certainty (the formulation is imprecise and affords scope for significant variations in interpretation of which bodies may have a legitimate interest in bringing individual cases) and is the test too wide? Should autonomous enforcement powers be granted to private bodies, or should they be reserved to a public body?

Given the deficiencies in legitimacy identified above, if individual groups across the Community are empowered to exercise quasi-regulatory functions, should they be subject to such similar controls as would apply to governmental authorities of democratic accountability, authorisation and ongoing supervision (for example by designated authorities or parliamentary mechanisms) on criteria of adequacy of representation, efficiency, and effectiveness, and possession of sufficient expertise? A parallel for such an approach is the notified body system that applies under EU New Approach product legislation. Notified bodies are private entities which are empowered with certain regulatory powers if they satisfy published criteria. They are subject to oversight by public competent authorities, and their approval may be withdrawn if performance falls.

Significantly, many national consumer organisations in the EU themselves appear reluctant to act as regulators. The evidence is that consumer organisations have not been active as enforcers. The position may not yet have been studied comprehensively, but longstanding anecdotal evidence from national consumer organisations and preliminary empirical evidence from the new Community mechanisms is in fact consistent here. This inactivity is partly because consumer organisations perceive their representative role as being inconsistent with that of a regulator, and partly because they do not wish to risk their limited funds on litigation, given high legal costs and 'loser pays' rules.

This reluctance can now be seen to raise the fundamental issue of whether consumer organisations are ineffective in exercising enforcement powers. The study on implementation of Directive 98/27 on injunctions for the protection of consumers' interests found that the legal and practical significance of injunctive actions is rather low, and described the picture across Member States as showing 'no coherent system'. Furthermore, it seems that only a single cross-border case has been brought.[41] Significantly, also, the case was brought by a governmental agency rather than a consumer organisation. Anecdotal evidence from

---

40 Directives 84/450/EEC, O.J. 1984 L 250, Art. 4.1, 93/13, Art. 7.2; 98/27, Arts. 1-3, 2005/29, Art. 4; Regulation (EC), O.J. 2006/2004 L 364/1, Arts. 4.2 and 8.3.

41 The case was brought by the UK's Office of Fair Trading, against a Belgian company that was sending unsolicited mail order catalogues to UK residents together with notification of a prize win, and the Belgian court issued an order banning the practice on the basis that consumers believed that they had to make a purchase in order to secure a prize, whereas winners were pre-selected and few recipients would receive a prize, usually £10,000. The company was reported to have received about 4,000 orders per day from its catalogues: press release at http://www.oft.gov.uk/News/Press+releases/2004/208-04.htm,

discussions with national consumer organisations in various Member States indicates that they are similarly inactive in the use of national enforcement powers, even where the powers have existed for many years. This is consistent with the UK government's comparative research, which showed that provision of funding to consumer groups to take legal action generally results in only marginal involvement by such bodies, since they are wary of the potential legal costs of launching litigation.[42]

It would be plausible to address the funding gap, for example either by providing consumer organisations with public funds to initiate legal claims or to pay opponents' costs if they lose, or by permitting the courts to excuse the organisations from having to pay opponents' costs if they lose. But either of these suggestions raises difficulties. Governments may be reluctant in the current economic climate to fully fund public regulators, so why should they provide funds to non-governmental bodies? Is it fair and just that certain litigants should be excused from the normal 'loser pays' rule, especially where the rule applies to prosecutions or civil claims brought by public authorities? What about distributive and corrective justice for defendants who are improperly sued?

2.3 Application of the 'responsive regulation' best practice

The above discussion has reached something of an impasse. However, a possible way forward appears if consideration is given to the implications of the findings of modern regulatory scholarship. Research has clearly established that the optimal policy for enforcing regulation is 'responsive': in short, this comprises a regulator with wide powers that are rarely used since persuasion, negotiation and co-operation are used as primary strategy instead of more aggressive and confrontational enforcement through court systems.[43] Regulatory strategies 'seek to link legal sanctioning to broader corporate incentive regimes, and involve demands that companies themselves generate explicit assurances on how they will proceed towards compliance.'[44] Such an approach has been seen to achieve both optimal compliance and minimal cost, for both regulators and regulatees. Yet 'responsive regulation' requires there to be consistency over time in the identity and policies of a regulator. Such consis-

and see Report from the Commission: First Annual Progress Report on European Contract Law and the Acquis Review, COM (2005) 456, 23.9.2005. *OFT v. D. Duchesne SA* referred to in *TS Today* (2006) February, p. 4.

42 *Comparative Report on Consumer Policy Regimes*, (Department of Trade and Industry, October 2003).

43 The approach is encapsulated in the classic phrase "the benign big gun syndrome whereby regulators with big sticks can speak softly": I. Ayres and J. Braithwaite, *Responsive Regulation: Transcending the Deregulation Debate* (Oxford 1992). A development of this approach is 'meta-regulation': C Parker, *The Open Corporation* (Cambridge 2002).

44 R. Baldwin, 'The New Punitive Regulation', (2004) 67(3) *MLR* 351-383, 382.

tency cannot be achieved where regulatory functions are split between multiple regulators, especially if they are infrequent repeat players. This conclusion undermines the empowerment of both consumer organisations (if they duplicate public agencies, or if they exist as multiples) and of regulation through litigation (where regulatory consistency is threatened by multiple claimants and court decisions).

The evidence that substantiates the 'responsive regulation' approach discredits a claim that deterrence justifies enforcement.[45] Baldwin has concluded that a punitive approach 'assumes a model of corporate behaviour that is unrealistic and, as a result, brings a number of dangers. It may fail to make best use of self-regulatory capacities, it may chill healthy risk-taking and it may make successful regulation more, rather than less, difficult to achieve.'[46] Baldwin's empirical research reveals that corporate behaviour is not driven by regulatory risks or fear but primarily by goals of running good quality enterprises and maintaining brand value. A punitive approach will fail to engage with how either responsible or crooked companies, and individuals within them, in fact operate. Thus, much regulatory policy (and tort law) may be being based on incorrect assumptions about what influences corporate behaviour and produces competitive markets.

It will also be seen that the exercise of enforcement powers by consumer organisations presents significant obstacles in fitting into a structure based on 'responsive regulation'. This is because the 'big stick' enforcement powers can only be realised effectively by public authorities, which have appropriate democratic accountability, expertise, resources, and flexibility over time. It is perfectly satisfactory to give consumer organisations a watchdog function as long as the bark is not a bite, and the biting is reserved to the public authority, which is the agent who is empowered to wield the benign big stick. Further, self-regulatory bodies which act under a regulator with a benign big stick can satisfy the requirements: this will be discussed further below.

2.4 Excessive litigation?

Pursuit of the goals of increasing access to justice, and providing for effective enforcement, do not necessarily involve an increase in litigation. Excessive litigation can be avoided on the 'responsive regulation' principle if sufficiently powerful enforcement forces exist which rarely need to be invoked since individual disputes are resolved through speedier, cheaper and less confrontational means. Importantly, however, care must be taken to avoid increasing incentives to litigate to such an extent that intermediaries can seek to maximise their own profits by generating excessive legal transactions. In other words, as Commissioner Neelie Kroes has said, the aim is to produce a competition

45 Conversely, the UK Competition White Paper announced a "strong deterrent effect" in attacking anti-competitive behaviour: *Productivity and Enterprise: A World Class Competition Regime* Cm 5233 (HMSO, 2001).

46 R. Baldwin, 'The New Punitive Regulation', (2004) 67(3) *MLR* 351-383.

culture but not a litigation culture,[47] and avoid both unnecessary transactional costs and transactions. In this connection, based on the experience of USA and elsewhere, moves in Europe towards class or collective actions, and contingency fees, may be viewed with alarm. Public opinion in the UK already believes that a compensation culture exists,[48] and although the government repeats that this is not the case it is taking strenuous steps to counter the perception.[49]

Private litigation could have a significant deterrent effect on business if its volume were permitted to rise significantly (as has occured in the USA), and this could be achieved by amending the financial incentives and risks, such as by permitting punitive or multiple damages, removing the 'loser pays' rule, introducing contingency fees, and so on. But it is certainly arguable that the adverse consequences of such changes would outweigh any advantages, and that it is not possible to fine-tune the blunt instruments involved so as to limit the effects. Above all, the risk is considerable that litigation would be controlled by intermediaries (lawyers or third party funders) for their own benefit. There is considerable evidence to substantiate such views from the USA.[50] The history of group litigation of product liability claims in England during the 1980s and 90s is further strong evidence.[51] Even within the past 6 years, an industry of claims-harvesting intermediaries ('claims farmers') developed in the UK, which gave rise to significant defrauding of consumer claimants,[52] leading to the financial collapse of various intermediaries,[53] and requiring the introduction of regulation.[54]

---

47 See Speech by Commissioner N. Kroes at the Harvard Club, 22 September 2005. Whether the Green Paper on competition damages is consistent with this aim is highly questionable.

48 See for example K. Williams, 'State of fear: Britain's "compensation culture" reviewed' (2005) *Legal Studies* 499; Better Regulation Task Force, *Better Routes to Redress* (2004).

49 Section 1, Compensation Act 2006, which the government has stated does not alter the standard of care, although this statement is controversial. The Business Plan 2005/06 of the Legal and Judicial Services Group of the Department for Constitutional Affairs included a section headed 'Tackling perceptions of a compensation culture and improving the compensation system'. See also 'Tackling the "Compensation Culture": Government Response to the Better Regulation Task Force Report 'Better Routes to Redress', (Department for Constitutional Affairs, 2005).

50 See especially R.A. Kagan, *Adversarial Legalism* (Harvard 2001); W.K. Viscusi, *Regulation through Litigation* (AEI-Brookings Joint Center for Regulatory Studies, 2002); D. Kelemen, 'Suing for Europe. Adversarial Legalism and European Governance' (2006) *Comparative Political Studies*, p. 101-127.

51 See C. Hodges, *Multi-Party Actions* (Oxford 2001).

52 The Better Regulation Task Force, *Better Routes to Redress* (2004) said: 'Media reports and claims management companies encourage people to "have a go" by creating a perception, quite inaccurately, that large sums of money are easily accessible.' However, there is little public understanding that the level of damages that apply to most claims is low: over 55% of county court awards in 2002 were for less than £3000.

53 The principal intermediaries were Claims Direct, and The Accident Group: see *'Improved Access to Justice – Funding Options & Proportionate Costs' Report & Recommendations*, Civil Justice Council, 2005.

54 The Compensation Act 2006, http://www.opsi.gov.uk/ACTS/acts2006/20060029.htm.

Underlying all of these problems is a concern to address the unresolved issue of what to do about *collectivism*. The concern is not so much with redress or the vindication of rights in individual cases, but with issues that affect multiple citizens and have significantly large economic impact. This problem manifests itself in two situations. In the regulatory sphere, there is the increasing empowerment of consumer organisations, whereas in the compensation sphere, there is the spread of 'class action' mechanisms within civil justice systems. How do we deal with situations in which many people are (or may be) adversely affected?

Survey results indicate that 67% of European Union citizens would be more willing to defend their rights before a court if they could join with other consumers who complain about the same issue.[55] BEUC therefore asserts that collective actions are particularly suitable to obtain compensation for damages that concern a large number of consumers but that, if handled individually, would never be brought to courts by the victim. However, as discussed above, it does not necessarily follow that consumer organisations are the best vehicle to co-ordinate any such action, even tough an efficient solution needs to be found to resolve a case where many consumers (or small businesses) suffer limited losses as a result of infringing activity by one or more businesses, which would not be cost-effective for them to pursue but if left unrectified would leave unjustified profits for the perpetrator(s).

2.5 Summary

To sum up the argument thus far, the seven policies identified in section I give rise to tensions, and a balance between them needs to be struck through political processes. Now that extensive mechanisms for consumer protection have been established, and new priorities and forms are emerging, there is an opportunity to assess whether new approaches may be required. Continuation of a consumer rights movement that is focussed on legislation now has diminished relevance. What role should consumers adopt in the new circumstances? The ultimate test is whether the approaches that are adopted deliver results that further the primary economic goal, rather than subsidiary goals: will the results prove to be effective, balanced, cost-effective, reduce regulatory breaches, increase competition, and increase profitability for business and the economy, and safeguard employment and pensions? The issue is not one of consumer interests but public and Community interest.

Is there a case for consumers to take a new holistic approach, and far greater interest in matters such as whether the costs of systems are justified (ie the 'better regulation' agenda) and whether systems are operated efficiently? Is the opportunity to participate in enforcement a mirage, and will it deliver effective compliance? Is the currently postulated involvement of consumers in enforcement merely just an attempt by governments to save money, and the policy of

55 Eurobarometer survey: European Union Citizens and Access to Justice, October 2004, p. 36.

empowering consumers merely empty rhetoric that will fail and give rise to a crisis of confidence? Will consumers' assumption of responsibility for regulation and enforcement merely be a poisoned chalice?

It is once again striking that many of the policies outlined above are based on theoretical grounds (that regulation through litigation, and increased aggression in enforcement, will enhance competitiveness), and that empirical evidence to support the underlying assumptions is lacking.

3 Some alternatives

Do alternative solutions exist to the opposed extremes of public regulation or private enforcement? How can society deal with the challenges of realisation of rights and collectivism? The following discussion identifies some possible options, first in regulation and then in litigation. The purpose is not to examine options in detail, but merely to identify ones that may repay further analysis.

3.1 Regulation

Two responses can be made to the issues involving regulation. Firstly, can agencies be made to operate on a more efficient basis, so as to reduce their costs? Secondly, do self-regulation or co-regulation present viable options?

3.1.1 Efficient Regulatory Agencies

If the objection to a continuation of public regulatory agencies is based on the ground that they are too expensive, it should be asked whether efficiencies could be made which would make them more attractive to governments. Governments may, of course, also respond to a clear political message from consumers that they do not seek extensive responsibility in regulatory enforcement (or in enhanced private litigation) but instead wish to see regulation delivered primarily through effective and properly funded public bodies.

It has been argued that increases in effectiveness and efficiency could be achieved through the creation of EU agencies, rather than continuing to rely on multiple national agencies.[56] The occurrence of events sometimes raises the arguments for creation of a coordinating European agency to have sufficient political force, as with the need for a European Food Agency. The point will not

---

[56] Arguments for a European product safety Agency are outlined in C. Hodges, *European Regulation of Consumer Product Safety* (Oxford 2005). See also C. Hodges, 'Do We Need a European Medical Devices Agency?' (2004) *Med.L.R.* p. 268-284. Some national agencies for medicinal products now carry out activities for governments in other Member States on a subcontract basis.

be pursued here, but the question that remains is whether governments should be encouraged to understand that a price for the provision of effective public regulation may be worth paying, and that other alternatives which may save treasury funds might not be as effective.

3.1.2 Self-regulation

Self-regulation, which has strong cultural roots stretching back to 19th century origins, has had a notable resurgence in the past decade in the UK,[57] after a period of giving ground to state regulation. A recent study found over 40 examples in a wide range of fields,[58] and concluded that this new wave should be seen not so much as part of a deregulatory agenda, but as a more efficient and effective mode of operation for the regulatory state – consistent with the 'better regulation' agenda.[59] Accordingly, British self-regulatory regimes are often associated with governing legislation. Indeed, both theoretical and practical experience supports the view that self-regulation will be most effective when subject to public oversight based on systems control, transparency and accountability.[60] These conclusions are precisely consistent with the separate research referred to above on 'responsive regulation'.

A wide range of distinct models can be identified which might be characterised as self-regulation or co-regulation, depending on factors such as the degree and nature of control and the powers involved, or the ability to impose sanctions. The advantages of self-regulation over classic state regulation lie in expertise, flexibility, speed, lower cost to the state (but sometimes internalised cost to the sector), potentially lower regulatory burden, and increased motivation. Disadvantages can include lack of accountability or transparency, failure to act in the public interest (and even continuation of anti-competitive rents), and lack of performance or inefficiency. Indeed, it was recognition that the superimposition of state oversight may address these deficits that led to the resurgence of the mechanism.[61] Further, reflexive law theory suggests that the oversight of the

---

57 *United Kingdom, Challenges at the Cutting Edge*, (OECD, Paris, 2002).

58 Including energy, telecommunications and transport networks, airports, professions, media content, environment protection, responsible drinking and universities.

59 I. Bartle and P. Vass, *Self-Regulation and the Regulatory State – A Survey of Policy and Practice* (Centre for the Study of Regulated Industries, University of Bath School of Management, 2005). The government's Better Regulation Task Force published a sequence of reports pressing the advantages of self-regulation between 1999 and 2005.

60 A.I. Ogus, 'Rethinking Self-Regulation' (1995) 15 *Oxford J. Legal Stud.*, p. 97-108; J. Black, 'Constitutionalising Self-regulation', (1996) 59 *Mod. L. Rev.*, p. 24-55; I. Bartle, cited above fn. 59.

61 Such a system is entirely consistent with the 'responsive regulation' system. As noted above, there are parallels with state regulation of notified bodies under the Community's New Approach system. The theory of autopoiesis also stresses the function of self-regulatory bodies as providing social integration between the multiple differentiated functional systems (such as law, politics, religion and the economy) that are found in modern society: G. Teubner, *Law as an Autopoietic System* (Blackwells, 1993).

self-regulatory body should be procedural, on the basis of controlling systems and transparency rather than intervening in individual outcomes.[62]

Responsibility for regulatory governance is often delegated by the state to a dedicated agency, the constitution of which is established by legislation.[63] Notably, the OFT has been given power to approve codes of practice,[64] and operates a Consumer Codes Approval Scheme.[65]

In summary, UK experience indicates that the conditions required for self-regulation to work best are:[66]

- the existence of a governmental supervisory body, with sufficiently strong background powers (such an the OFT; the Australian ACCC even has power to impose a Code);
- genuine ownership by the regulated community, including detailed understanding of the purpose and benefits of the regulation and of compliance, hence enhancing brand value;
- separation of the functions of representation from regulation, through the formation of separate entities, so as to avoid conflicts of interest;[67]
- power to monitor and investigate (often fudged);
- taking action and imposition of sanctions, without which public confidence will evaporate.[68]

3.2 Compensation

In the area of compensation, three alternative mechanisms deserve attention as possible ways forward: court 'class action' rules, ADR mechanisms, and special schemes.

---

62 J. Black, cited above fn. 60; I. Bartle, cited above fn. 59.

63 Examples include the OFT, Financial Services Authority, Advertising Standards Authority, Ofcom, Otelo, Oftel, Ofwat, Ofgem, Offer, Qualifications and Curriculum Authority. Bodies operating outside a statutory framework include the Press Complaints Commission, the Mobile Operators Association (planning of cell phone masts), the Association of British Travel Agents, the Portman Group (responsible drinking).

64 Section 8, Enterprise Act 2002.

65 *Consumer Codes Approval Scheme: Core Criteria and Guidance* (OFT, 2004).

66 These views are based on many conversations with regulators and industry over many years, but I would like to thank particularly K. Richards of ABTA, and C. Banks, former Director of Consumer Affairs, OFT.

67 When the Association of the British Pharmaceutical Industry decided to assume responsibility for regulating the content of advertising of proprietary medicinal products it established the Prescription Medicines Code of Practice Authority as a separate entity.

68 It is noticeable that ABTA imposes high fines for infringements.

3.2.1 Class actions

European judges and legislators are increasingly realising that it is necessary for courts to have powers to manage multiple claims effectively. Modern mass trading can lead to many people who wish to bring similar claims. Traditional court systems, based on resolution of individual claims, risk being overwhelmed unless judges have powers to combine claims and manage them efficiently. Exactly this same rationale has underpinned, amongst others, the introduction of Group Litigation Orders in England,[69] of the Capital Investors' Model Proceeding Law in Germany,[70] and recent proposals for collective actions in Italy.[71]

Whilst 'class action' rules may offer a necessary response to collective compensation claims, they suffer from a serious disadvantage in being open to being dominated by intermediaries whose interests' conflict with those who own the underlying claims. Strong examples of failures in consumer protection and in the provision of solutions which involve proportionate costs for compensation claims can be seen in the experience of class actions in the USA, English group actions up to the mid-1990s, and the Australian 'tort crisis'. Important lessons include that consumer interests need to be strongly protected, that lawyers' costs require firm regulation, and that the activities of any intermediaries need to be strongly regulated. As mentioned above, recent activities of claims intermediaries in England involved such scandalous behaviour that regulation had to be rushed through.[72] Ireland has recently tried to reduce delays in legal processes by requiring personal injury claims in which liability is agreed must be referred to a public body in order to speed up assessment of quantum.[73]

There is a real risk of drawing the wrong conclusions here. Although class or collective action mechanisms may be necessary in the contemporary world, a need for courts to manage multiple claims effectively should not be confused with justification for creating uncontrolled new collective remedies or rights. The unfairness of insulating claims brought by or for consumers from the 'loser pays' rule has been referred to above. The risk that well-intentioned collective mechanisms may be hijacked by intermediaries needs to be taken seriously, and consideration given to how a system can deter bad claims from being brought, and can identify good and bad claims so that bad claims can be swiftly weeded out and good claims settled.

---

69 Civil Procedure Rules, Part 19.III; see C. Hodges, *Multi-Party Actions* (Oxford 2001).

70 *KapitalanlegerMusterverfahrensgesetz* (KapMuG), following 15,000 individual claims against Deutsche Telecom, that the company overvalued assets before a share sale in 2000.

71 See statements in the Illustrative Reports of Bills introduced by Deputy Maran, Senator Benevento and Minister Bersani in June 2006, which all refer to the need to provide a solution to the rise of multiple similar claims, such as for financial crashes (Cirio, Giacomelli, Parmalat, Argentine bonds) and breakdown in energy supplies (as occurred on 28 September 2003).

72 Compensation Act 2006.

73 Personal Injuries Assessment Board.

Might there be an alternative mechanism in relation to provision of compensation? In some Member States, regulatory action can involve a supplementary redress mechanism under which settlements are encouraged, or courts empowered to award compensation, for people adversely affected by illegal activity, without requiring unnecessary initiatives to be taken, or costs to be incurred, by those adversely affected. Such a mechanism avoids lawyer-led actions and the potential for sizeable legal transaction costs, which are associated with private court actions. A regulatory function would still be required, so any reduction in costs would remain speculative, and there would be an increase in costs on the court systems. This is the Australian Federal model of consumer regulation through the Australian Competition Compensation Commission. It is the inverse image of the European competition proposals for privatised enforcement. The ACCC, as regulator, is empowered to institute civil compensation claim, and distribute proceeds to consumers. Thus, a public body exercises this collective function, rather than a private consumer organisation, with likely advantages in relation to accountability, efficiency, expertise and the ability to act proportionately (i.e. the freedom not to act in some circumstances).

3.2.2 ADR

The advantage of ADR mechanisms is that they are essentially outside national court systems, and can offer low cost, speed, and direct contact between consumer and business. These considerations, plus some jurisdictional limitations imposed by the EC treaty, have recommended ADR mechanisms to the Community. The main EU initiatives are an Extra-Judicial Network (EEJ-NET) launched in 2001,[74] a consumer claim form,[75] the Proposal for a Directive on certain aspects of mediation in civil and commercial matters,[76] and the establishment of a European small claims procedure (which does not require representation by a lawyer).[77]

These mechanisms have had insufficient time to bear fruit, but could offer promising solutions, whether at EU or national levels. Consumer organisations or self-regulatory bodies should be encouraged to investigate possibilities, noting that ADR is essentially outside the public court system and is less likely

---

74 Council Resolution, (EC) OJ C 155/1, 6.6.2000.

75 http://www.eejnet.org/filing_complaint.

76 COM(2004) 718 final, 22.10.2004. This http://europa.eu.int/eur-lex/LexUriServ/site/en/com/2004/com2004_0718en01.pdf is proceeding through the European Parliament. A voluntary European Code of Conduct for Mediators was launched in July 2004: http://europa.eu.int/comm.justice_home/ejn/adr_ec.

77 Proposal for a Regulation of the European Parliament and of the Council establishing a European Small Claims Procedure, COM(2005) 87, 15.3.2005, see Art. 7; the procedure would apply to claims under €2,000, although the legal basis under Art. 61 EC for coverage of domestic disputes as well as cross-border ones is, however, a matter of debate.

to be subject to expensive legal costs. Thought should be given to mechanisms of dealing with collective claims – perhaps through existing official bodies or Ombudsmen, with the addition of a power to coordinate? The Swedish model of the Ombudsman referring claims to a Public Consumer Complaint Board, or some other extra-court, low-cost mediation facility, seems attractive.

3.2.3 Compensation schemes

Dedicated compensation schemes can provide speedy and low-cost solutions. In Sweden, virtually no medical or drug claims have been made in the courts since the 26 years since schemes were introduced for medicinal product or medical accident injuries.[78] France introduced a compensation scheme for medical accidents (ONIAM) in 2004,[79] and the UK is to introduce a similar scheme (NHS Redress).[80] Schemes are, of course, antithetical to aggressive litigation remedies.

4 Conclusions

The starting point for these thoughts was that changes are occurring in Community policy, priorities and arrangements. Accordingly, a reappraisal of consumer policy and arrangements is called for. In particular, this raises the role and involvement of consumer organisations in enforcing regulation, and in regulation by private litigation.

The most fundamental question is whether an overview is being taken. This prompts the question whether it is enough to be 'consumer' or 'business' in the current environment? Should responsible opinion be pressing for holistic analysis, challenging as that may be to achieve? If so, does this imply new joined-up links or even institutions?

The evidence is that consumer involvement in regulatory enforcement is ineffective and inefficient. The data may be limited, and further empirical research is called for. But if this conclusion is correct, it has profound implications for Community policy on regulation and enforcement, and tort law. The 'responsive regulation' structure deserves to be far more widely understood – applied in practice. Theoretical considerations indicate that we should be suspicious both of regulation of business by consumer interests, and equally of consumers by business interests. If consistency, quality of output, and account-

78 See C. Hodges, 'Nordic compensation schemes for drug injuries', (2006) *Journal of Consumer Policy* 29, 143-175.

79 Titre IV du Livre Ier de la Première Partie du Code de la Santé Public, tel qu'il result de la loi n° 2002-303 du 4 mars 2002 relative aux droits des maladies et à la qualité du système de santé et de la loi n° 2002-1577 du 30 décembre 2002 relative à la responsabilité civile médicale: http://www.oniam.fr/.

80 NHS Redress Bill 2005.

ability are important, balanced regulation through public institutions seems the optimal solution, although self-regulation under a 'responsive regulation' structure. If costs are a barrier to current public policy in strengthening public regulatory bodies, then it needs to be understood both that these are necessary costs but also that solutions can and should be made to make regulatory systems more efficient. Further EU harmonisation, the involvement of approved consumer bodies in surveillance (but not in enforcement), and extension of co-regulation within defined parameters, all appear to offer potentially useful ways forward.

In the area of resolving multiple private damages claims, there is a need for civil justice systems to have efficient collective mechanisms. However, experience clearly raises concerns about enforcement of regulation through civil litigation. The development of excessive and disproportionate transactional costs, self-interested lawyer-led litigation and excessive claims culture, would appear to harm the economy rather than encourage competition, decrease prices, and increase employment or innovation.

There are many similarities between the functions and powers of the British OFT, a German, Austrian and now Dutch Consumer Authorities, and the Nordic Ombudsmen. Although some may differ in the extent to which they are formally part of government, they essentially operate as public authorities, rather than consumer organisations. If this observation is correct, there is considerable scope for proceeding by way of ensuring that such bodies operate as public authorities in the 'responsive regulation' mode. Further, an important part of their functions could be to facilitate low cost, extra-court mediation systems, rather than expensive and aggressive enforcement actions. One matter that deserves further scrutiny is the current interest in empowering public authorities with sanctioning powers that can be operated under their own authority without going to court. Such a mechanism adds to the 'big stick' but needs to be controlled wisely in a balanced fashion.

The analysis presented here also prompts concern over the extent to which policy is evidence-based. Has Europe understood and applied the 'responsive regulation' theory and the finding that deterrence is all but irrelevant as a justification for regulation and tort law? The ongoing absence of empirical data, or of systems that would produce relevant data that could be evaluated over time, is a serious problem. Given the revolutionary, transformational nature of some of the trends and changes that are taking place, there would seem to be a strong case for investing in ongoing analysis and research. Mechanisms for undertaking these activities are notably absent from current policy. The testing of some of the more revolutionary proposals might also be done though undertaking pilot studies. There should also be *post hoc* evaluation of Impact Assessments, so as to determine what the costs and effects of new regulation have in fact been, and whether they were higher or lower than was anticipated.

Europe seems to be at something of a crossroad, and to have greater opportunities and risks than have been widely realised in relation to policy options. Will sufficient re-evaluation be undertaken? Will the right choices be made?

CHAPTER 10

Effective enforcement of consumer law in Europe

Private, public, and collective mechanisms

Willem van Boom and Marco Loos[1]

Abstract

In this chapter, we draw together the main issues discussed and arguments presented by the authors to this book. We provide insight into the questions why there is a need for the collective enforcement of consumer law and what legal instruments have been developed to this end in European law and domestic legal systems. Furthermore, we make some suggestions for finding the right balance between private and public enforcement efforts.

1 Introduction

Individual consumers are ill-equipped to enforce their legal rights. They stand isolated against companies and organizations which often have better legal support and resources. This may result in individual consumers abstaining from pursuing their legal entitlements. Moreover, whereas the individual consumer stands to gain from legal action in only one or few particular cases against a particular trader, that trader faces the cumulative risk that a detrimental outcome of a particular case may affect many other transactions. As a result, the trader can by simple economic calculation justify greater expenditures on litigation than the individual consumer can.[2]

Conversely, *organized* consumers, be they represented by private organizations or public authorities, may challenge traders on more equal footing. Centralization of individual consumers' interests and aggregation of individual consumers' claims may help create bargaining power that isolated individual consumers lack when complaining and claiming for themselves. Collective enforcement of consumer law may therefore be more effective.

In this book, the contributions are centred on the idea of private, public and collective mechanisms for enforcement of consumer law. In this chapter, we draw together the main issues discussed and arguments presented by the authors to this book. We provide an insight into the questions why there is a need for the collective enforcement of consumer law and what legal instruments to this effect have been developed in European law and domestic legal systems. Furthermore, we make an attempt at suggesting a framework for finding the right balance between private and public enforcement efforts.

---

1 Willem van Boom is professor of private law at Rotterdam Institute of Private Law, Erasmus University Rotterdam (the Netherlands). Marco Loos is professor of private law at the Amsterdam Institute of Private Law, University of Amsterdam (the Netherlands).

2 Cf. William C. Whitford, 'Structuring Consumer Protection Legislation to Maximize Effectiveness', *Wisconsin Law Review* 1981, 1020, reprinted in: Iain Ramsay (ed.), *Consumer Law* (New York 1992), 459.

2 A short summary of the contributions

First, we give a short summary of the contributions to this book. In this book, authors representing a wide spectrum of expertise have presented the reader with information and insights regarding the challenges of collective enforcement of consumer law.

Gerrit Betlem gives a detailed account of the possibilities of transnational collective enforcement and the legal loopholes that both public and private collective enforcers may face. He notes that the present EU legislation roughly follows the *OECD Guidelines for Protecting Consumers from Fraudulent and Deceptive Commercial Practices Across Borders* as regards the provision of an institutional framework, the provision of mutual assistance concerning evidence gathering and information sharing and coordinating actions against 'rogue traders'[3] in multiple jurisdictions. However, in Betlems opinion the EU legal framework is somewhat incomplete. He argues that the EU legislation is not detailed enough as regards the legal action that can be taken by watchdogs against traders based in other countries, including in particular the possibility to allow for assets of rogue traders to be frozen on demand of foreign watchdogs. Moreover, as Betlem states, the legal framework in the EU fails to impose any duty on watchdogs to assist individual consumers who litigate against foreign traders, even though there may be collective consumer interests at stake.

Betlems paper shows that European policy is gradually shifting legislative attention to cross border cooperation in the enforcement of European consumer law, and that although the 1997 Injunctions Directive does not properly address any of the complicated cross-border enforcement issues, the Cooperation Regulation has increased the possibilities for both private and public enforcers to lodge cross-border complaints.[4] Indeed, as Betlem shows, the Unfair Commercial Practices Directive has potentially made competitors into private enforcers of the Directive, as they have a 'legitimate interest' in the cessation of unfair practices of their counterparts in competition. Moreover, they will also have a competitive interest in taking action, as unfair practices give rogue traders an advantage over competitors who do stick to fair market practices.

Howell's paper shows that the role of a public enforcer such as the Office of Fair Trading (OFT) is not merely to enforce substantive law but also to collect and provide information, to grant licenses for consumer credit companies and

3 The term is used in the 2002 Annual Report on handling of cross-border advertising complaints of the European Advertising Standards Alliance (EASA) and quoted by the European Commission in its proposal for the Unfair Commercial Practices Directive, COM (2003) 356 final, p. 4-5 and in its press release of 18 June 2003, IP/03/857. The term will be used throughout this paper.

4 Directive 98/27/EC of the European Parliament and of the Council of 19 May 1998 on injunctions for the protection of consumers' interests; Regulation 2006/2004 of the European Parliament and of the Council of 27 October 2004 on cooperation between national authorities responsible for the enforcement of consumer protection laws (the Regulation on consumer protection cooperation).

to stimulate self-regulation. So, stimulating consumer awareness seems to be as much a part of public enforcement as wiping out rogue traders' practices. The OFT's strategy appears to have evolved from a fundamentally criminal law oriented approach into one of responsive and cooperative enforcement. The OFT has grown from a reactive into a proactive authority using market analysis rather than specific complaints as a guideline for policy. It works with businesses where possible and uses administrative fines where required. This evolution seems to reflect the 'benign big stick' approach presented in this book by Chris Hodges and bears resemblance to the 'tit for tat' strategy as appears in the regulatory policy theory and negotiation theory.[5]

In his paper, Hodges puts forward the case for responsive regulation in the field of enforcement of consumer law. He shows that there is little empirical evidence of the relative costs and effects of either 'privatising' enforcement by empowering private actors to collectively pursue 'regulation through litigation' or centralising enforcement effort into a public authority using the 'benign big stick' approach. Hodges argues that private litigation is a diffuse mechanism that raises questions of consistency, expertise, efficiency, accountability and transparency. His overall conclusion is that enforcement should be best placed in the hands of public authorities rather than in those of private enforcers and that stimulating self-regulation by industry and trade should be at the top of the priority list of such authorities.

In their paper, Jansen and Ammerlaan appraise the reasons for the recent introduction of a Consumer Authority by the Dutch government. These reasons first of all include that the government recognised that some traders did not only fail to comply with consumer legislation, but actually made use of unfair commercial practices precisely to undermine consumer legislation. Moreover, the expansion of the European legislation regarding the internal market required the government to set up an instrument to deal with cross-border breaches of consumer legislation. The government decided that it would be illogical if consumers would be better protected in cross-border infringements of consumer law than in case of purely domestic infringements. As a result, recently the *Wet handhaving consumentenbescherming* (Consumer Protection Enforcement Act)[6] was enacted. The Dutch Consumer Authority's primary tasks are to increase the knowledge of both consumers and suppliers of their rights and duties and of options for obtaining legal redress, and to enforce consumer legislation in case of collective infringements in order to protect the economic interests of the consumer. However – as is the case with the OFT-model – the Dutch Consumer Authority will not be the only public enforcer of consumer legislation in the Netherlands: it will operate as a mere secondary enforcer in areas where another public enforcement authority is active, such as the Competi-

5 E.g., Ian Ayres and John Braithwaite, *Responsive Regulation – Transcending the Deregulation Debate* (Oxford 1992).

6 Act of 20 November 2006, *Staatsblad* 2006, 591, effective as of 29 December 2006.

tion Authority or the Food and Consumer Product Safety Authority. In determining its initial priorities, the Consumer Authority focuses on the impact of non-compliance with consumer law. In particular, the Authority will take action where the total economic loss (potentially) suffered by consumers is the highest, where consumer confidence is most at stake and where market behaviour jeopardizes competition and fairness on a particular market. On this basis the Consumer Authority announced it will focus in 2007, its first year of operation, on unilateral, unfair standard contract terms, the compliance with the obligations to inform and the right of withdrawal in the area of distance selling, on misleading lottery and price schemes, unclear pricing in the travel and tourism sector, and on information as to the rights and obligations of parties in case of non-conforming goods.[7]

Viitanen presents the reader with the Nordic 'acquis' concerning enforcement of consumer law and the settlement of individual and mass consumer claims. From his contribution follows that the Scandinavian approach reflects a regulatory culture of negotiated rulemaking, informal pressure on non-compliant business, and a proactive stance of public authorities. Court interference and criminal prosecution seem to play a secondary role in the enforcement process. Viitanen concludes that during the years the use of soft law methods has shown to be extremely effective. Possibly, the Nordic model meets most of the demands that Hodges sets for an effective 'benign big stick' approach.

Micklitz provides the reader with an in-depth analysis of the legal position of interest group organisations in European and domestic consumer law. He pays special attention to the contours of a possible group action for compensation and disgorgement, confronting the advantages and disadvantages of recent national legislation such as the *Kapitalanleger-MusterverfahrenGesetz* (KapMuG; the Financial Investors' Model Proceeding Act), the Swedish *Lag om grupprättegång* (Group Proceedings Act 2003), and the recent Dutch *Wet Collectieve Afwikkeling Massaschade* (Mass Damage Collective Settlement Act). These statutes are notable legislative attempts at designing efficient procedures for collective consumer compensation. Micklitz goes on to discuss the tension between procedural economy and the fundamental right to be heard under the European Convention on Human Rights, and he also deals with problems of financial incentives for lawyers, and the possible shift from private litigation to public authorities claiming compensation on behalf of consumers.

The direct link between enforcement of consumer legislation and competition law, put forward by Betlem, is also emphasised by Cseres. She analyses the competition law implications of finding effective means for the enforcement of consumer interests. In her paper, she indicates the possibilities competition law offers to consumers in order to enforce their rights. She also shows the other side of the coin by focusing on the competition law perspectives of enforcing consumer interests by applying consumer protection rules, in particular with

7 Press release of 15 January 2007, available at www.consumentenautoriteit.nl.

respect to the existing system of remedies and sanctions. She shows that when individual consumers face costs and burdens that are disproportionate to the value of their complaint they will decline to seek redress and resolve disputes.[8] This is problematic in particular with regard to 'trifle losses' – cases in which overall damage is widespread but individual losses are nominal – because in such cases the injured individuals will not claim for economic reasons, even though the total economic loss may be high. As private actors are much more influenced by costs and benefits than public bodies enforcing the law, this is an indication that public agencies are better equipped to enforce consumer rights than private parties in case of 'trifle losses'. Moreover, Cseres finds that private interests do not always coincide with public interests. In her view, collective actions – where consumers may bundle their fragmented individual claims and divide litigation costs over a large group of consumers instead of over just one person – may provide solutions to both the individual incentive problem for trifle loss and to the public policy concern. This can also considerably enhance law enforcement, Cseres argues. It is necessary, however, to limit the potential adverse effects of collective actions, such as excessive litigation and excessive fees for attorneys. Ultimately, competition authorities, consumer organizations and courts need to cooperate in order to make enforcement of collective consumer interests a success, she concludes.

Finally, Van den Bergh relates consumer law enforcement to the principles of law and economics and he too gives the reader valuable insight into the analogies between the enforcement of competition law and the enforcement of consumer law rules. For instance, the problem of trifle losses – the concept will be dealt with more extensively *infra*, § 3 – and how policymakers deal with these issues, show that consumer law can learn from competition law. Van den Bergh argues that both private and public enforcement of consumer law should aim at redressing market failures and should heed excessive enforcement which may stifle innovation. Van den Bergh also shows that as consumer law values are likely to be underenforced by individual consumers, the intervention of public authorities is vital. So, finding the right mix and quantity of enforcement instruments seems to be the challenge ahead. In § 9 we will address this matter in some detail.

3 Why collective action is needed

Consumer law gives individuals substantive rights with ancillary remedies – varying from claiming performance and damages, to rescission of the contract, suspending payment or invoking a cooling-off period and thus

[8] In a similar vein, William C. Whitford, 'Structuring Consumer Protection Legislation to Maximize Effectiveness', *Wisconsin Law Review* 1981, 1026 f., reprinted in: Iain Ramsay (ed.), *Consumer Law* (New York 1992), 465 f.

withdrawing from the individual contract concluded by the consumer. Such remedies start from the idea that individuals autonomously enforce their legal rights and that they seek individual access to justice.[9] But do they? It seems that they do not, or to quote Hadfield c.s., "consumer protection laws which give a private right of action to harmed consumers are notoriously underutilized".[10] If individuals do not invoke the available remedies, the underlying substantive rights may suffer from a state of underenforcement. This underutilisation boils down to too few complaints reaching the pinnacle of the complaints pyramid described by Cseres in her contribution, causing but a few consumers to take their case to court.

Naturally, claiming that consumers invoke their legal rights 'too little' or 'too much' needs a yardstick, which is difficult to offer.[11] Especially yardsticks such as 'the social optimal', 'economically efficient' and 'welfare optimising' level of enforcement may be appropriate in theory but difficult to use in practice. The evidence, however, does point towards a lack of enforcement of consumer law.[12] The obstacles for consumers to access justice are manifold: lack of information on legal rights, the costs of acquiring such information, the legal cost, time and effort, et cetera, all impede access to dispute resolution and stand in the way of enforcing consumer rights.[13]

Moreover, consumer losses could be large but tend to be small. The smaller the detriment to the individual consumer, the more likely he will be to abandon his complaint at the lower level of the complaints pyramid in the face of the cost of climbing up. The smallest of these complaints are what we called earlier 'trifle losses'. Trifle loss may be incidental but may also be of a more structural nature. Whenever an infringement of consumer law gives rise to such a dispersal of detriment to a great number of consumers endowed with individual but uneconomically viable claims, these consumers may show what is sometimes called 'rational apathy'.[14] The possible benefits of claiming for trifle loss are

9 The complaints pyramid presented by Cseres in her contribution to this book is not necessarily in conflict with this idea. It seems natural that consumers try to settle their dissatisfaction with their counterpart in an amiable way.

10 G.K. Hadfield et al., 'Information-Based Principles for Rethinking Consumer Protection Policy', 21 *Journal of Consumer Policy* 1998, 161. Cf. Iain Ramsay, 'Consumer Law, Regulatory Capitalism and the 'New Learning' in Regulation', 28 *Sydney L.Rev.* 2005, 33.

11 See especially Van den Bergh in his contribution drawing attention to this most relevant point.

12 See e.g., Anthony Ogus et al., *Best Practices for Consumer Policy: Report on the Effectiveness of Enforcement Regimes*, OECD (2006).

13 Cf. Stephen Weatherill, *EU Consumer Law and Policy* (Cheltenham 2005) 227.

14 William M. Landes and Richard A. Posner, 'The private enforcement of law', 4 *J. Legal Stud.* 1975, 33; Hans-Bernd Schaefer, 'The Bundling of Similar Interests in Litigation. The Incentives for Class Action and Legal Actions taken by Associations', 9 *European Journal of Law and Economics* 2000, 195. Cf. Geraint G. Howells and Stephen Weatherill, *Consumer Protection Law* (Aldershot 2005) 604 f.; Yves Picod and Hélène Davo, *Droit de la consommation* (Paris 2005) 321. For empirical underpinning of this

outweighed by the transactional cost of pursuing a complaint.[15] Not complaining then seems the rational thing to do. The result may be that trifle loss is in fact amplified by a structural consumer 'apathy', which in turn may well lead to structural non-enforcement of substantive rules of consumer law.[16] This turns enforcement into what economists would consider a 'public good'.[17]

Apart from the issue of trifle loss, there is a more fundamental question: what is, if any, the effect of individual consumers pursuing their legal rights on corporate behaviour? Are consumer claims mere isolated events that are dealt with as such by businesses, or does claiming by individual consumers actually lead to change in corporate behaviour and quality improvement of their products and services? The former seems to be the case, Cseres argues in her contribution to this book, whenever businesses operate on the basis of a cost-benefit analysis, violation of consumer rights is considered to be the price of doing business and a degree of wrongdoing is considered to be incidental to marketing and promotional activities. In any case, in changing corporate behaviour the law and its enforcement are but one factor. The net effect of individual enforcement efforts on corporate behaviour may be substantial, but may also turn out to be insignificant. Imagine for instance a retail chain of consumer electronics sellers using unfair terms in its general conditions. If a specific consumer is faced with such clauses he may successfully contest the invocability of such clauses. However, he will typically not request an injunction forbidding the seller to use similar clauses in future transactions with other consumers. As a result, the unfair clauses remain in circulation, thus sustaining illicit practices with regard to other, less informed or persistent consumers.[18] This is characteristic for indi-

---

'apathy', see, e.g., Hazel Genn, *Paths to Justice – What people do and think about going to law* (Oxford 1999) 67 ff. Note that the extent of the 'apathy' in part depends on financial arrangements concerning legal aid, litigation fees and civil procedure cost allocation. Cf. WRR, *De toekomst van de nationale rechtsstaat*, Wetenschappelijke Raad voor het Regeringsbeleid (2002) 63 205 ff.

15 Cf. Ianika N. Tzankova, *Strooischade – Een verkennend onderzoek naar een nieuw rechtsfenomeen* (Den Haag 2005), 19 f.

16 Cf. Anthony J. Duggan, 'Consumer access to justice in common law countries: a survey of the issues from a law and economics perspective', in: Charles E.F. Rickett and Thomas G.W. Telfer (ed.), *International Perspectives on Consumers' Access to Justice* (Cambridge 2003) 48 ff; N. Frenk, *Kollektieve akties in het privaatrecht (diss. Utrecht)* (Deventer 1994) 286; Hans-Bernd Schaefer, 'The Bundling of Similar Interests in Litigation. The Incentives for Class Action and Legal Actions taken by Associations', 9 *European Journal of Law and Economics* 2000, 185; Peter Cartwright, *Consumer Protection and the Criminal Law – Law, Theory and Policy in the UK* (Cambridge 2001) 16.

17 On public goods, e.g., R. Cooter and T. Ulen, *Law & Economics* (Reading 2004) 42 f. A similar obstacle is identified by Cseres with regard to consumer action against competition law infringements, where individual consumers lack both the tools and the incentives to lodge complaints. Moreover, it has been argued that consumers suffering from anti-competitive cartels should not be allowed to claim compensation for indirect purchase detriment (see the discussion by Cseres in her contribution to this book).

18 Hugh Collins, *Regulating Contracts* (Oxford 1999) 233. Cf. Hugh Beale, 'Legislative Control of Fairness: The Directive on Unfair Terms in Consumer Contracts', in: Jack Beatson and Daniel Friedman (ed.),

vidual action in consumer law: the individual consumer may have been helped, but society as a whole may be left untouched. Who will ensure that unfair terms will be deleted from contracts with other consumers?

Furthermore, whereas consumers typically invoke their legal rights after the event, there may be room for some form of additional *ex ante* enforcement. Later in this paper, we will tag a number of such ex ante instruments. Suffice to say at this point that the effectiveness of consumer claims as such may be insignificant if it is an isolated claim and does not raise any threat to business reputation. Media attention therefore seems an important ingredient for effectiveness, although it is also clear that fly-by-night operators and rogue traders in general tend to be relatively immune to such negative exposure.

4 Private law instruments filling the enforcement gap

Currently, there is no common European core regarding enforcement in private litigation.[19] There is no across-the-board right to injunctive relief for individual claimants reinforced with recurring penalty payments such as *astreinte, Zwangsgeld* or *dwangsom*. The effects of non-compliance with injunction orders, stop and desist orders and the like may therefore vary from country to country. As a result, the impact of such orders may vary. Moreover, there is neither a European class action nor a common group action for disgorgement or compensation of the interested backing of organisations. On the contrary, most member states are just beginning to discover the need for efficient and effective mass damage settlement.

As the contributions to this book make clear, the most significant pieces of European legislation in this respect are the Injunctions Directive[20] and the Cooperation Regulation.[21] Moreover, some other directives contain relevant but scattered provisions for both domestic and cross-border enforcement. So, the

Good Faith and Fault in Contract Law (Oxford 1995) 254. See also, with regard to respective roles of legislation and case law, Paul Burrows, 'Contract Discipline: In Search of Principles in the Control of Contracting Power', 2 *European Journal of Law and Economics* 1995, 141.

19 See, e.g., Hans Schulte-Nölke et al., *EC Consumer Law Compendium – Comparative Analysis* (Bielefeld 2006) 583 ff., for a telling overview of the state of domestic laws in Europe prior to implementation of Directive 98/27/EC.

20 Directive 98/27/EC of the European Parliament and of the Council of 19 May 1998 on injunctions for the protection of consumers' interests. On this Directive, see, e.g., Peter Rott, 'The Protection of Consumers' Interests After the Implementation of the EC Injunctions Directive Into German and English Law', 24 *Journal of Consumer Policy* 2001, 401 ff.; Geraint G. Howells and Stephen Weatherill, *Consumer Protection Law* (Aldershot 2005) 592 ff.

21 Regulation 2006/2004 of the European Parliament and of the Council of 27 October 2004 on cooperation between national authorities responsible for the enforcement of consumer protection laws (the Regulation on consumer protection cooperation).

existing European legislative framework is far from comprehensive. Moreover, as Betlem rightly observes, none of the pieces of European enforcement legislation addresses purely internal cases (although admittedly the Injunctions Directive is not clear in this respect). So, cross-border enforcement seems more at the forefront of European policymaking than the unification of procedural law of collective enforcement in general.[22]

Moreover, none of the European legal instruments deal with (let alone change, reduce or harmonize) *the cost* of cross-border private litigation,[23] which may explain the apparent lack of increase in collective private enforcement across the borders of EC member states.[24]

5 Compensation of mass consumer damage

One of the issues not regulated at a European level is the compensation of mass consumer damage. Few European jurisdictions allow compensation claims instigated by interest group organisations on behalf of consumers (other than by means of assignment of individual claims). As Micklitz reports, there are some important issues that would have to be dealt with if such collective compensation actions were to be allowed. The first psychological barrier to overcome, however, seems to be the fear of American scenes in European courts. There is serious scepticism concerning the phenomenon of *class actions*. The US example indeed seems to show that with class actions lawyers win and consumers and businesses lose out.[25] This unfair distribution of proceeds may well be caused by traits of the legal system (*e.g.*, contingency fees, punitive damages, settlement practice and jury bias) rather than by the phenomenon 'class action' as such.[26] Be that as it may, the concept of class action in itself

[22] Note the policy considerations for the Dutch government to extend the scope of the Consumer Authority's activities to purely domestic situations as to prevent that consumers would be better off in cross-border contracts then in domestic contracts.

[23] See Hans Schulte-Nölke et al., *EC Consumer Law Compendium – Comparative Analysis* (Bielefeld 2006) 582.

[24] Cf. Hans-W. Micklitz, 'Legal Redress', in: Geraint G. Howells et al. (ed.), *European Fair Trading Law* (Aldershot 2006) 220.

[25] Cf. Deborah R. Hensler et al., *Class Action Dilemmas – Pursuing Public Goals for Private Gain (Study)*, RAND Institute for Civil Justice (1999) 1 ff.; for a recent overview of advantages and drawbacks, see, e.g., James M. Underwood, 'Rationality, Multiplicity & Legitimacy: Federalization of the Interstate Class Action', 46 *S. Tex. L. Rev.* 2004, 397 ff.

[26] Cf. J. Basedow et al. (ed.), *Die Bündelung gleichgerichteter Interessen im Prozeß* (1999) 49; Per Henrik Lindblom, 'Individual Litigation and Mass Justice: A Swedish Perspective and Proposal on Group Actions in Civil Procedure', 45 *Am. J. Comp. L.* 1997, 822 ff.; Rachael Mulheron, *The Class Action in Common Law Legal Systems* (Oxford 2004) 72 ff.; on fundamental differences between the U.S.A. and Europe in this respect, see, e.g., Christopher Hodges, 'Multi-Party Actions: A European Approach', 11 *Duke J. Comp. & International Law* 2001a, 339 ff.

does not enjoy popularity in Europe. The gap left by failing private enforcement is usually filled by some form of public enforcement rather than by the after the event class action for damages.[27] This alternative intervention may take the form of state-driven intervention, self-regulation, or something in between. For instance, by subsidizing private claims or setting up alternate dispute resolution boards or small claims courts with low financial thresholds, governments sometimes successfully activate private enforcement.[28]

However, as Micklitz shows, all these efforts still start from the idea that individual claims for compensation are to be dealt with on an individual basis. Compensating individuals thus in essence remains a tailor-made procedure rather than mass justice. As already mentioned, the issue of designing *mass* compensation procedures is slowly becoming the centre of legislative attention in Europe.[29] Although a common approach is not yet found, this evolution should be applauded. *Group* actions instigated by authorized interest groups – rather than class actions instigated by lawyers – may indeed overcome the lack of enforcement in cases of trifle loss and may empower large groups of people otherwise suffering from rational apathy.[30] Having said that, the actual design of a European group action should be carefully contemplated and adverse experience in other jurisdictions should be heeded.

With regard to the introduction of a European group action for consumer compensation, several relevant questions would need answering.[31] First, who

[27] Harald Koch, 'Non-Class Group Litigation under EU and German Law', 11 *Duke J. Comp. & International Law* 2001, 358.

[28] Anthony J. Duggan, 'Consumer access to justice in common law countries: a survey of the issues from a law and economics perspective', in: Charles E.F. Rickett and Thomas G.W. Telfer (ed.), *International Perspectives on Consumers' Access to Justice* (Cambridge 2003) 50 ff.

[29] Cf. N. Frenk, *Kollektieve akties in het privaatrecht (diss. Utrecht)* (Deventer 1994) 289 ff.; W.D.H. Asser et al., *Een nieuwe balans – Interimrapport Fundamentele herbezinning Nederlands burgerlijk procesrecht* (Den Haag 2003) 173 ff.; Astrid Stadler, 'Gruppen- und Verbandsklagen auf dem Vormarsch?' in: Birgit Bachman et al. (ed.), *Grenzüberschreitungen – Beiträge zum Internationalen Verfahrensrecht und zur Schiedsgerichtsbarkeit (Festschrift für Peter Schlosser zum 70. Geburtstag)* (Tübingen 2005) 939 ff. See also European Commission, *Report from the Commission on the Application of Directive 85/374 on Liability for Defective Products (COM (2000)893final)*, European Commission (2000) COM (2000)893final p. 34: "Other areas where the Commission intends to launch initiatives concern measures to make it easier for consumers to take legal action collectively and the definition of the applicable law to non-contractual obligations." See also the historical notes by Stephen C. Yeazell, *From Medieval Group Litigation to the Modern Class Action* (New Haven 1987) 10 f.

[30] In a similar vein (with regard to trifle loss), I. N. Tzankova, *Strooischade – Een verkennend onderzoek naar een nieuw rechtsfenomeen* (Den Haag 2005) 128 ff.. Cf. Gerhard Wagner, *Neue Perspektiven im Schadensersatzrecht – Kommerzialisierung, Strafschadenersatz, Kollektivschaden (Gutachten zum 66. Deutschen Juristentag Stuttgart 2006)* (München 2006) A107 ff.

[31] Generally, see Neil Andrews, 'Multi-actions proceedings in England: representative and group actions', 11 *Duke J. Comp. & International Law* 2001, 263 ff.

should be representing the individual consumers?[32] A class action would empower private individuals and/or their lawyers, whereas a group action would authorize acknowledged[33] interest groups with a certain degree of representation to instigate claims. A pressing argument against the possibility of individuals starting group compensation claims would be that scheduled fees would give lawyers rather than stakeholders the incentive to start proceedings.[34] A possible modified model, identified by Micklitz, is the current Swedish law, where a consumer who has a claim which is typical for the whole group as regards the financial and other interest in the case, is chosen to represent the group. In such a case, the group members' interests would be represented in a manner as similar as possible to the situation where they would individually claim themselves.

There are several reasons why group actions may have to be preferred over class actions instigated by lawyers working on the basis of a (usually rather high) contingency fee. In the case of class actions, the risk of frivolous claims – fed by too much media attention and the fear of businesses for bad publicity and the accompanying fear of detriment to the business reputation[35] – seems higher than in the situation where the lawyer does not have a personal (financial) interest in the outcome of the claim. Furthermore, the problem of 'sweetheart settlements' or 'sell-out settlements' may rise: if the lawyer's fee is not based on the amount of time he invested in the procedure, but merely on the amount of damages that is obtained on behalf of the individual consumers, the lawyer might be inclined to settle prematurely and at a 'bargain' rather than to invest much time and effort in lengthy legal proceedings – once the claim is settled and the lawyer has obtained his fee, he may try to start yet another claim and thus obtain a more substantial income than would have been the case if the original claim would have been followed up in court.[36]

Yet another issue is whether individual consumers should be required to *opt in* or *opt out* regarding a collective action scheme. Should all consumers in a similar case automatically be represented in the group action, even without their consent and possibly without them knowing of the group action? Or should they rather be required to actively join the group action? In the latter case the free rider problem emerges: individual consumers may be inclined *not* to join the

[32] Cf. Emmanuel Putman, 'Scénario pour une class action à la francaise', 58 *La revue des idées* 2005, 322.

[33] It should be noted, however, that where *ad hoc*-interest groups created upon the initiative of lawyers are allowed to act as claimant in a group action, there does not seem to be much difference between class actions and group actions as regards the matter of representation.

[34] There is some evidence that multi-party actions are essentially 'lawyer led'; see, e.g., Christopher Hodges, *Multi-Party Actions* (Oxford 2001) 83.

[35] Cf. Ianika N. Tzankova, *Toegang tot het recht bij massaschade (thesis Tilburg)* (Deventer 2007) 113 f.

[36] Cf. Hans-Bernd Schaefer, 'The Bundling of Similar Interests in Litigation. The Incentives for Class Action and Legal Actions taken by Associations', 9 *European Journal of Law and Economics* 2000, 204; J. Basedow et al. (ed.), *Die Bündelung gleichgerichteter Interessen im Prozeß* (1999) 27 f. Cf. also the contribution by Cseres in this book.

group action but nevertheless benefit in the pursuit of their individual claim from the research conducted on behalf of the group action. On the other hand, in the former case, individual consumers would have to opt out in order to not be bound by the judgement in the group action. Clearly, such a scheme would require stringent norms as to the question whether the leaders of the group action are actually representative of the group. It would also require safeguards to prevent 'fake group actions' instigated with insufficient funding or incompetent and inadequate legal representation with the hidden purpose of failing the claim, thus freeing the tortfeasor from otherwise successful individual claims.[37] Apart from that, it should be recognised that opting out in cases of trifle loss may be illusory: rational apathy will probably also lead to acceptance of the default position (i.e. opt-in).[38]

Moreover, how would damages have to be calculated? Would a group action include heads of damage that are usually not considered to be individual damage, such as damage to the 'consumer surplus'?[39] Perhaps the best way to proceed here is to experiment with group actions for specific types of trifle loss and to evaluate after a period of some years what the added value of group actions is in that particular field.[40] In any event, the criteria set by Micklitz are essential in making any system of mass claim settlement work: are the claimants numerous, are their claims common or similar, are the claims typical for all claimants, is the group adequately represented, is a mass claim superior to individual settlement?

---

37 Cf Ianika.N. Tzankova, *Toegang tot het recht bij massaschade (thesis Tilburg)* (Deventer 2007) 148 f.

38 Cf. Hans-Bernd Schaefer, 'The Bundling of Similar Interests in Litigation. The Incentives for Class Action and Legal Actions taken by Associations', 9 *European Journal of Law and Economics* 2000, 195. Moreover, Theodore Eisenberg and Geoffrey P. Miller, 'The Role of Opt-Outs and Objectors in Class Action Litigation: Theoretical and Empirical Issues', *NYU, Law and Economics Research Paper No. 04-004; Cornell Law School Research Paper No. 04-019* 2004, 1 ff. point out that in the U.S.A. legal practice a considerable number of people may actually fail to opt out, even in cases where the loss sustained is more than trivial.

39 On this point, see, e.g., Clifford A. Jones, *Private Enforcement of Antitrust Law* (Oxford 1999) 153 ff. With regard to similiar issues in compensation of environmental damage, see Edward H. P. Brans, *Liability for damage to public natural resources standing, damage and damage assessment* (The Hague 2001). Note that the 2003 Swedish Group Proceedings Act – considered by some to be the most inclusive of European statutes on class action – is very cautious in allowing claims for damages.

40 In this respect, the recent changes to the German UWG present a possibility of experimenting with group actions for profit disgorgement. For references, see, e.g., Rolf Sack, 'Der Gewinnabschöpfungsanspruch von Verbänden in der geplanten UWG-Novelle', *Wettbewerb in Recht und Praxis* 2003, 549 ff.; Markus Burckhardt, *Auf dem Weg zu einer class action in Deutschland? Eine Untersuchung des Art. 1 § 3 Nr. 8 RBerG im System zwischen Verbandsklage und Gruppenklage* (Baden-Baden 2005) 36 ff.; Hans-W. Micklitz and Astrid Stadler, 'Der Reformvorschlag der UWG-Novelle für eine Verbandsklage auf Gewinnabschöpfung', *Wettbewerb in Recht und Praxis* 2003, 559 ff.

6 Self-regulation and public supervision: two ends of the spectrum?

How can collective consumer interests be served best? A number of instruments of enforcement are relevant here. In this section, we will make some remarks on self-regulation on the one hand, and supervision by public authorities on the other. They seem to be on two opposite ends of the spectrum, but in practice they may well converge.

At a European level, self-regulation through so-called codes of conduct seems very popular: in EU private law, policy trade associations and professional associations are encouraged to develop such codes.[41] This instrument may not only help to empower interest groups, but can also facilitate concrete rulemaking on the basis of vague private law standards such as 'good faith' and 'unfair' terms or 'unfair' commercial practices. As Viitanen, Hodges, and Van den Bergh rightly emphasize, the use of self-regulation may add to private and public enforcement.[42] Under specific conditions self-regulation, either on a fully voluntary basis or stimulated by state intervention or committal, can be a very effective instrument of both standard-setting and reaching compliance by business. For this reason, voluntary arrangements such as codes of conduct are stimulated in, e.g., the Unfair Commercial Practices Directive.[43] State supported negotiations concerning standard contract terms are a good example of such self-regulation.

Contrastingly, public authorities may step in where self-regulation fails. Remember the case of unfair contract terms: consumers may enforce their rights *ex post*, namely by avoiding the unfair term from the contract as soon as the professional counterpart using the term invokes it. This does not seem to be the most effective way of stamping out unfair contract terms.[44] In such cases

---

41 See, e.g., Article 17 *Directive 2004/48/EC of the European Parliament and of the Council of 29 April 2004 on the enforcement of intellectual property rights*. Cf. OFT, *Enforcement of consumer protection legislation – Guidance on Part 8 of the Enterprise Act*, Office of Fair Trading (2003) 5 ff.

42 For an overview of self-regulation amidst possible alternative instruments of regulation, see, e.g., Anthony Ogus, 'Comparing Regulatory Systems: Institutions, Processes and Legal Forms in Industrialised Countries', in: Paul Cook et al. (ed.), *Leading Issues in Competition, Regulation and Development* (Cheltenham 2004) 146 ff., (p. 157 ff.); Anthony Ogus, *Regulation: Legal Form and Economic Theory* (Oxford 1994) 107 ff. Cf. Peter Cartwright, *Consumer Protection and the Criminal Law – Law, Theory and Policy in the UK* (Cambridge 2001) 40 ff.; Peter Cartwright, *Banks, Consumers and Regulation* (Oxford 2004) 121 ff.

43 Cf. 'whereas' no. 20 and Article 17 of the Unfair Commercial Practices Directive.

44 It is doubtful whether the sanction of avoidability is sufficient to meet the requirements of the Directive. It may be doubted, in particular, whether a Member State that requires the consumer to *invoke* the unfairness of a clause, has properly implemented the Directive, as in such a case the clause is binding until the consumer has avoided it, even though Article 6 (1) of the Directive provides that unfair terms used in a contract concluded with a consumer by a seller or supplier 'shall ... not be binding on

a more direct instrument of enforcement of the underlying private law values – although not necessarily a perfect one – would be an ex ante evaluation of standard terms of trade either by a government agency or private interest group or a procedure facilitating forced erasure of the clauses altogether.[45] Indeed, Article 7 of the Unfair Contract Terms Directive provides that the Member States must ensure that 'adequate and effective means exist to prevent the continued use' of unfair general clauses.[46] Moreover, in *Commission/Italy*, the ECJ emphasised that under this article, the Member States are required to facilitate the possibility of a procedure against unfair terms even before they are used in practice.[47] This leads public authorities such as the OFT and the recently instated Dutch Consumer Authority to actively pursue enforcement against businesses that continue to use unfair contract terms.[48]

A slightly different approach is the setting up of a negotiation process between representatives of consumer groups and business and trade organisations leading to balanced contract terms in consumer contracts. This reflects the Nordic as well as the Dutch approach, but to some extent it also bears resemblance to the French monitoring process. In France, the governmental *commission des clauses abusives* can recommend erasing or adjusting unfair clauses. Although the commission does not have regulatory powers, it can publish its findings and it has some informal influence over courts and legislature.[49]

---

the consumer'. In any case it is clear that the national court may not wait for the consumer to invoke the unfairness of the clause. In a recent case (ECJ 26 October 2006, case C-168/05, not yet reported (Mostaza Claro/Centro Móvil Milenium), nos. 36-38, the ECJ stated that this provision is a mandatory rule of consumer protection which aims to re-establish equality between the parties. Such measure, the ECJ explains, is essential to accomplish the tasks entrusted to the Community under Article 3 (1) under (t) of the EC Treaty. The nature and importance of the public interest underlying the protection which the Directive confers on consumers justify, according to the ECJ, the national court being *required* to assess of its own motion whether a contractual term is unfair, compensating in this way for the imbalance which exists between the consumer and the seller or supplier. This seems to imply that where a case is heard before a national court, the court *must* apply any means it has in order to set the unfair clause aside.

45 Cf. Hugh Beale, 'Legislative Control of Fairness: The Directive on Unfair Terms in Consumer Contracts', in: Jack Beatson and Daniel Friedman (ed.), *Good Faith and Fault in Contract Law* (Oxford 1995) 251 ff.; Robert Bradgate, 'Experience in the United Kingdom', in: (ed.), *The integration of Directive 93/13 into the national legal systems (Proceedings of the Conference 'The Unfair Terms Directive: 5 years on – 1-3 July 1999')* (Brussels 1999) 29. On this problem, see also EC, *Report from the Commission on the implementation of Council Directive 93/13/EEC of 5 April 1993 on Unfair Terms in Consumer Contracts*, Commission of the European Communities (2000) COM(2000)248 final 20 ff.

46 See Stephen Weatherill, *EU Consumer Law and Policy* (Cheltenham 2005) 126.

47 ECJ 24 January 2002, case C-372/99, ECR 2002, p. I-819 (Commission/Italy).

48 E.g., Geraint G. Howells and Stephen Weatherill, *Consumer Protection Law* (Aldershot 2005) 597.

49 Jean Calais-Auloy and Frank Steinmetz, *Droit de la consommation* (Paris 2003) 208 f., no. 185 ; no. 548. Moreover, authorized consumer interest groups can instigate an 'action civile'; Jean Calais-Auloy and

Authorized consumer interest groups are allowed to request for injunctive relief.[50]

Another example of such *ex ante* supervision that may lead to adjustment of corporate behaviour at an early stage is the Nordic 'advance opinion'. Viitanen describes the practice of 'advance opinions' under the Danish Marketing Act, which makes it possible for businesses to submit at an early stage the legal question to the Consumer Ombudsman whether the planned marketing arrangement is in conformity with consumer law. Such advance opinions have the obvious advantage of creating clarity and legal certainty for businesses at an early stage, thus avoiding possible overcautious marketing strategies. In most legal systems, however, the problem with such a system would be that civil courts judging ex post are not bound by such advance opinions.

7 Injunctive relief by collective private action

It has been said that individual and private claims differ in many respects from public enforcement. A relevant difference is that the latter does not concern itself with redressing the wrongs committed vis-à-vis individual persons, but with protecting the general interest. This does not imply, however, that it is impossible for private law to focus on collective well being.[51] In fact, in recent years a number of jurisdictions have given interest groups standing in court to file specific claims, notably claims for declaratory and injunctive relief. Nevertheless, the European picture with regard to interest group actions is one of diversity.[52] For instance, in the Netherlands there was already a very generous position on interest group standing with regard to both mandatory and prohibitory injunctions and declaratory relief.[53] In Germany, *Verbandsklagen* are

Frank Steinmetz, *Droit de la consommation* (Paris 2003) 597 ff, no. 556 ff. For an overview of the European 'styles' of reagulatory policy in consumer affairs, see, e.g., DTI, *Comparative Report on Consumer Policy Regimes*, Department of Trade and Industry (2003).

50 Jean Calais-Auloy and Frank Steinmetz, *Droit de la consommation* (Paris 2003) 211 ff., no. 188.

51 Hugh Collins, *Regulating Contracts* (Oxford 1999) 8, even goes as far as to argue that 'welfarist regulation' is transforming contract law regulation.

52 For an in-depth comparative review of these jurisdictions, see Hans-W. Micklitz and Astrid Stadler (ed.), *Das Verbandsklagerecht in der Informations- und Dienstleistungsgesellschaft* (2005) 57 ff.; cf. Hans Schulte-Nölke et al., *EC Consumer Law Compendium – Comparative Analysis* (Bielefeld 2006) 583 ff.; Ulrike Docekal et al., *Rechtliche und Praktische Umsetzung der Richtlinie Unterlassungsklagen 98/27/EG in 25 EG-Mitgliedstaaten*, Bundesministerium für Soziale Sicherheit, Generationen and Konsumentenschutz (2006) 1 ff.

53 Walter van Gerven et al., *Cases, Materials and Texts on National, Supranational and International Tort Law* (Oxford 2000) 273-275. An example of this generous position is a case in which the Dutch Consumer Association successfully filed for a declaratory judgement for the benefit of victims of a mass tort (legionnaires disease outbreak at a flower exposition); see Rechtbank Alkmaar 12 december 2002, *Nederlandse Jurisprudentie* 2003, 68.

only allowed to file for injunctive relief on the basis of specific statutory provisions.[54] Recently, however, suggestions for a more general statutory framework have been voiced.[55] A similar picture emerges from England and Wales.[56] In France, specific statutory provisions (mostly concerning consumer law) present interest group organisations with the right to file an 'action civile' or a request for injunctive relief.[57] In theory, this 'action civile' can be the basis of a group claim for compensation, but in practice the 'action' is confined to cases of criminal offences and the damage may not consist of the total of individual damage.[58] It seems that with regard to multi-party *compensation* proceedings, up to now England and Wales seem to be the most receptive.[59]

As noted earlier, collective private action has become a deliberate choice of instrument in European consumer law enforcement. We refer to the access to private enforcement by organizations with a 'legitimate interest' as dealt with in Article 4 (1) Directive 84/450/EEC (as amended by Directive 97/55/EC on misleading and comparative advertising), Directive 98/27/EC on injunctions for the protection of consumers' interests, Articles 4 (2) and 8 (3) of Regulation 2006/2004 on consumer protection cooperation, and Article 11 of the Unfair Commercial Practices Directive. However, standing in court of private groups and organizations is not boundless. It may be subject to acknowledgement of the consumer interest group by the national executive, as the list of qualified entities according to the Injunctions Directive shows. Such lists may come a long way in redressing the lack of guarantees for accountability of such private organisations. If private collective group actions were to become a more important instrument of enforcement, we feel that issues of accountability and transparency would have to be dealt with more intensely. Already, in jurisdictions that allow the consolidation of claims for compensation in mass tort cases, the question may be raised how the intermediary interest groups and their lawyers

54 Walter van Gerven et al., *Cases, Materials and Texts on National, Supranational and International Tort Law* (Oxford 2000) 272-273. See currently the *Unterlassungsklagengesetz (UKlaG)*, outlining the specific cases in which injunctive relief can be pursued. Cf. Ellen Schaumburg, *Die Verbandsklage im Verbrauchserschutz- und Wettbewerbsrecht* (Baden-Baden 2006) 143 ff.

55 See, e.g., Hans-W. Micklitz and Astrid Stadler (ed.), *Das Verbandsklagerecht in der Informations- und Dienstleistungsgesellschaft* (2005) Cf. several authors in *Österreichisches Anwaltsblatt* 2006/2 discussing the "*Sammelklage*".

56 OFT, *Enforcement of consumer protection legislation – Guidance on Part 8 of the Enterprise Act*, Office of Fair Trading (2003) 1 ff.

57 Yves Picod and Hélène Davo, *Droit de la consommation* (Paris 2005) 330 ff.

58 See, e.g, Emmanuel Putman, 'Scénario pour une class action à la francaise', 58 *La revue des idées* 2005, 322; Jean Calais-Auloy and Frank Steinmetz, *Droit de la consommation* (Paris 2003) 597 ff., no. 556; Yves Picod and Hélène Davo, *Droit de la consommation* (Paris 2005) 332, no. 529. Cf. Geraint G. Howells and Stephen Weatherill, *Consumer Protection Law* (Aldershot 2005) 593.

59 Christopher Hodges, 'Multi-Party Actions: A European Approach', 11 *Duke J. Comp. & International Law* 2001a, 328; Geraint G. Howells and Stephen Weatherill, *Consumer Protection Law* (Aldershot 2005) 647 f.

are funded and what percentage of the proceeds actually end up in the hands of the injured parties. Similar concerns would have to be addressed in cases where collective actions for disgorgement were acknowledged. Having a procedure for listing and blacklisting may then prove helpful, but we should not forget that issues of accountability and transparency are even more pressing when it comes to public authorities. The level of democratic control of such authorities largely depends on national constitutional arrangements, which in itself is not a complete guarantee of effective, proportionate, and dissuasive enforcement effort.

Granting private group organisations standing in court is one thing, making them use their right to actually start civil proceedings is quite another. In practice, interest groups have little resources to spend on costly litigation.[60] The Netherlands, for instance, seems to be one of the most permissive jurisdictions when it comes to interest group standing in court. Any incorporated interest group, even if it has been founded on an *ad hoc*-basis, has standing to sue in the interest of their backing and may file for injunction and stop and desist orders.[61] Hence, the legal position of such organisations seems excellent. In reality, however, they hardly ever appear in civil court.[62] This is caused at least in part by the fact that the consumer organisation is obliged to try to reach an out of court settlement ('prior consultation') before the organisation can be heard by the court,[63] which fits perfectly with the consensus-model that dominates the Dutch (legal) culture but in practice may function as a hindrance to effective enforcement of consumer law.[64] To sum up Viitanen's conclusion: competitors are more likely to enter the courtroom than consumer organisations.[65] However, the most plausible reason for this absence of consumer organisations in civil procedure is

60 Klaus Viitanen, 'The Crisis of the Welfare State, Privatisation and Consumers' Access to Justice', in: Thomas Wilhelmsson and Samuli Hurri (ed.), *From Dissonance to Sense: Welfare State Expectations, Privatisation and Private Law* (Aldershot 1999) 552. Contra: I. N. Tzankova, *Strooischade – Een verkennend onderzoek naar een nieuw rechtsfenomeen* (Den Haag 2005) 92 f.

61 See Article 3:305a Dutch Civil Code; note that the fact that The Netherlands has only put one private organisation on the list of the Injunction Directive is relevant for access to courts abroad but not for access to courts in domestic proceedings.

62 See, critically, G.J. Rijken, 'De Wet algemene voorwaarden na één jaar: een trieste tussenbalans', *NJB* 1994, 643 ff. Cf. also Hodges in this volume.

63 Cf. Article 6:240 (4) Dutch Civil Code for proceedings combatting unfair contract terms and Article 3: 305a (2) Dutch Civil Code for other proceedings. Legal persons governed by public law, including the Consumer Authority, have to comply with the same rule of obligatory prior consultation (Article 3:305b (2) Dutch Civil Code). These provisions apply also to foreign consumer organisations on the list of the Injunction Directive. They apply as well in the case of an alleged infringement of Community law, cf. Art. 3:305d (3) Dutch Civil Code.

64 Cf. Ianika N. Tzankova, *Toegang tot het recht bij massaschade (thesis Tilburg)* (Deventer 2007) 137.

65 This is the more remarkable given the no-cost rule, as explained in the contribution by Viitanen to this book.

the lack of funds to pursue civil litigation. In a sense this is fortunate because limitless resources of consumer organisations will certainly not help finding enforcement equilibrium. Nevertheless, from a political perspective there might be good reasons for supporting 'collective relief' in areas where private enforcement lags behind and political pressure to intensify public enforcement is mounting.

So, rational policy may demand that governments identify in which areas private enforcement could add to or substitute public enforcement, and then provide incentives – be it financial or otherwise – for collective private enforcement. The Finnish proposal for a *State Group Action Board* as reported by Viitanen goes a long way in this direction, but this proposal was abandoned for reasons of budgetary constraints. Somehow, the politics of public finance do not always reflect rational policy.[66] The fact that public policy seems reserved when it comes to spending money on group actions seems even more curious when we consider that most European jurisdictions do have some sort of national scheme helping *individuals* in need of legal aid, but obviously forget the economies of scale when they refuse interest groups to benefit from similar arrangements.[67] Moreover, it has been argued that it would be unfair to abandon the 'loser pays'-rule in consumer cases. On the other hand, it could be argued that it may seem equally unfair to deny respectable private organisations a subsidy that each and every individual claimant whose interests are at stake does receives. And in any case, would this not be cheaper for the government than subsidizing many individual claimants? In other words, governments may be acting penny-wise but pound-foolish, in this respect.[68]

There is also the matter of monitoring. Injunctive relief obtained by a consumer organisation does by no means guarantee voluntary compliance with the court decision. So who will monitor the implementation of the court decision? Clearly, full monitoring could be too expensive and inefficient.[69] Therefore, incentives have to be built into civil procedure for voluntary full compliance by the respondent and some monitoring by the claimant at the same time. There are several instruments in the various jurisdictions that can help in this respect. The European legislature could introduce a *recurring penalty payment* – *i.e.*, the provisional obligation to pay a designated sum of money in the event of non-

---

[66] Cf. Klaus Viitanen, 'The Crisis of the Welfare State, Privatisation and Consumers' Access to Justice', in: Thomas Wilhelmsson and Samuli Hurri (ed.), *From Dissonance to Sense: Welfare State Expectations, Privatisation and Private Law* (Aldershot 1999) 561 ff.

[67] Cf. Hugh Collins, *Regulating Contracts* (Oxford 1999) 89.

[68] Cf. Matthias Arkenstette, 'Reorientation in Consumer Policy – Challenges and Prospects From the Perspective of Practical Consumer Advice Work', 28 *Journal of Consumer Policy* 2005, 361 ff. See also the education efforts by the EU (cf. European Commission, *Consumer Policy Strategy 2002-2006*, EU Commission (2002) 25).

[69] S. Shavell, 'The optimal structure of law enforcement', 36 *J. of Law and Economics* 1993, 271-272; G.S. Becker, 'Crime and punishment: an economic approach', 78 *J. Political Economy* 1968, 193.

compliance with the original court decision – ancillary to injunctive relief under the Injunctions Directive.[70] Thus, the respondent would forfeit a considerable sum of money clearly exceeding the value of his obligation if he does not comply with the court order.[71]

In some legal systems injunctive relief is already combined with this *penalty payment*.[72] This has proved to be a useful incentive for compliance, even more so in conjunction with media attention.[73] On the other hand, incentives for the respondent to comply may not be enough. Then, the consumer organisation may be given financial or reputational incentives to develop monitoring activities, for instance by allowing the consumer organisation to benefit directly from the penalty payment instead of requiring the respondent to make such payment to the State, as is the case in some Member States. Finding the appropriate incentive for private groups to develop the right level of monitoring activity is one of the more challenging assignments for European legal doctrine.

8 Bundling actions for trifle loss?

The Roman legal expression that people should not complain to the judicial authorities about small nuisances – *de minimis non curat praetor* – seems outdated. In modern Europe the insight has grown that trifle loss and minor detriment to individuals as such may equal large detriment to consumers as a whole on the one hand and substantial benefits accruing to the wrongdoer on the other hand. Hence, from a deterrence point of view such detrimental infringements of consumer law should be remedied. But is it possible to secure compliance through individual damages actions? The 'rational apathy' we mentioned earlier leads to less than maximal individual enforcement efforts. However, forced bundling of trifle claims – as experienced in the typical Ameri-

---

70 Cf. Directive 2004/48/EC of the European Parliament and of the Council of 29 April 2004 on the enforcement of intellectual property rights.

71 Christian von Bar and Ulrich Drobnig, *The Interaction of Contract Law and Tort and Property Law in Europe – A Comparative Study* (München 2004) 114.

72 A recent Dutch case serves as an example. In the Dutch case of HCC (a small consumer organisation of computer hobbyists) against Dell Computers, the Court of Appeal of The Hague found several provisions in the standard contract terms of Dell to be unfair (Court of Appeal The Hague 22 March 2005, *Landelijk Jurisprudentienummer* AT1762 (HCC/Dell Computer B.V.)). The court awarded conditional penalty payments in case Dell would not implement the required changes within three months time. HCC was of the opinion that Dell had not sufficiently performed its obligations under the court ruling and indicated it would start proceedings to execute the penalty payments. Dell tried to prevent HCC from this by ordering a prohibition of such proceedings. The Court denied the order (Court of Appeal The Hague 24 October 2006, *Landelijk Jurisprudentienummer* AZ0734 (Dell Computer B.V./HCC)).

73 Perhaps media attention (e.g., publication of the court decision) should also be a more prominent part of the private law enforcement toolbox.

can class action leading to 'sell-out' and 'coupon settlement' – does not seem an attractive alternative either. As Cseres argues, such settlements do not seem to bring meaningful compensation to consumers and mainly appear to be in the interest of the lawyers involved.

So, perhaps the proceeds of claims for compensation of trifle loss should not be distributed? For instance, it has been suggested that interest groups should be allowed to claim exemplary damages or some other form of damage in excess of individual damage (e.g., damage to 'consumer interests') and put these into a fund. With this fund these interest groups could then finance future litigation in the common interest.[74] To some extent this is already allowed by § 10 of the German *Gesetz gegen den unlauteren Wettbewerb (UWG)*, according to which consumer interest groups can claim profit disgorgement in some cases of unfair trade practice. The disgorged profits accrue, however, not to the consumer organisation that commenced the enforcement action but to the State after deducting the cost of claiming.[75] Under the influence of debated changes to the current EU legislation of competition law this may, however, change.[76]

9 Mixed instruments: private and public enforcement

It has been argued that public enforcement is superior to private enforcement and that having a public authority retaining control ensures a balanced and responsive enforcement process whereas private collective enforcement raises not only issues of accountability, legitimacy, and transparency, but may also bring about frivolous and disproportionate enforcement activity and cause overdeterrence.[77] In short: public watchdogs are to be preferred over private watchdogs. In this respect Hodges suggests a working mode in which private entities do the 'barking' (e.g., by lodging complaints in an administrative procedure before a public authority) while the 'biting' (fining, claiming, injunction) remains the public authority's prerogative.

---

74 Cf. D. Collins, 'Public Funding of Class Actions and the Experience with English Group Proceedings', 31 *Manitoba L.J.* 2005, 236-238. See also Edward H. P. Brans, *Liability for damage to public natural resources standing, damage and damage assessment* (The Hague 2001).

75 On this topic, see, e.g., Rolf Sack, 'Der Gewinnabschöpfungsanspruch von Verbänden in der geplanten UWG-Novelle', *Wettbewerb in Recht und Praxis* 2003, 549 ff.; Markus Burckhardt, *Auf dem Weg zu einer class action in Deutschland? Eine Untersuchung des Art. 1 § 3 Nr. 8 RBerG im System zwischen Verbandsklage und Gruppenklage* (Baden-Baden 2005) 36 ff.; Hans-W. Micklitz and Astrid Stadler, 'Der Reformvorschlag der UWG-Novelle für eine Verbandsklage auf Gewinnabschöpfung', *Wettbewerb in Recht und Praxis* 2003, 559 ff.

76 Cf. *European Commission, Green Paper "Damages actions for breach of the EC antitrust rules", EU Commission (2005) COM (2005) 672 final* 1 ff., in particular p. 8 f. Cf. J. Kessler, 'Cui bono? Schadensersatzansprüche der Verbraucher im Kartellrecht', *Verbraucher und Recht* 2007, 41 ff.

77 See also the contribution of Cseres to this book.

Admittedly, however, public authorities have their limitations as well. Public authorities may lack information that private enforcers do have. Moreover, much like private consumer organisations, they too have limited resources, need to prioritise and therefore cannot enforce all rules with equal vigour.[78] Furthermore, public authorities may or may not maximize enforcement efforts (we cannot really know as a result of the principal/agent phenomenon).[79] Additionally, public authorities are in danger of suffering from 'agency capture' when taking a 'responsive enforcement' stance.[80]

Undeniably, if we consider consumer law to be part of the free market design in Europe, then the state's role in setting up and enforcing the market structure is essential.[81] Naturally, the state can rely on criminal law and the common framework for the enforcement of criminal law. Administrative law sanctions and procedure is also used as a tool for implementing and enforcing some parts of consumer law. More recently, there have been experiments with in-between solutions for the benefit of generating compliance with consumer law. A notable form of such a solution is the empowerment of public agencies to enforce private law rights for the benefit of the public. For instance, the Office of Fair Trading (OFT) can file for injunctive relief with regard to unfair terms in consumer contracts for the benefit of consumers at large.[82] Not surprisingly, the same applies for its Dutch counterpart.[83]

So, public enforcement is important, but we would not go as far as to suggest that it is superior to private law. We feel that public and private enforcement should instead coexist or continue to do so. In both public policy theory and law

---

78 Cf. Ian Ayres and John Braithwaite, *Responsive Regulation – Transcending the Deregulation Debate* (Oxford 1992) 103.

79 On that topic, e.g., Joseph E. Stiglitz, *Economics of the Public Sector* (New York 2000) 202 ff. Cf. Keith Hawkins, *Law as a Last Resort* (Oxford 2002) 16 ff., p. 415 ff.

80 See, e.g., Michael Faure and Roger van den Bergh, *Objectieve Aansprakelijkheid, Verplichte Verzekering en Veiligheidsregulering* (Antwerpen 1989) 148; Sally S. Simpson, *Corporate Crime, Law, and Social Control* (Cambridge 2002) 86 ff.; see also Catherine Albiston, 'The Rule of Law and the Litigation Process – The Paradox of Losing by Winning', in: Herbert M. Kritzer and Susan S. Silbey (ed.), *In Litigation – Do the "Haves" Still Come Out Ahead?* (Stanford 2003) 174.

81 Cf. Peter Cartwright, *Consumer Protection and the Criminal Law – Law, Theory and Policy in the UK* (Cambridge 2001) 7.

82 Regulation 8 Unfair Terms in Consumer Contracts Regulations 1994; Regultion 12 of the Unfair Terms in Consumer Contracts Regulations 1999; Part 8 of the Enterprise Act 2002. Cf. J. Basedow et al. (ed.), *Die Bündelung gleichgerichteter Interessen im Prozeß* (1999) 15, p. 126; OFT, *Enforcement of consumer protection legislation – Guidance on Part 8 of the Enterprise Act*, Office of Fair Trading (2003) 18 ff., p. 76 f. Usually, the threat of OFT seeking an order is sufficient to prompt businesses to change their general clauses.

83 Cf. Article 3:305d Dutch Civil Code. The Dutch Consumer Authority is required to give the infringing party a reasonable period to stop the infringement and to obtain a copy of the data on which the Consumer Authority bases its intention to act against the infringing party.

and economics the arguments in favour of *combined* public and private enforcement efforts are well articulated.[84] We feel that consumer law may profit from a similar combined approach and that there is no need for strict adherence to either public law or private law enforcement.[85] Having said that, it must be admitted that overzealous enforcement on both sides – or rather: the setting and maximal enforcement of unnecessary high standards of care – may stifle innovation and cause counterproductive corporate behaviour. Hence, the real challenge is finding the *optimal* quantity of private litigation and responsive public enforcement against the background of the goals of substantive consumer law.[86] In this regard we second Hodges' call for a balanced approach. Using the 'fine-tuning' process proposed by Van den Bergh in a trial-and-error setting may indeed give a valuable starting point for such an approach. Admittedly, however, what is lacking are data on costs, benefits, effects, and side effects of consumer empowerment. Obtaining a clearer picture of these data is crucial in finding the optimal level of enforcement.

Having said that, we think we can already see from the contributions to this book a picture emerging of the road ahead. This road is one of a balanced and multifaceted approach. This is an approach in which individual consumers are encouraged to make use of the available civil law remedies and consumer organisations serve the consumer interests at large by filing for injunctive relief and claiming compensation for trifle loss, and in which one or several public authorities are entrusted with the supervision over the proper functioning of consumer markets. Hence, in this approach the use of criminal law is reserved for combating rogue traders, who usually have little reputation to lose but may be sensitive to imprisonment. In such cases, directors and executives of such companies should be exposed to imprisonment to repair the judgement proof-problem. The balance is found in the extent to which these powers are used and the net effect on consumer markets.

So, the challenge for EU member states is to find the right balance in the light of the unfolding European legislative approach. As Van den Bergh rightly observes, the member states have different starting points in this respect. Traditionally, the national approaches to enforcement diverge: some jurisdictions trust on enforcement by private consumer organisations (e.g., Germany), others emphasize the role of public authorities (e.g., United Kingdom, Scandinavian countries) or the criminal justice system (e.g., France), and some prefer

84 Seminal S. Shavell, 'A model of the optimal use of liability and safety regulation', 15 *Rand J. of Economics* 1984, 271 ff. Cf. Susan Rose-Ackerman, 'Tort Law in the Regulatory State', in: Peter H. Schuck (ed.), *Tort Law and the Public Interest – Competition, Innovation, and Consumer Welfare* (New York 1991) 80 ff.

85 Cf. Harald Koch, 'Non-Class Group Litigation under EU and German Law', 11 *Duke J. Comp. & International Law* 2001, 360.

86 In a similar vein, see Anthony J. Duggan, 'Consumer access to justice in common law countries: a survey of the issues from a law and economics perspective', in: Charles E.F. Rickett and Thomas G.W. Telfer (ed.), *International Perspectives on Consumers' Access to Justice* (Cambridge 2003) 64 ff.

soft instruments of negotiated and self-regulatory market balance (Scandinavia, the Netherlands). However, from whatever enforcement culture the EU member states may come, administrative or criminal law now seem to be indispensable. This follows from the more recent European legislation such as the Cooperation Regulation and the Unfair Commercial Practices Directive that designates 'competent administrative authorities' and 'public bodies' with the task of enforcing and cooperating in the collective interest of consumers.[87] So, the mix of enforcement instruments is here to stay, challenging national policymakers to find the right balance between the different instruments against a background of the need for effective, proportionate, and dissuasive sanctions.

10 Concluding remarks: On the way to creating (slightly less im)perfect markets

Making consumer law work is not all about sticks and carrots. We conclude from the contributions by Hodges and Viitanen that 'soft approaches' may have an important impact as well and should be used where possible. Moreover, as Van den Bergh rightly points out, any regulator should consider it to be its priority to address the causes of market failure, e.g., by making sure that consumers have adequate information on quality and essence of the offered products. A certain level of information symmetry is an important prerequisite for any market to function properly.[88] This is especially true for infrequently bought experience and credence goods. With regard to these goods, consumers are not fully able to learn from their mistakes and 'vote with their feet'.[89] As a result there may be a lack of incentives for producing above average quality and consequently good quality may not be signalled to consumers. This may result in consumers being forced to choose on the basis of price alone rather than on a mix of relevant properties of the product.[90] Such imperfections

87 Cf. Hans-W. Micklitz, in: Geraint G. Howells et al. (ed.), *European Fair Trading Law; The Unfair Commercial Practices Directive* (2006) 227.

88 Seminal George A. Akerlof, 'The Market for "Lemons": Quality Uncertainty and the Market Mechanism', 84 *The Quarterly Journal of Economics* 1970, 488 ff. Information on legal rights and dispute resolution options seems crucial as well; cf. Peter Cartwright, *Consumer Protection and the Criminal Law – Law, Theory and Policy in the UK* (Cambridge 2001) 17 ff.

89 Cf. G.K. Hadfield et al., 'Information-Based Principles for Rethinking Consumer Protection Policy', 21 *Journal of Consumer Policy* 1998, 140 ff.

90 Note that the assumption underlying this theory is one of rational consumer choice; this assumption has been criticised from the viewpoint of behavioural science; see, e.g., Christine Jolls et al., in: Cass. R. Sunstein (ed.), *Behavioral Law & Economics* (2000) 14 ff.; David A. Statt, *Understanding the Consumer – A Psychological Approach* (London 1997) 227 ff.; Incardona Rossella and Poncibò Cristina, 'The average consumer, the unfair commercial practices directive, and the cognitive revolution', 30 *Journal of Consumer Policy* 2007, 21 ff.

– Van den Bergh mentions relevant examples – are conceivable in financial and insurance markets especially, where quality is not easy to measure or evaluate by individual consumers and reputation is based on trust and brand reputation rather than on intrinsic value. The complex task of public authorities serving consumer interests here is to try to create informational transparency (without overloading consumers with information), comparability and other conditions for markets to function as perfectly as possible. No private consumer organisation can fulfil that task alone. It can, however, fulfil the role of 'side-kick' to the regulator by bringing collective actions to civil courts on the basis of general private law. This may lead the regulator to step in and regulate the litigated issue by means of legislation.[91] The recent EU legislation thus paves the way for a productive coexistence of the needed mixed approach of public/private enforcement. As is shown above, it appears to be essential that two more steps are taken. On the one hand, more elaborate study should be made of the possible benefits and drawbacks of granting consumer organizations the right to obtain damages on behalf of consumers and to put these into a fund to finance future litigation in the common interest. On the other hand, as Betlem suggests, public watchdogs should be obliged to assist individual consumers who litigate against foreign traders in a situation where a collective interest is at stake.

One final remark is in order. However detailed or elaborate a public or private scheme for the enforcement of consumer law is, in practice it all comes down to the determination and stamina of the parties enforcing the law. As Whitford concluded as early as 1981, the commitment of public authorities to the enforcement of the legislation is far more important in determining the level of compliance than the statutory powers they may have.[92] If collective enforcement of consumer legislation is to truly work in Europe, any piece of legislation empowering consumer organizations or public authorities needs to provide sufficient (and in any case not adverse) incentives for enforcing such legislation.

In sum, there is still a lot the European legislator may do to improve enforcement of European consumer law. We hope that this book has provided fuel for such future action.

91 G.K. Hadfield et al., 'Information-Based Principles for Rethinking Consumer Protection Policy', 21 *Journal of Consumer Policy* 1998, 154, rightly observe that legislative intervention may come too late when media attention has already made consumers very cautious.

92 William C. Whitford, 'Structuring Consumer Protection Legislation to Maximize Effectiveness', *Wisconsin Law Review* 1981, 1041 f., reprinted in: Iain Ramsay (ed.), *Consumer Law* (New York 1992), 480 f.

14W68091/ T8/ 9789076871806